TROPIC OF
CAPRICORN

For Anya

TROPIC OF CAPRICORN

A remarkable journey to the forgotten corners of the world

Simon Reeve

BBC
BOOKS

This book is published to accompany the television series entitled
Tropic of Capricorn, first broadcast on BBC2 in 2008.

1 3 5 7 9 10 8 6 4 2

Published in 2008 by BBC Books, an imprint of Ebury Publishing,
A Random House Group Company.

This paperback edition published 2009

The Random House Group Limited Reg. No. 954009
Addresses for companies within the Random House Group
can be found at www.randomhouse.co.uk

A CIP catalogue record for this book is available from the British Library.

ISBN 978 1 846 07386 1

The Random House Group Limited supports The Forest Stewardship Council
(FSC), the leading international forest certification organisation. All our titles that
are printed on Greenpeace approved FSC certified paper carry the FSC logo. Our
paper procurement policy can be found at www.rbooks.co.uk/environment

Mixed Sources
Product group from well-managed
forests and other controlled sources
www.fsc.org Cert no. TT-COC-2139
© 1996 Forest Stewardship Council

Commissioning editor: Martin Redfern
Project editor: Eleanor Maxfield
Copy-editor: Justine Taylor
Designer: seagulls.net
Production controller: David Brimble

Printed and bound in the UK by CPI Cox and Wyman, Reading, Berks

CONTENTS

TROPIC OF

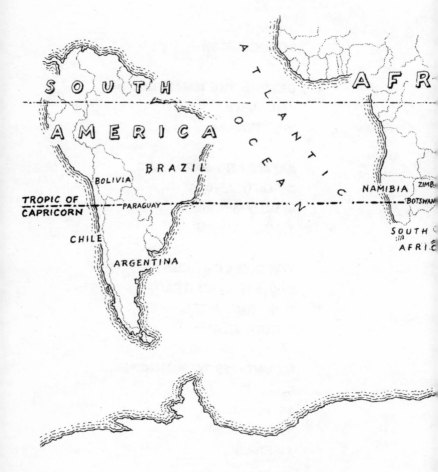

CAPRICORN

INTRODUCTION

I N THREE days I will leave home to begin an extraordinary journey following an imaginary line around the planet. With a crack film crew from the BBC, I will spend months tracking the Tropic of Capricorn through some of the wildest and least-known areas of our world. Capricorn cuts through Namibia, Botswana, South Africa, Mozambique, Madagascar, three country-sized regions of Australia (Western Australia, the Northern Territory and Queensland), Chile, Argentina, Paraguay and Brazil, where my adventure will end on the Atlantic coast.

Along the way I will cross the stark Atacama Desert in Chile, perhaps the driest place on Earth, and the Kalahari Desert of southern Africa, which isn't really a desert at all. The line will take me over the Andes mountains, across remote valleys, sun-kissed beaches, rusting railway lines, dusty roads, between homes and hovels, through farms, forests, villages and towns.

The BBC team and I have been planning this Capricorn journey for an age, but we know there will be problems ahead. On many stretches of the line we will be travelling in remote areas and our medical backup will be limited. To deal with unexpected emergencies our arms have been repeatedly jabbed with vaccines to prevent diseases the comfortable West has long forgotten. We will carry packs of antibiotics and emergency pills, sterile needle kits, and a trauma pack stuffed with wound dressings and other kit I pray we will never need. Although we have had medical training, none of us is a medic.

As I begin my final preparations for months of travel I'm a bag of excitement and nerves. There is the thrill of an epic new journey with a clear direction, beginning and end. But there is also the uncertainty of a true adventure. On my last major trip, following the Equator around the planet, my temperature rocketed and I began vomiting blood. I was diagnosed with malaria and spent weeks recovering.

I know there will be life-sapping heat and humidity while following the Tropic of Capricorn. If my last trip is anything to go by, there will also be landmines, sleep deprivation, stroppy border guards, dodgy food, altitude sickness, poisonous snakes, killer electrical sockets, roving robbers, government bureaucracy, recalcitrant donkeys, punctures and the sheer logistical challenge of travelling through some of the most remote regions of the world. And merciless cockerels; the dawn chorus in every village.

I look at the map of our planet that covers my desk at home and my stomach leaps and turns at the thought of the journey ahead. The Tropic of Capricorn is 22,835 miles long. The distance is vast, the challenge enormous. I know this will be a tough and exhausting adventure. So what is the point?

Although the precise position of Capricorn moves by tiny amounts over the years, according to *Whitaker's Almanack* and the *Encyclopaedia Britannica*, the Tropic lies at roughly 23° 27' south, or 23.5 in digital. Many think of Capricorn as just an imaginary mark on a map. But the line is actually the most southerly latitude at which the sun can appear to be directly overhead during the summer and winter solstices, just as the Tropic of Cancer is in the north. As such, map-makers identify Capricorn and Cancer as the southern and northern boundaries of the tropics, a region of huge political and environmental importance for the planet, with a climate that drives the ecosystem of our entire world.

Half the surface of the planet is in the tropics. Between Capricorn and Cancer is a band of life 3,222 miles wide, a home to extraordinary natural biodiversity, but an overwhelming concentration of human suffering. Outside the tropics every country in the temperate zone has either middle- or high-income economies. Researchers at the Harvard Centre for International Development identify only three tropical economies, Singapore, Hong Kong and part of Taiwan, as 'high-income'. Even in states straddling a line of the tropics, such as Brazil and Australia, wealth is concentrated in the temperate areas. Nature blesses the tropics with resources and riches, but bedevils it with brain-boiling heat, hurricanes, poor farmland and demonic diseases. Despite the enormous natural wealth and endless potential of the tropics, sullen heat crushes expectations and suppresses human enterprise.

Yet I fell in love with the sultry, sweaty tropics when I passed through the middle of the zone while following the Equator for the BBC in 2006. It is a raw, edgy and beautiful part of the world. Now I want to know more about life in the remote parts of countries on the southern edge of the tropics. The climate on Capricorn will vary, but travelling along the line will take me through some of the world's great deserts. Intense heat at the Equator causes warm air to rise and spread outwards towards the North and South Poles. The warm air cools on the journey and slowly sinks back down to the surface at a latitude of 30°S and 30°N, near Capricorn in the southern hemisphere and the Tropic of Cancer in the north, producing areas of high pressure and a drier climate.

Four trips will take me around Capricorn, each at least a month long, with short gaps in between to plan the next leg, remind loved ones I still exist and prepare for my wedding. For not only am I going on a life-changing journey, but I am marrying my fiancée Anya halfway through the trip. It is going to be a busy six months, so there will be no time for dawdling on the journey. This book will need to be a journalogue, written on my laptop while on the move, in the early morning, or before bedding-down at the end of the day. Writer's block can normally be resolved by a trip to the pub, but there will be no time to lubricate the mind with a pint of Guinness during this adventure. My fingers need to burn across the keyboard.

It is getting harder to find such a unique journey. Mr Palin has bagged many of the best, and I will not be the first to travel around the Tropic of Capricorn. The great African explorer Kingsley Holgate stuck closely to the line on his Capricorn journey. But I will have more latitude, zigzagging along the line in search of interesting stories and people. Brazil is the only line that I have visited before. I was in the far north, now Capricorn will take me to the south. This is the sort of adventure I dreamed about as a child. Growing up in west London, I lived on the periphery of the most international of world cities, and spent wonderful summers in Dorset. Yet my foreign travels were limited to a school trip to Paris and a couple of spectacular family holidays on sunny campsites between Acton and Italy. I flew for the first time when I started work, and my world began to expand. I have never lost the thrill of travel, but a young Somali woman helped me to recognise it as an awesome privilege.

While tracking the Equator, I dropped out of the sky to meet Fatimah and a thousand others in a refugee camp on the Kenyan –Somali border. It was a positive camp run by caring aid workers. But it was also a forgotten prison. Nobody was going anywhere. Fatimah was 23, and had been there for most of her life. She was literate, well educated, fluent in English and bursting with capability and promise. All of it wasted out there in the desert. While an accident of birth and my British passport allowed me to travel the world, for nearly two decades, Fatimah had been forbidden from travelling more than a few kilometres from the camp. Her story haunts me.

When we leave our borders we should remember travel is a desire of many, but an honour for a few. As such it carries certain responsibilities. For the time has long gone when we could happily settle for weeks on a sunny beach without considering the environmental impact of our travels, or the fact that our boutique hotel is owned by the son of the local dictator. None of us should now be travelling blind, and learning more about the places we visit makes for a more interesting experience, a more rounded adventure. So following the Tropic of Capricorn closely is important to me, but the real idea is to use it as the central thread of a journey that teaches me more about issues and places of which we hear little in the West. There will be no time for lazing on beaches. This journey should confront issues, not confirm stereotypes. It should agitate my senses, not dull them. It should be a visual feast but also a political eye-opener.

I am making my Capricorn journey at an extraordinary time for our world. Our climate is changing. It is an age, perhaps, of reckoning, an era of consequences. The random nature of the journey should afford me unique insights into the southern hemisphere and a wider view of the world. But what will I learn about the great issues of our time? About our changing environment, about poverty, globalisation, AIDS, about the rise of China and the suffering of Africa? I wonder how this journey will affect me. Will it alter my outlook on life?

Before my trip can begin there are the inevitable last-minute hassles and problems. I have my maps and a natty hat to keep the sun off my pink neck. But will the government of Paraguay allow us to enter the country? Where is my water filter? I am thrilled, nervous and humbled by the prospect of a unique adventure. I leave soon. I had better start packing.

Simon Reeve
London, June 2007
www.shootandscribble.com

BEYOND THE
NAMIB DESERT

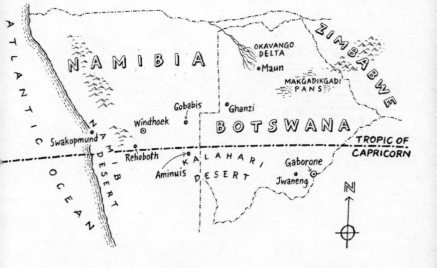

1 · NAMIBIA

THE TROPIC of Capricorn hits the coast of Namibia in south-west Africa on a remote beach in the Namib-Naukluft National Park, next to a small colony of noisy seals reeking of rotten sushi.

The weather is cold and drizzly, and the wind blows a gale, so in the best British tradition the BBC team and I eat soggy sandwiches by the seaside sitting in a four-wheel drive and toast the beginning of our journey. Even the grey clouds overhead cannot dampen our spirits.

It was a challenge to reach this starting line. A flight from London took us to Windhoek, the inland capital of Namibia, north of Capricorn, where we hired two drivers and Toyota 4WDs, drove west to the coast for four hours, then turned south towards Capricorn and the seals. Plenty of time to bond with assistant producer Simon Boazman, and *Equator* veterans Sophie Todd, the resourceful director of this first leg of our Capricorn trip, and Brian Green, a relaxed South African cameraman.

Our first target after starting this extraordinary journey around the planet is Swakopmund, a Namibian coastal town just a notch to the north of Capricorn. To get there we need to leave the seals and skirt the edge of the Namib Desert, crossing some of the biggest sand dunes in the world. They loom in the distance, challenging us with their size.

Dune driving is difficult and dangerous. Vehicles can roll over and frag-ment as they somersault. I fear it will be a nerve-racking ride.

There is no ceremony or fanfare to mark our launch, no cham-pagne, flags or bunting, but I say a few words wishing us a safe journey, almost a traveller's prayer. We finish our picnic, toss a few crusts to the gulls circling outside and start the engines. Here we go. Deep breaths. We are off.

Golden sand dunes run right down to the sea just a few miles from the Tropic of Capricorn, and the only way of crossing them is to head inland a few hundred metres and go over the top, one by one. Our drivers, Doug and Jacques, both originally from South Africa, are old hands at travelling through this remote corner of the world, but I still find the dunes intimidating. Initially they rise gently and the Toyota engines purr. Gradually the height increases and the slopes become frighteningly steep, soon they begin to soar. I grip my seat and our engines scream as we battle our way up a dune hill hundreds of metres above sea level. We reach the top, balance precariously on the sandy crest and the Namib Desert unfolds before my eyes. I gaze in awe. The landscape of the desert, running 2,000 kilometres from South Africa to Angola, is simply out of this world. Mountainous glowing dunes rise from the very edge of the deep blue Atlantic. Inland, endless ripples of sand snake into the empty distance. I laugh out loud. Any lurking doubts I have about this Capricorn journey evaporate instantly. From the very beginning this random line has already brought me somewhere ethereally beautiful, somewhere remote I would never normally be able to visit.

Then Jacques, a tough adventurer with tousled hair and a stubbly beard, guns the engine, and we slide down the other side of the dune, the fine sand making a mournful grating growl as it cascades like liquid ahead of our bumper. I have stood atop dunes in the Empty Quarter of Saudi Arabia as the sun sets and been awed by their luminous beauty. But the Saudi hills are minnows compared to the giants of the Namib, the oldest desert in the world. Is any environment more fundamentally alien to a Brit? As a child, my family rented a small holiday cottage in Wareham, Dorset, for summer holidays on nearby Studland Beach. My brother James and I would run into dunes behind the beach and play hide and seek. The dunes were perilous, even then. The air was stiller, the sun hotter. And the dunes were the furthest bit of Studland from the ice-cream shop. A terrifying place to get lost.

We stop in the shadow of one huge, light terracotta Namibian dune. I listen to the sound of the desert. Gentle wind pushes dazzling sand that responds, shifts and transforms. I spot a jackal trotting along, eyeing us nonchalantly, his fresh tracks pocking the surface. Overhead, pelicans are fishing the bountiful ocean along the coast. The desert is a place of order, every grain neatly stacked. But despite these rare sightings of wildlife it appears sterile, with little life.

We rollercoaster over more dunes, up one ridiculously steep side, down the other, with the sea glistening to our left. In past centuries vicious wars were fought along this remote coast over huge deposits of bird droppings, which provide phosphorus and nitrogen for gunpowder and fertilizer. Namibian guano, in some places 30 metres deep, was especially prized thanks to high levels of nitrates.

Then suddenly we are passing freshwater springs and pink flamingos in a saltwater lagoon at remote Sandwich Harbour, a strange sight in the wilderness. Jacques takes us over the top of a particularly tricky ridge. As we race down the side even I can see we are going to get stuck. I throw out a hand to brace myself against the dashboard and shout a warning, but the next dune is too close and there isn't enough room at the bottom for us to level out or turn. We slam into the sand at the bottom, throwing us forward in our seats. Jacques tries spinning the wheels then curses lightly in Afrikaans and radios for Doug in the other car to help. 'I am a driving expert,' he says with a shrug, 'not a recovery expert.'

Doug, a short, ruddy man with a lobster tan, comes to the rescue, but his car gets stuck on the sharp edge of the dune above us. Initially, of course, this is fun. I sit on the dune taking photographs and making helpful comments as Jacques and Doug use brute driving force on the sticky sand. But then Jacques mentions extracting cars from bunkers can take so long he carries a golf club and balls and practises his game while waiting to be rescued. That encourages me to help. The prospect of spending a cold night or two out in the desert without food does not appeal.

Digging out the wheels and letting air out of the tyres proves futile, so we add extra weight to each corner of the car as the wheels spin. Nothing works. Then Jacques and Doug jack up the front of the vehicle, but the jack just sinks into the sand.

'The problem is there's no place for it to really grip,' says Jacques gloomily as he peers at the sand under the car. He finds a thick wooden running board in the back and slips it under the jack, but as soon as weight is applied it sags, then snaps in half with a noise like the crack of a bullet.

Stacking the two pieces together, we start to jack again, finally lifting the car off the sand. Then we all push the front of the car until it topples to one side. But the front moves no more than eight inches. We jack and push, over and over again. It is knackering work and soon we are all damp with sweat. It takes a full hour before the front of the car has turned enough for the wheels to bite on firmer sand and we can escape. We roar our way up the side of the dune, throw a rope around the back of the second car, and tug it free of the crest.

After another few hours of hard driving, mercilessly free of major incidents, we leap over the final high dune and head down to a flat beach that opens before us. Doug stops his car above the high tide for a cigarette break and shows us fossilized oysters. Despite the icy sea, this region is experiencing a tourist boom as wealthy foreigners are drawn to the desert for adventure sports such as sky-diving, quad-biking and sandboarding. Some travel writers have even suggested the Namibian coast can be reached from London on a long weekend break. The Green Party must love that. But who am I to talk?

We drive on, over small dunes turned a dark reddish hue by a layer of garnet dust. We pass vast pans where 650,000 tons of salt are harvested each year, before we eventually find ourselves on a tired piece of tarmac and finally reach the town of Swakopmund late in the evening. We are tired, hungry and thirsty. But we've made it. Time for a cold beer.

SWAKOPMUND IS not your usual African coastal town. This is a corner of Africa that is forever Germany. It is bizarre. Think Bavaria, with sand, sun, and a vicious wind. The town is stuck in a time warp, with old German colonial architecture and gothic writing advertising shops, services, even the local plumber. Colonized by Germany in the late nineteenth century, Namibia used to be called South West Africa, and outside Café Anton at the Schweizerhaus Hotel on Bismarck Street, *kaffee und kuchen* still comes in steaming mugs with thick slices of Black Forest Gateau. There are German shops, bakeries, packs of German tourists, and thousands of retirees from the old country.

Like most transplanted Europeans, many of the local German–Namibians, even those who have been here for four or five generations, have kept their Teutonic identity. In a foolhardy bid to understand the pioneering spirit necessary to survive on the edge of the desert, I arrange to join a local swimming club known as the *Krampfadergeschwader*, or the Varicose Vein Squadron, for one of their morning dips. The squadron, membership of which seems limited to mildly eccentric Namibians of advancing years and sturdy German stock, gathers at seven in the morning. I overlooked one crucial fact: they spurn the attractive facilities at the Swakopmund Municipal Baths for a swim in the bracing waters of the southern Atlantic, normal temperature a bone-chilling 13 degrees Celsius.

Crossing the beach towards the water, I shiver in the morning chill. From behind the camera, Brian stifles satanic chuckles. I contemplate fleeing but Sybille Meintjes, a sprightly 78-year-old, and Wulf Von Teichmann, a mere 71 years old, emerge from beachside changing rooms. There will be no escape. Wulf, a retired farmer of captivating bearing, manages the extraordinary feat of looking aristocratic in trunks and a fluorescent bathing cap. I stand next to him in my shorts, knock-kneed and shivering.

The sea is freezing. Or at least close to freezing. But after the initial shock it is not entirely unpleasant and I keep telling myself that cold baths and cold swims are great for the circulation. Wulf occasionally has trouble sleeping, but his daily dip clears his mind for the day. 'It helps me to be focused,' he says.

We swim in shallow water for 20 minutes, but then I plead for a return to warmth. Sybille and Wulf are made of stronger stuff, but graciously join me back on the beach. I chat politely, then Sybille notices I am turning blue. She orders me home, then goes beachcombing for stones for her pot plants; Wulf probably went jogging along the beach. I creep back to my guest house, teeth chattering incessantly, in search of a hot shower.

After a warm wash and flagons of hot coffee I head out again and wander along the seafront, this time fully clothed. It is winter in southern Africa, and the seaside town is quiet. Rain is so rare that few houses have gutters or drainpipes. Sprinklers, water clipped green lawns and an elderly white woman and her broom fight a losing battle against sand blowing across the steps to her bungalow. I walk along a short pier, obeying officious signs telling visitors where to stand, walk and fish, and look back. The town is small, white, neat and prosperous.

But there is a darker side to both Swakopmund and Namibia. In a local café I meet Johanna Kahatjipara, a 55-year-old former nurse now working as a historian. Johanna is a bubbly woman with a broad, sincere smile. As we eat fish salads, gritty with sand, she talks me through a chapter of Namibian history that includes a genocide the former colonizers, and even many locals, have tried to forget.

In 1884 the European powers decided to carve up Africa. Germany took control of Cameroon, German East Africa, Togo, and South West Africa. Germany had not been an aggressive empire-builder in the fashion of Britain or France, but at the end of the nineteenth century German cities were over-populated and riddled with disease. Hundreds of thousands fled the country for a new life in America. German politicians decided if people were going to emigrate, they should be encouraged to emigrate to a German colony. By 1903 a few thousand Germans had settled in South West Africa, buying cattle and renting farms from the Herero, a powerful and well-organized tribe who owned the best land. But soon Germans were seizing land and cattle by force. When the Herero fought back, they were annihilated. General Lothar von Trotha, the German Commander, read an extermination order, or *Vernichtungsbefehl*, to his troops: 'Within the German borders every Herero with or without a gun will be shot. The Herero people must leave the land.'

Ethnic cleansing developed into what some consider the first genocide of the twentieth century. One German officer wrote in his diary: 'We had been explicitly told beforehand that this dealt with the extermination of a whole tribe; nothing living was to be spared.'

Herero survivors were forced to flee east into the Kalahari Desert, where German troops poisoned water holes and continued to shoot men, women and children.

'It was a genocide,' Johanna says vehemently, 'because the order was to exterminate the Herero people. They should be wiped off from the face of the so-called German protectorate, that's what they said.'

An outcry back in Germany eventually forced Kaiser Wilhelm II to stop the killing. So German troops then herded many of the remaining Herero and people from the Nama tribe into labour camps. Thousands became units of work with numbered metal tags around their necks, just entries in a ledger. Vast numbers were beaten or starved to death.

Johanna finishes her salad and we walk down to the seafront. She tells me that thousands of Herero, mainly women and children, were imprisoned in two concentration camps in Swakopmund.

'What do you mean,' I ask, 'by the term "concentration camp"?'

'Well, they were put in camps where they could not run away, where they were watched by German soldiers, where they were being flogged and beaten regularly.'

She pauses. Her own relatives suffered in the camps.

'They lived half-naked in the camps in shacks made from poles with material over them to give the simplest of covering from the wind and the weather. And they had to do forced labour for the Germans.'

I nod slowly. It is a shameful past. We pause in front of the pier, standing among beautifully tended gardens. Sprinklers are whirring away.

'They unloaded ships and worked as slaves right here,' says Johanna. 'The women, even the children, had to push wagons loaded with materials that came from the ships. Here, where we're walking right now, this was the concentration camp.' She stops for a moment, then adds quietly, almost to herself. 'People died here. It feels like I am walking on the bones of my ancestors.'

Eighty per cent of the Herero people and half the Nama people, around 65,000 men, women and children, were exterminated and their land and cattle stolen.

'In the concentration camps most people died from exhaustion,' says Johanna. 'It even stated that on death certificates.'

Techniques used by the Second Reich against the Herero, such as shipping prisoners in cattle cars and moving them to isolated locations for systematic disposal, were copied by the Third Reich for use against Jews. Events in Namibia helped to lay the logistical and intellectual foundations for the Holocaust. Professor Eugen Fischer and General Franz Ritter von Epp, who both shaped Hitler's racial and political thinking, had their own views shaped by their involvement in the South West African genocide. It is a terrible and incredible story. A tale of forgotten genocide we stumble across because Capricorn takes us through remote corners of this far-off land.

European colonial rule in Africa was, of course, rarely benevolent. The Brits were hardly better than the Germans, using extraordinary force even into the 1950s, during the Mau Mau revolt in Kenya, when at least 100,000 Kikuyu were either killed or died in British concentration camps. But Namibians were spectacularly unlucky with their colonial occupiers. The Germans were followed by the South Africans, who entered the country during World War One and administered it until after World War Two, when they made it a South African province and enforced apartheid. The new state of Namibia finally won independence in 1990. Throughout the South African occupation, black and white Namibians were never taught about the genocide. The slaughter was airbrushed from history.

That has only begun to change recently. In 2004 a German government minister travelled to Namibia and apologized to the Herero, asking Namibians to 'forgive us our trespasses and our guilt'. But the German state has never really acknowledged the enormity of the Namibian genocide. To do so might require Germans to accept that the Holocaust, rather than being a freakish stain on their character that can be blamed entirely on the Nazis, has deeper roots within their history and culture.

The Herero are a pragmatic lot. To reclaim land stolen from their parents and grandparents, they are pursuing the German government through the courts, asking for $3 billion in compensation so they can buy their land back legally. But the Namibian leadership is reluctant to back the Herero. Germany is the largest investor in Namibia. German tourists contribute millions to the economy. Best not to rock the boat.

In Swakopmund today historians believe a supermarket stands on the site of a concentration camp. Black Namibians work in the shop as cheap labour on a site where their families were worked to death. Opposite the supermarket more gothic lettering announces a dusty and smelly antique shop. There are books about Namibia's stunning wildlife and landscapes, new Namibian flags and leaflets extolling the glories of this open and liberal new society. There is African art from across the continent and antique German coins. But there are also several copies of Hitler's *Mein Kampf*, and even the odd photo of a smiling Hitler greeting tousle-haired Aryan kids. I found it kitsch and creepy, just like the town.

On the outskirts of Swakopmund, as streets give way to scrub and sand along the Swakop River, the cemetery for local whites is well tended, well watered and verdant, with palm trees creating the feeling of an oasis in the desert.

The path through the cemetery passes scores of graves bearing German names, then a small Jewish quarter, and then, as desert and scrub beckon beyond low bushes, the path comes to an abrupt halt. Leaving the oasis, Johanna and I walk 50 metres across harsh open land, and come to an area where the bodies of hundreds of Herero and Nama people, worked to death by their masters, were unceremoniously wrapped in simple cloth and dumped in shallow graves. Desert plants grow on the low mounds, sustained by what lies within. Stretching into the distance, tyre tracks show quad-bikers have shown their respect for the dead by riding over the bodies.

At the edge of the graveyard is a tall, black granite monument, erected just a few months before our visit, commemorating the thousands of Namibians who perished under 'mysterious circumstances' in concentration camps in Swakopmund during the years between 1904 and 1908. There doesn't seem much mystery to me. They were worked or beaten to death, raped, abused and generally treated as disposable batteries that could be used for their energy and then discarded.

As a thick mist crawls in from the Atlantic, swallowing Swakopmund, Sophie, Brian, Simon and I take Johanna for dinner.

Our choice of restaurant, recommended by the German Namibians who own our guest house, is perhaps unfortunate. Zur Kupferpfanne, The Copper Pan, used to be Haus Altona, the home and office of the head of the Woermann shipping line, which was closely linked to the colonization of Namibia and the slaughter of many Herero slave-workers in Swakopmund. The house is now a restaurant cum museum, with colonial-era photos on the walls and display cases of memorabilia from the days of German South West Africa. But it has a benevolent, friendly air. With tinkling faux crystal chandeliers, a table I can't quite get my legs under, and cork place mats displaying exotic varieties of fruit, it reminds me of going for dinner at my gran's.

Perhaps eating at Zur Kupferpfanne seems a tad insensitive, but Johanna is a fan of Germany, and the two of us wander from room to room examining old sepia photos.

'Even though they killed my ancestors, I love everything about the country,' she says, idly tapping a photo of a German settler wielding a spade and impressive facial hair. Johanna first visited Germany in 1985 on a German government bursary programme. 'It was beautiful. I fell in love with the place.'

Johanna is remarkably forgiving. At a diplomatic party during her trip, the wife of a prominent German journalist asked her where she had found her clothes.

'I bought them at the airport,' she deadpanned.

But what on earth did she wear on the plane?

'I wrapped myself in a blanket to keep warm.'

I find this feisty woman confusing. She campaigns for Herero rights, but also admires the German culture that swamped and subdued her people. The Herero have developed a wary respect for German efficiency and supremacy. Perhaps this has helped them to accept their crushing defeat. The Herero are a proud people. They cling to the belief that any tribe that can defeat them must be truly extraordinary.

But the consequences of genocide, and the apartheid that followed it, are still evident in Namibia. Around 4,000 white farmers own roughly half of Namibia's arable land. Much of it was acquired from locals under dubious circumstances, or simply confiscated.

'These are farms on land taken away from my ancestors, their grazing land,' says Johanna angrily. 'So I cannot say this is history, let's just forget it.'

She paces her words. 'Today, even though we are in an independent Namibia, we are really just a robbed nation.'

ACROSS ARID ground from the wealthy, overwhelmingly white centre of Swakopmund is Mondesa, a sprawling black township of small huts and shacks that exists to serve the basic needs of the white town.

The township lies behind a salt depot, a building supplies merchant, and an ore crusher, on the other side of the tracks, quite literally, beyond a railway line that helps separate blacks from whites. Many of the thousands living in Mondesa manage without sewers or even communal latrines. At the edge of the township the Swakopmund side of the railway tracks is used as an open toilet. I step carefully through a squalid, stinking minefield of human waste and ribbons of toilet paper that flap in a bitter wind blowing in off the sea.

The shock for me here is not that conditions are tough. The shock is that poverty exists in such close proximity to wealth. Out of all proportion to their numbers, white Namibians seem to run the businesses, own the farms and drive the nice cars. Anyone serving, waiting, walking, riding buses, or driving service vehicles is likely to be black. Perhaps this is no surprise. 'Black Africans are poor' is hardly a newspaper shock story. But I have not seen such a staggering economic and racial divide in any other country I have visited. According to studies, Namibia has the highest level of economic disparity in the world. At times it feels like Namibia still suffers under apartheid.

Most people in Mondesa who work for whites do so for a pittance. Henry Shilongo, a labourer working on a holiday apartment block on the Swakopmund beach front, told me he walks for nearly an hour each way to and from his small home on the far side of the township. He cannot afford a bus ride to or from work. 'I do not earn enough,' he said simply.

I am watching men and women like Henry stumbling across the open rocky ground between town and township when a couple of kids come power-walking down the railway track. The young engine driving the train has a serious face, set on a destination. The child behind giggles at the sight of a television crew standing among crap beside the tracks.

As dusk arrives, a convoy of buses appears over the horizon and turns towards the township. They carry the lucky few from Mondesa who work at Rossing, a huge uranium mine, the largest of its type in the world, forty minutes outside Swakopmund. A few years ago much of the workforce at the mine was laid off when nuclear power fell out of favour and the price of uranium plummeted. But global energy trends are fickle. With oil running low, nuclear power is back in fashion. The price of uranium has rocketed skywards, and Rossing has re-hired workers. Namibia now sees itself as a major uranium supplier to the world. Another uranium mine has opened, another is about to open, and 13 more are in various stages of development. Namibia could soon be making a killing because the world demands power. It is a safe bet that only a fraction of the money will trickle down to the residents of Mondesa.

On the very edge of the township, Rose Hadebe, a large, matronly woman wearing a long and voluminous thick skirt, is supervising two young men putting plastic sheeting over the roof of her small rented house. It is a basic structure, if not downright primitive. Rough wooden posts form one side of the house. With spaces in between the posts, it is more of a fence than a wall. Rose gestures towards a piece of cardboard.

'I will put this wood over the wall to keep the wind out,' she says optimistically.

I ask Rose why she thinks all the white Namibians live in the town, and black Namibians live in the township.

'That's the way it is,' she says. 'White Namibians have the money while we are poor. The white people they have money to do everything. But our black people – we have no money.'

'Do any white people live in the township?' I ask.

'No.'

'None? Not one white person lives here?'

'The owner of the houses is a white person. And we see tourists coming here to look around.'

'But surely things have improved since independence?'

Her answer is exquisitely accurate.

'What use is independence if you have no money? If you have money you can feel independent anyway.'

After enduring the Germans, black Namibians fought for freedom from South Africa behind the banner of the South West African People's Organization, SWAPO. It was a bitter struggle.

Independence finally came in 1990 and SWAPO now runs the Namibian government. But national independence does not soften the pain of black poverty. Rose tells me jobs are few and unemployment is high. She sells clothes door-to-door, but struggles to put food on the table and pay school fees. To be comfortable, Rose says she would need just £60–80 a month. Tourists in Namibia are often unaware most people in this country survive on less than £2 a day. The government plans to improve the townships, promising every household water, sewage and electricity. But progress is slow. Conditions in Mondesa are a disgrace. No wonder many black Namibians are disenchanted. Whites in Swakopmund must exist in a moral bubble if they are able to live so close to such hardship. I sense that if things do not start to improve, whites in this country may find their wealth being taken by force, just as it has in Zimbabwe.

As I talk to Rose the lads on the roof bang nails into the plastic sheeting forming her barrier against the elements. But Rose's small house is on the edge of the township, across a flat, arid plain, and her fence and cardboard wall will not keep out the wind roaring in from the Atlantic.

WE LEAVE Swakopmund the next morning and take the Trans Kalahari road east towards the capital, Windhoek. I am relieved to see the seaside town fade in the rear-view mirror. It is an apartheid-era town stuck in a painful past. Within half an hour of leaving the coast, Atlantic clouds lift and we are bathed in bright sunshine.

There are few trees amid the baked scrubland and with Kevin and Terence, wise-cracking local drivers, now behind the wheels of our two cramped four-wheel drives, we race through the harsh terrain, overtaking a film crew on their way to a set in the desert. Hollywood has discovered Namibia, and the country is currently doubling as the Middle East for an American television mini-series about the war in Iraq. It might be a nice earner for Namibia, but I find it disconcerting to see a vanload of American soldiers in full battle-dress on their way to level Falluja.

There are few diversions along the road. Long fences set just back from the road mark the edge of vast farms and dry scrubland. Apart from birds and occasional herds of cattle, there appears to be no life in the undergrowth. But Namibia has wildlife treasures. The country has the largest population of wild and healthy cheetahs in the world, with around 6,000 of the cats running free. Farmers are not best pleased with large predators roaming their land and nabbing calves. They treat them as vermin, killing the territorial cats by trapping, shooting and even burning them alive. So on the road to Windhoek we take a short detour to a hillside lodge, where Olivier Houalet and his father Alain run a cheetah sanctuary protecting cats captured on Namibian farms.

Olivier, a tanned, lean and ridiculously cool young Frenchman known by admirers as 'Catman', aims to save, rehabilitate and re-introduce cheetahs on to farms across the country. With Anyway, a stocky Jack Russell and fox terrier cross, at his feet, and a young meerkat called Qwick-Qwick on his shoulders, he takes me on a tour of the sanctuary.

Nicky, CP, Anya and Nanoushka, four hand-reared cheetahs, are permanent residents at Amani, living in an enclosure known as 'cheetah paradise'. As Olivier and I walk over to the gate the lanky racers inside spot their man and begin to purr. Apparently he sleeps with them. As I sit on my haunches and gaze into their hypnotic eyes, I can see why.

The cheetahs at Amani are magnificent. Anya, the most aloof of the four, rejects my offer of a stroke and swats me away with a great paw. But I never feel at risk. Although no wild animal can ever be completely tame, cheetahs are the safest big cat for a low-risk encounter.

The four hand-reared cheetahs are Olivier's sleeping partners, but he also has five other male rescued cats, orphaned as small cubs after their mothers were shot by hunters, that have learned to hunt, trap and kill. Olivier plans to release them in the south of the country. In his old open-top Toyota Land Cruiser we drive through two sets of gates on a bushy, beautiful corner of his estate.

'In this area the cats are completely wild,' says Olivier in his soft French accent. Windhoek is just visible on the horizon. 'Can you believe we have cheetahs so close to the city?'

The five cats here pursue and eat anything meaty and edible that slips under the farm fences and strays into their killing ground.

'We wanted to raise them all together, as a group, in order to give them the chance to build up a hierarchy and the strengths of coalition, and that worked perfectly,' says Olivier. 'And in a coalition the weaker personality is pulled along by the stronger personality to help with survival and hunting. We put them in a wild situation and their instincts took over.'

We stop at the bottom of a hill and Olivier begins carving snack-sized chunks from a slab of raw meat. His plan is to leave the meat in the open, retreat, and wait for the cheetahs to appear.

'Maybe they will come, but if they have eaten something wild, maybe they won't.'

'So they could be anywhere out there?' I ask nervously.

'They could be anywhere.'

'Watching us now?'

'Yes.'

'Well, I've got my trainers on so I can run if necessary.'

'No,' says Olivier. 'Don't ever run, that's the biggest mistake. Even with lions, the only way to survive a lion encounter is to stand your ground. If you are strong enough, if you manage to control your energy and your fear, that's your best chance of survival, otherwise you have no chance.'

As Olivier finishes his sentence there is a low thunder, like a herd of soft-shoed horses galloping through the bush. Five hungry cheetahs come racing down the hill.

'No, this is wrong!' says a shaken Olivier. 'They should not be coming yet, quick, back in the car!'

Brian and I are standing on the ground next to Olivier. He hustles us towards the Land Cruiser, over which I can see hungry heads launching their raid. Olivier looks genuinely worried. Brian and I pull each other on to the front seats and glance back to see cheetahs surrounding Olivier. He lobs the smaller pieces of meat a few metres away from the vehicle and throws the thick slab of meat back into our car. The top of it is clearly visible, and the cheetahs can smell the blood. They wolf down the smaller pieces and swarm around Olivier hissing, spitting, growling and snarling. Emboldened by the pack, each goads the other into more aggressive behaviour.

For a moment I fear they will jump into our car, devour the slab of meat, and then take a fancy to a few other tasty morsels. Like Brian. Or me. But Olivier holds them back, dropping into a karate stance with one arm out, and making a snapping star shape with his hand as three cheetahs nip at him with their teeth.

'They are wild guys, they are able to hunt and kill for themselves for survival, and I'm standing right in their territory,' says Olivier, keeping up a running commentary. 'It looks like they haven't killed anything so they're pretty hungry, and it's now all about body language and no fear at all.'

His karate pose works. Olivier pushes them away from the car, the meat, and us. My left hand grips the windscreen, while my right digs into Brian's flesh, holding him from falling into the pack as he tries to film. Two cheetahs turn. The other three snarl and retreat. Olivier is annoyed.

'When cheetahs feel threatened,' he says, 'or when they have enough of things, and have to fight, they are very powerful from the front and they will stand on their back legs and basically whack whatever is in front of them. And cheetahs, you see, their claws are always outside. They cannot retract their claws.'

One of his wardens should have watched the cats and warned him. Although it is unlikely the cheetahs would harm us, they do not normally live in packs, they are large, wild animals, and their sharp claws are always ready. It is hard to predict their behaviour when a few gangly humans come between them and a meal.

We drive 50 metres away, with the pack watching closely. Olivier hurls the meat slab on to rocks and they descend and tear it to pieces, sucking and licking the meat with sandpaper tongues.

'They are beautiful, and part of the African ecosystem for thousands and thousands of years. We need them here and everywhere in Africa, but farmers are still putting down traps for them,' says Olivier with a shake of his head. He is desperate to see cheetahs protected, and supports a new scheme exporting cheetah-friendly beef to Europe. It guarantees farmers higher prices for their beef if they allow cheetahs to live on their land and take an occasional cow. 'We must work to change the minds of farmers. We must protect these incredible animals.'

I leave Olivier's lodge vowing to adopt my own wild cats. On the outskirts of one village I see a lion moving through the undergrowth. Closer inspection reveals a golden labrador. Another member of the team sees giraffes in the distance. They are horses. Best to leave the wildlife to the experts.

WE COULD see the Namibian capital Windhoek from Olivier's lodge, and head towards a hotel in the centre of town late in the evening.

Driving through the outskirts of Windhoek, the team and I see dozens of women and young teenage girls in mini-skirts and heels loitering on pavements or in doorways. A taxi stops directly in front of us so the white passenger can call a girl over to his car. There are increasing numbers of sex tourists in Namibia, helping to fuel the devastating spread of HIV, and Windhoek is a magnet for the trade.

'Older men are coming from Germany to get women and young girls,' Rodrick Mukumbira, a local journalist, tells me the next day over a meal in a popular Portuguese restaurant. But sex with a stranger is a deadly risk in a country where the adult HIV/AIDS rate is a staggering 21 per cent.

After lunch and a chat, Rodrick takes me to meet Herman Klein-Hitpass, an elderly Catholic priest who has spent years helping sex workers. With donations from German churches, Klein runs a centre called Stand Together, and provides food and clothes to desperate girls and women at his small one-storey centre in the poor township of Katutura on the outskirts of Windhoek. Katutura means 'we won't go there'. Many residents were moved here when the former apartheid regime decided to clear the Pioneer Park area for wealthy whites. Even after independence, they are still here, and the whites are still there.

Nine sex workers are hanging around, chatting and hoping for help, as I walk through the security gate at Stand Together and nearly lose my eyes to low-hanging razor wire. 'People keep breaking in,' says Father Klein apologetically, pointing to the wire and grilles over the windows. The women he helps are always desperate for more. They broke through the roof while Klein was sleeping inside. He caught them red-handed trying to steal half a case of tinned fish.

Klein sees prostitutes as young as nine years old at the centre, some pimped by their mothers. I ask whether he sees child prostitutes occasionally or regularly.

'Sometimes regularly,' he says. 'Sometimes the mother takes the children to the street and I say "you will not be helped".'

'What's their response?'

'"Doesn't matter, my child makes money."'

Inside the centre is chaos. Boxes of flour and powdered milk are stacked on shelves. An entire room has been given over to tins of fish. Klein is losing a battle against clutter. He is brave and caring, but he is also old and fragile, and he cannot trust the women to help him clean and organize the food or clothes, because they keep stealing the supplies. Nearly 1,300 prostitutes are members of the centre. They are women who have fallen to the bottom and have nothing to lose. Seventy-five per cent have HIV. Of those carrying the virus, 40 per cent have passed it to their children. I run the figures around my head and swallow hard. AIDS is like a medieval plague, I say to the priest. He nods. He has lived with the consequences for years.

Tessa Peri is an impish woman with bright eyes and a cheeky grin. She sits next to me wearing a dirty red sweater, threadbare pyjama trousers and a dusting of foundation on her face. She looks younger than her 40 years, and her face alternately crumples and blooms with intense expressions. Abandoned as a baby, Tessa left a care home at 13 and lived with a gang of boys under bridges and in storm drains, hustling for food and money, then sold her body for a pittance.

'I was young, small and pretty and the men were looking for young girls.' She smiles as she tells me, perhaps to put me at ease.

'Sometimes they would pay me with just food, such as chips and sausages. A chicken leg to have sex with me. I was young and did not know any better and that is why I accepted it. And this is how I grew up – with different men picking me up and having sex with me.'

Tessa works the streets for one simple reason: money.

'I have tried to stop, but when I need money I start again.'

Sometimes men refuse to pay her. 'And they would often refuse to use a condom. And this is how I got AIDS.'

When Tessa discovered she had HIV she went crazy, sleeping with clients without caring.

'I did not care about my life anymore and I had the attitude that I would destroy!'

Like all of the prostitutes at the centre, Tessa has friends and family who have died from AIDS. She knows what it does.

'I still weep for some of my friends,' she says sadly. And she knows she has infected clients. 'This man I met was healthy and then I made him sick. And now that man goes and destroys other lives.'

But even now, despite publicity campaigns warning clients that Namibian prostitutes are ravaged with AIDS, men will not use condoms.

There are few phrases that do justice to the impact of AIDS on southern African. A holocaust. A vindictive plague, taking the most productive members of a family and society. More than 60 per cent of all HIV/AIDS cases are in sub-Saharan Africa. According to figures for 2006, 25 million Africans are HIV-positive and 2.8 million are infected each year. AIDS kills 2.1 million every 12 months.

Condoms can help to stop the spread, and Father Klein has 5,000 of the latex lifesavers, made in Alabama and covered with spermicide, sitting in white cardboard boxes on his shelves. He has already given away thousands more, which has caused him one or two problems with Rome. Women at Stand Together usually earn between one and eight pounds when they sleep with a client. But the prostitutes get more money, up to £20, if they agree not to use a condom. Both parties to the transaction appear to be suicidal. Tessa is now trying to stop younger girls from taking her path.

'I say to them, the men look for young women, but the men are totally ruining you, they are killing you. You are not going to get money, you are going to get AIDS. I tell them they can choose between life and death. They earn nothing and have no life if they become prostitutes. To give your body to the streets is looking for your own death. You drift between the living and the dead.'

Tessa now gets treatment and anti-retrovirals, but is vague on details. I ask when she had her last client. 'Not for several months.' Father Klein listens but wants Tessa to be honest. He heads back to his cluttered office. I ask Tessa again. She just giggles.

We chat at the centre, then Tessa takes Father Klein and me back to her home in the Babylon area of the township. She lives in a simple square shack about ten square feet. The walls are scrap sheet metal and old car bonnets, and the roof is a thin piece of leaky plastic. Next to her is a woman who treks into Windhoek every day to work as a cleaner, but also earns a pittance. Their shacks are just two of thousands in the township made of breeze-blocks, rusting metal skeletons, shiny new corrugated iron or wood. Better than living rough, says Tessa. Each shack has a small space around it, but there are few homely touches and the earthy smell from communal latrines is pervasive.

Tessa has a padlock and chain on her door protecting her paraffin cooker. 'People know I am a woman all on my own; they will try to take anything.'

I feel a welling sense of sadness for Tessa, the sickness she carries, and the suffering she has endured in her life. A knot rises in my throat, so I swallow hard, trying to be businesslike. She is not asking for my pity, just my attention. I ask more questions while she draws water from a stand pipe provided by a water company a few minutes' walk from her house. She pays with a small blue plastic charge card pushed into the pump. General living conditions are not far removed from refugee camps, where charities often provide water for free. Here people are being charged for it. The overall disparity with the lives of white Namibians is utterly depressing.

The government says most of Babylon is 'informal housing'. I call it a shanty town. Hundreds of families arrive in the townships around Windhoek every week from rural areas of Namibia and from strife-torn countries abroad. It is a pathetic way to live, but it is the future. Every single week a million people around the world move into shanty towns that are growing at a phenomenal, unstoppable rate. Urbanization is one of the great global trends. More than 90 per cent of population growth in the twenty-first century is predicted to be in cities. In sub-Saharan Africa more than 70 per cent already live in slums, and over the next 30 years the population of African and Asian cities will double, adding another 1.7 billion people to the world. That's more than the combined populations of China and the US. We will be living on a planet of slums. How will our cities cope? Here in Babylon the government is trying to provide for new arrivals, building roads, primary schools and communal latrines, and collecting rubbish once a week. Yet it is a desperately slow process. Tessa is optimistic about the future, but it will be a long time before lives improve.

Back in my bland hotel I sleep fitfully, disturbed by what I have seen and heard. But the next morning I venture out in bright sunshine, on to clean streets full of bustling shoppers, hawkers and purposeful commuters.

Charitable visitors call Namibia 'Africa for beginners'. The capital is clean and soulless. Like Slough in the sunshine. But a brisk walk reveals independent Namibia has chosen revolutionary friends. At a roundabout graced by the sandstone Lutheran *Christuskirche*, Fidel Castro Street meets Robert Mugabe Avenue, home to the British High Commission. The Foreign Office must be delighted.

The West has ignored Namibia for decades, and the country now has a new suitor. In the last few years China has arrived in Namibia, signing exclusive agreements for minerals and tons of uranium. Deals have been lubricated by lucrative payments and by China paying for the construction of a new presidential palace in Windhoek. China is getting the raw materials feeding its extraordinary economic growth. Heading in Africa's direction are products flooding out of Chinese factories in search of new markets and eager buyers.

To find out more, I take a taxi to the Chinatown trading estate in Windhoek, a small empire packed with cavernous shops rented to enterprising Chinese. Bruce Lee, the pistol-packing 32-year-old son of owner Leonard, takes me inside the huge sliding security gate that marks the entrance to the estate. Black Namibians are shopping for quilts, toys, shoes, handbags, tools, generators, tacky clocks, and cheap clothes. Traders come from towns in China that specialize in specific products. They buy in bulk and barter prices ever lower. I find a natty handbag for less than 50p, and a denim jacket for under £1. This is both the democratization of consumer goods, making the luxuries we take for granted in the West available to poor Africans on a low wage, and consumerism gone mad, as the Chinese churn out endless mountains of often shoddy goods and dump them on Africa.

Leonard Lee invites me for a meal at his restaurant Yang Tse and produces a strong Chinese liquor in a blue fluorescent glass container with curves of a perfume bottle and the taste of anti-freeze. Business is going well for the 5,000 Chinese in Namibia, who have become the second biggest employers after the Namibian government.

Across Africa, the Chinese are gaining power and influence. China now gets one third of its oil from Africa and has huge investments in oilfields, mines, railways, forestry and retailing across the entire continent. The IMF forecasts China's trade with Africa will double to around £50 billion a year by 2010. China has already passed the UK as a trading partner, and is rapidly closing on France and the US.

Europe and the US seem blind or unconcerned by these developments, but locals on the ground have spotted the changes. In Namibia, Chinese language courses have been heavily oversubscribed.

At the University of Namibia, Professor Yan Gan Fu is teaching a Chinese class. Uda Nakamhela, a young Namibian lawyer wearing academic glasses and a crisp shirt, has seen the writing on the wall: 'I think 10 or 15 years down the line Chinese will be rivalling

English as the language of the world, and I want to get in with Chinese businesses from the start.' Uda hopes to make a packet drafting contracts and legal documents for new Chinese firms in Namibia. Smart chap.

A few hours from Windhoek, on the edge of a backwater African village, I find a new brickworks owned and run by a Chinese construction firm and staffed by Chinese and local workers. I arrive unannounced and unexpected, but as I walk towards the main building, a small dilapidated house now rented to the Chinese, Daniel Xiu appears buttoning his shirt. The fresh-faced and bespectacled 24-year-old reminds me of a Chinese Tintin. He is running a fever but has leapt off his sickbed to greet me. He is wearing thick white gloves, black trousers and shirt, and a black jacket that would pass muster in a nightclub.

'You're looking very smart,' I say.

'I'm very young, that's why I'm very smart,' he replies. And we both chuckle.

Daniel is the group's translator. He tells me they are making 100,000 bricks for more Chinese construction companies operating in the north of Namibia.

'They get a lot of tenders from the government and also they are building private houses for local people,' says Daniel.

Across Africa, state-owned Chinese construction firms are deliberately under-bidding for contracts, because China's long-term objective is not profits but to get a foot in the door and secure access to natural resources.

On the ground in Namibia, standing with Daniel, I feel I am witnessing history. The hair on the back of my neck actually stands on end. For these are momentous events, both a new 'scramble for

Africa', and proof of China building a global business empire, reclaiming the superpower position it held for centuries.

What this means for this continent is unclear. There are now around one million Chinese in Africa and they are not here for altruistic reasons. Chinese firms operating in Africa prefer to employ Chinese workers and buy Chinese equipment. More worryingly, the Chinese have signed deals with repressive governments such as Sudan, Zimbabwe and Eritrea, ignoring their records on human rights, saying they want 'a new type of strategic partnership', according to their official Africa policy, which 'respects African countries' independent choice of the road to development'. It means China is giving African dictators huge sums of money and loans, free of conditions, without worrying about where and how it is spent, even when the money they have given Sudan has sustained the war in Darfur and helped end 300,000 lives.

But China was supporting anti-colonial liberation struggles in Africa while the West was still supporting appalling dictators such as Mobutu. So perhaps China's arrival might bring positive benefits. The West has failed to save the continent. Four decades and $570 billion of aid have done little to improve the lives of many Africans. Their lives are getting shorter and poorer. After security, a salary is high on the list of what most poor Africans want. They are queuing to apply for jobs with Chinese firms. Conditions are poor, and pay is lower than in China. But it is still more than most Africans earn. Perhaps this could lift some Africans on to the bottom rung of the ladder. Chinese money and construction workers are also starting to build infrastructure in struggling African countries such as Angola and Nigeria, a development policy that has helped transform China. Perhaps it could just help to transform Africa. At least that's the hope. Either way, the arrival of Daniel and the Chinese has huge implications for Africa and Africans, and quite possibly the rest of us as well.

HEADING SOUTH from Windhoek takes us towards the town of Rehoboth, close to Capricorn. The weather is perfect, with clear blue skies and crisp sunlight, and we speed along the edge of giant farms. Miles of scrubby grassland follow miles of scrubby grassland. Simple fences prove everything is owned.

Capricorn crosses Namibia just outside Rehoboth. Two Tropic of Capricorn signs flank the road. We stop briefly for group photos and then head into Rehoboth, a small, well-kept, town home to some 35,000 Basters, the self-named mixed-race descendants of white Afrikaaner colonizers and local San Bushmen and Nama women.

Vera Tune, a local Baster teacher, has agreed to show me around. She waits for us at the local petrol station despite feeling poorly with flu. Tall, 40-something, with tousled blonde hair, caramel-coloured skin, and a long, infectious, throaty laugh, Vera is the happy offspring of a Baster mother and a 'Cape-Coloured' father, who fled South Africa after the Second World War when the racist government decided 'coloureds' could no longer vote.

The Basters are a curious people, trapped between blacks and whites in southern Africa. They fought alongside the Germans against the Herero, but then found the colonizers turning on them. Independent Namibia has little time for them.

'Children born from marriages between white settlers and black natives were not white enough for the white community and not black enough for the black community,' says Vera. 'So they were on the outskirts.' They still consider themselves to be a unique tribe, and celebrate their connections with the old Boer settlers. Shy mixed-race kids in the local school perform a traditional dance for us wearing outfits the original Boer trekkers would have recognized.

We are to spend the night by Lake Oanob, formed by a new dam high in the Rehoboth hills, and we carry our bags to a group of simple dry-stone lodges spread out around the edge of the water. My kit is an essential annoyance. I carry a expedition duffel bag for my clothes, sleeping bag, mozzie net and other equipment. My gadgets and gizmos – laptop, camera, chargers, phone, GPS and a satellite phone – are stuffed into a hardened Pelican case. I love the Peli case. It could be air-dropped from a plane and would only suffer minor scratching. But the damn thing weighs a ton. I drop it on to the wooden floor of the cabin and the whole hut shakes.

Back in the lodge kitchen, Vera and her friend Charlotte Blom are preparing dinner.

'We want to give you a taste of Baster cooking,' says Vera, shooing me out when I try to check the pots.

By the time Charlotte emerges from the kitchen carrying a huge, steaming, cast-iron cooking pot I am suspicious about the menu. Trying local dishes on camera can be a perk of the job. I get to eat while the rest of the crew salivate. But I am also the group guinea pig, and jokes about 'cockroach cake' have been bandied around most of the evening. With a flourish, Charlotte lifts the pot lid and a cloud of steam parts to reveal a full sheep's head stuffed inside a sheep's stomach. I would have preferred cockroach cake.

'Go on, Simon, tear it open with your fingers,' Charlotte says with glee.

The stomach has been baked to a crisp. I tug it apart, and an eye rolls into sight. It looks revolting.

Charlotte takes over. She lifts the head out from the stomach and expertly carves the sheep cheeks, considered to be the best meat. She beams at me expectantly. I expect the worst, but the cheeks are delicious: delicate texture and a subtle flavour. Eyes are considered the real treat, but I find the idea of eating them repulsive. My meat and fish usually comes in anonymous chunks and wrapped in plastic. It certainly doesn't stare back at me. Charlotte tips an eye on to my plate. I pop it into my mouth, expecting the texture of an egg and the taste of ... well ... whatever foulness an eye tastes like. But it begins to dissolve on my tongue. The sensation is pure fat. Not unpleasant at all. Actually rather tasty.

I eat the other eye with a new sense of confidence, then move on to the tongue and pancreas, which tastes like strong liver. It is an offal feast. The finale comes with a crack. Charlotte snaps open the back of the skull to dig out the brain. A creamy pâté. Charlotte says she cooks sheep head regularly.

'I had it just last weekend. It's like a traditional Sunday lunch for us.'

Trying it is one thing. Eating it regularly is another. It doesn't beat a good roast chicken.

Cold dawn the next morning and I am standing outside my lodge looking around the edge of the lake, numb with shock. Overnight the lodge kitchen and dining room has burned down. The stone structure underpinning the building is still standing, but the wooden floor, walls, bar, kitchen and thatched roof have all gone. The floor and wall beams are still on fire.

Christy, the stocky Baster owner of the lodge, is upset but pragmatic. 'Ach, these things happen,' he says. He is not blaming us for the blaze, which is a relief. We left the restaurant by 10 p.m. and the doors were closed half an hour later. The fire started around 3 a.m. Several beers ensured I slept soundly. Even three exploding gas canisters failed to wake me.

Christy is astonishingly cool, inviting us to drive around the lake to his own home, where his wife and daughter are preparing breakfast. We eat toast and scrambled eggs while a pet meerkat and puppy play together on the lawn and Christy and his Swiss wife Helena chat about how they will rebuild the restaurant. Christy has already rung the local thatched-roofer, who is able to start work in a few days. 'He's ready to go,' says Christy. 'We'll clean the stonework and get the place built again.'

'They're very practical around here,' says Helena. 'That surprised me when I first arrived from Switzerland. I was used to things taking ages.'

It is no wonder Basters have become good at getting things done. They feel left out of the new independent Namibia and are pushing for a degree of self-governance for the Rehoboth region. They are already self-reliant, and by investing money in small, intensive farms are trying to make themselves self-sufficient. Some even hope to secede from Namibia and create their own state.

We drive further east, through a scrubby, empty landscape and along wide, flat, dusty tracks bleached by the sun, each vehicle throwing up a cloud of fine dust that billows behind and blows through the cab of our car. Back home I cannot even glance at my map in a car without my stomach starting to turn. Out here my senses are already toughening. I wrap a shemagh shawl around my head to keep dust out of my nose and read.

After four hours we stop for a group call of nature on a small hill by a tree packed with the huge nest of social weaver birds. The nest looks like a bale of straw has been dumped in the gnarled branches. Dozens of birds work together to build the nests, which can be three metres high and five wide, and may contain hundreds of chambers, like a housing block. We have not seen another car for more than 150 kilometres. So of course as soon as we were all peeing a truck shoots past, covering us in dust.

We pat ourselves clean, then watch silently as a black-chinned weaver darts out of the communal block and skips along the top of a low hill that joins the road from the left. The hill is packed with fine reddish soil that trickles through my fingers like sand. The landscape is changing. Camelthorn trees, already a careful distance apart to secure the maximum amount of precious liquid for their roots, are creeping further from their neighbours. I spread my map across the bonnet of the car. One word dominates the land to the east. We are getting closer to the western edge of the Kalahari Desert.

Few crops enjoy these harsh conditions. But a succulent triffid-like cactus called hoodia seems to thrive.

'These are our little soldiers,' says Kirk Bassingthwaighte, the 28-year-old son of a tough, pioneering farmer, as we stand in a nursery containing thousands of tiny hoodia plants. Anyone using email may be familiar with the word. Or at least you will be if you check your junk mail folder. Hoodia is the new great hope of the diet industry that wants to offer terminally chubby Westerners a slim waistline in tablet form, and Internet snake-oil salesmen spamming billions in the hope of a quick buck.

For centuries the San Bushmen have eaten hoodia growing wild in the Kalahari Desert to stave off hunger and thirst. Dougal, Kirk's father, ate it as a lad while out searching for horses on the vast estates dotted around his current farm near Mariental, close to Capricorn.

This is outback territory, reached on long, straight roads, a place where farmers fly small planes around their country-sized estates, mustering cattle and sheep.

We arrive at the Bassingthwaighte farm just as a group of black Namibian farmers are finishing a tour. Black farmers receive preferential loans thanks to affirmative action policies designed to push more land into the hands of the majority community. This particular group wants to join with Bassingthwaighte and form a hoodia association. By uniting forces, they hope to create momentum and a serious global market for hoodia, which can already sell for prices of £20 an ounce.

Close to their farm estate, Dougal and Kirk have 130,000 seedlings that will each weigh roughly two kilos in a couple of years. The crop could become a huge earner, a solid reward for years of hard work. Dougal and his wife Bobbie have spent four decades transforming their farm from a single building into a huge estate of 10,000 hectares, an area of nearly 40 square miles. My eyes widen at the scale.

'But land is cheap out here,' laughs Dougal. He puts a value of £400,000 on his buildings and vast lands.

That evening Bobbie generously cooks us a delicious feast of local game in their huge open kitchen, and I ask what the family thinks about land reform in Namibia. I had thought of Dougal as a leathery, no-nonsense soul, an image softened by his excessively comfortable slippers, and by Bobbie calling him Peanut. Yet he is completely in favour of the 'willing buyer, willing seller' policy of the current government, which encourages wealthy whites to sell their land to black farmers. His brother has sold the neighbouring farm. I ask whether the reforms are moving quickly enough.

'It will take time. Things aren't going to change overnight. They shouldn't change overnight,' says Dougal with a nod to the chaos in Zimbabwe, where farms have been forcibly taken by the Mugabe regime.

I suggest the pace of reform in Namibia is moving too slowly, and Dougal does not disagree. How long is it since independence? Fifteen years? Twenty? I cannot remember. But neither can the Bassingthwaightes, which infuriates Kirk.

'How come we can't remember the date of independence of our own country?' he says later, reproaching himself and his family.

'Well, there was a slow transitional period,' Bobbie says thoughtfully, 'but also, in truth, the change didn't affect us very much.'

We hunt for the exact date in reference books, and then ask Kevin and Terence, our black drivers, who are sprawled on sofas watching a garish soap opera. They answer in unison: 21 March 1990. Independence was one of the most important days of their lives.

I WAKE AT 4 a.m. in north London to the sound of cockerels crowing. What are they doing here? Then I dozily remember I am on a farm in southern Africa. I try to block the noise, but the cockerels sense my rejection of their call to rise. They wander closer to the outbuilding where I am sleeping and crow louder. I suffer for an hour, slipping in and out of sleep. Then I crack. I leap out of my sleeping bag, grab my torch and explode out of the door ready to slaughter breakfast. The cockerels run off cackling. Now completely awake. No point in going back to sleep. Cockerels 1, Reeve 0.

Two hours later we are all up and on the road, heading east from the Bassingthwaighte oasis towards the town of Aminius. We go from a track to wide roads carved straight across the western edge of the Kalahari. We race along, two clouds billowing behind our four-wheel drives, until nature follows our lead and a fierce wind whips sand and dust into the air, filtering the sun and blanketing our path.

Four hours later we arrive in Aminius, a small and depressing collection of Herero homesteads scattered over a huge area next to a salt pan, blindingly white under the sun. The Herero are not out here by choice. At the end of their genocidal campaign against the tribe, German troops pushed the few survivors out to the bleak lands around Aminius, and left them here to suffer. We are nearly at the end of our journey across Namibia and have reached one of the most remote corners of the country. On my map Aminius looks like a substantial town. But the 'Corner Supermarket' is a shack, and it is closed. We have a few supplies left over in the back of the cars and eat a late breakfast of eggs boiled on a small stove and some slightly stale bread, while standing around our cars at the edge of the salt pan. Or at least the rest of the gang eat. My guts are churning, so I sip water. Perhaps the sheep is taking revenge. I dread the thought of carrying an upset stomach further east, across the Kalahari Desert.

As the others eat I call back to London on our satellite phone. Time to make contact with my real world. Anya, my fiancée, who will be working and travelling with me on the second and third legs of the Capricorn adventure, says she needs my list of invites for our wedding and the roof is leaking in our flat.

Back to the road. Outside the spartan local government offices in Aminius, Peter-Hain Uaakiza Kazapua, a Herero guide from Windhoek with family roots in this area, has been waiting for us patiently. A muscular man wearing a sports top, jeans, trainers and carrying a small rucksack, he looks younger than his 32 years. I try calling him Peter, but Peter-Hain corrects me. He was named after the British politician who at the time of writing is the UK secretary of state for work and pensions. When Peter-Hain was a young lad, Peter Hain was a leading campaigner against apartheid.

'He was a hero in my family. It is my life's dream to meet him, just to shake his hand,' says the Namibian namesake, with touching sincerity.

With Peter-Hain leading, we drive to the tiny Aminius settlement where one of the great Herero generals lived and organized a final, failed campaign to save his people from annihilation by the Germans. Mbahuurua Mungendje now owns the general's former house. Tall, imposing, and wearing a dark trilby hat, sunglasses and a thick coat despite the mid-morning sunshine, Mbahuurua looks more like a New Orleans jazz legend than a cattle-farmer and local headman. His sturdy mud home has a rusty red corrugated roof topping two open windows and a door, out of which a delicate long white cable trails for eight metres across the sandy front porch to a cream telephone wrapped in a clear plastic bag. The phone is flat on the ground next to a jacaranda tree and a checked umbrella on a stake that provides shade for a large, solemn, middle-aged lady, who sits working triangles of bright fabric on an ageing Singer sewing machine that is propped upon a large blue washing bowl. She is wearing what looks like a relic from Victorian times, an enormous, billowing dress and a horned hat. It is a surreal scene.

Professor Mburumba Kerina, a Namibian historian with a home in the area, sits with me on fragile plastic school chairs under the tree and explains that most rural Herero woman still wear their traditional dress, inspired by the clothing worn by the wives of German missionaries in the 1800s, at least once or twice a week. A huge dress is worn over an apparently endless series of petticoats. Some suggest between six to twelve metres of material. I glance at the sewer on my right. She appears to be sitting on a small chair, but perhaps solid petticoats provide the support. I am intrigued, but an inspection might be deemed impolite.

The top half of a Herero dress is no less impressive. Fabric cascades off shoulders, which are topped by a large hat folded to resemble two horns. How the wives of those original German missionaries survived out in this baking and arid land wearing such a confection, I cannot imagine. But many Herero still wear the dresses, which vary widely and wildly in style, every day. I have already seen elegant ladies wearing 1970s curtains, lurid tartan and fluorescent green elsewhere in Aminius.

The lady sewing outside Mbahuurua's house is wearing grey with brown polka dots. Her outfit looks incredibly impractical. Wearing it in the midday winter sun must be deeply uncomfortable. Wearing it in the heat of an African summer must be unbearable. To me at least, it seems utter madness.

As we chat I feel familiar low rumbles starting in my stomach. I wince and shift uncomfortably. Professor Kerina, a jolly man wearing a patterned jumper, nods sagely. 'Try this,' he says, producing a mysterious yellow bottle from his leather bag. I take a slug of alcoholic ginger with a taste so intense I am knocked sideways. I cough and splutter. 'Bush medicine,' says the Professor with a laugh. I prod my insides. All seems calm.

We finish discussing Herero clothing, then Professor Kerina explains his disappointment at the state of modern Namibia. He is uniquely qualified to comment. The professor named the country while living in exile during the years of South African occupation. 'I was completing my doctorate in Indonesia and one day the president asked me about my country, and I said it was called South West

Africa. He said, "That's no good, Angola is also in south west Africa."' The professor leans towards me, lowering his voice. 'And do you know what he said next?'

I shake my head.

'He said to me, "only dogs and slaves are given names by their masters. Free men invent their own names."'

The professor leans back in his chair and puts his hands triumphantly on his knees.

'Well, I tell you it made a huge impact on me. Huge. I had been thinking about the riches in the coast off the Namib Desert, and so I started writing about this fictional country called Namibia.'

Simple, really.

Suddenly the phone on the ground rings loudly next to Mbahuurua. The noise seems so completely out of place. Mbahuurua answers, chats, then laughs and passes the phone to his incredulous white visitor. It is Mbahuurua's niece calling from Colchester in Essex – of course – where she is studying travel and tourism at college. Just ringing to chat to the family. I stick to the obvious. Apparently it is sunny in England and her studies are going well. She is very excited the BBC is in her village.

That afternoon we drive back to the small homestead of Peter-Hain's brother Moses, just east of Aminius, where we will spend the night among his livestock. Including a few cockerels. The land out here is poor and cattle walk deep into the bush to graze, so Peter-Hain takes me out on horseback to find the family cows and drive them back into the kraal for nightly protection against hungry African carnivores. If this sounds like something out of *Rawhide*, think again. I am on a gentle old nag who recognizes my inexperience and plods along slowly. It would have been faster to walk and takes us hours to find the cattle.

By the time we do, my bum is saddle-sore. But as we turn the cattle back towards the setting sun and the family hut, my horse-with-no-name picks up his pace and even manages a canter. It becomes a perfect end to a fascinating day. As a cold wind sweeps in, we layer jumpers and then coats. Tents fold out on solid bases on top of our Land Cruisers. We light a wood fire in the open and scoff stringy local sausages and rubbery old potatoes in a heavenly, thousand-star restaurant.

I climb the short ladder to my small tent and bed down on a corner of Moses's land. I dream of Mbahuurua's niece becoming the boss of Thomas Cook, before the dreaded cockerels wake me at four in the morning (cockerels 2, Reeve 0), and we go in search of Holy Fire.

HERERO LIFE is centred on families, fire and cattle. Those three pillars of life are all venerated by the Holy Fire, a small, simple fire lit in the morning that burns until the night. The fire is where male elders sit while talking to their ancestors, appealing for help or advice. It burns on a strip of land separating the homestead from the cattle in the kraal, and is sparked by an age-old daily ceremony. Not every family, or even every settlement, has the Holy Fire. 'It's a great honour that's inherited,' says Peter-Hain.

Julius Ndukireepo, the *Ondagare,* or keeper of the holy flame at Otjongombe, a tiny Herero settlement close to the Botswanan border, has asked us to be at his village before sunrise to witness the Holy Fire ceremony.

We are up early, but in truth, I hardly slept all night. Bitter cold, cockerels, 45 flatulent, mooing cows in an adjoining kraal, and a herd of noisy, stroppy goats just metres from my head saw to that. I also slept on a hard metal surface that rolled around on the car-suspension whenever I breathed. It was like being on a waterbed.

We find the *Ondagare*'s one-room hut by torchlight and Peter-Hain knocks softly. Julius answers from his bed. It turns out he wanted us there before sunrise to check we were serious about witnessing the ceremony. He will not be rising for nearly another hour. So Peter-Hain and I stand around in near-zero temperatures, flapping our arms and stamping our feet while waiting for Julius to emerge and the ceremony to begin. I mutter a few choice phrases under my breath, I can tell you.

As with many traditional African ceremonies, women actually do most of the preparation work for the Holy Fire. Batseba, the daughter of Julius, emerges into the biting cold 20 minutes before her father, gathers some wood, starts a fire close to the house, then takes embers around the inside of the hut and out on to the dung-strewn land between the homestead and the kraal, where three short fat tree trunks are arranged as a triangle. Kneeling in the sandy soil, Batseba blows on to the fire and the wood begins to smoke.

The sharp sun rises, bathing us in early warmth and light, and taking my breath away with its clarity. The cattle begin to stir, their hot breath hanging in the cold air, and steam slowly rising from the heat of their bodies. Then a door scrapes open and Julius, a distinguished 82-year-old, emerges from his hut wearing an old South African army officer's dress uniform. Supported by two ancient wooden crutches and with utter dignity, he limps towards the smoking fire at a stately pace. It is a sight I will treasure.

I had thought of Peter-Hain as a city-boy aloof from the traditions of the village. But he watches silently and treats the whole ceremony with solemnity and respect. Julius lowers himself on to a log in the triangle.

'The fire can bring good luck if you treat it correctly, and bad luck if you do not respect it,' whispers Peter-Hain. 'If I buy a new car, I will drive it here from Windhoek and it will sleep here, next to the fire, and my father will sit by the fire and bless it and ask the ancestors to protect me.'

A look of bemusement crosses my face.

'Simon, it is all about belief. If you believe in something it can be so. If you jump over the Holy Fire, it could either make you sick, or give you bad luck and we really do believe in that.'

'So you're quite careful around the fire?' I ask.

'Not *quite* careful, Simon. Very much careful. I mean, this is God.'

Venerating the fire, ancestors and cattle I can understand. But I still struggle to understand why Julius and other male Herero elders treasure uniforms of their oppressors, and why Herero women wear their elaborate Victorian-era missionary dresses, even to the shops. Surely victims should not adopt the clothing of their oppressors?

I try to get an explanation from Julius, but he just gives a snort, and asks whether I have seen the Himba people of northern Namibia. Many Herero think the Himba still wander around virtually naked and view them with unbridled contempt.

'Until the Germans arrived our people were dressed like the Himba. Now we dress like you,' says Julius.

It seems the Herero originally started wearing European clothing because it made them feel superior to other tribes. The notion makes me feel uncomfortable. But it is easy to forget just how much tribalism still dominates this continent.

We leave Julius sitting by his fire and arrive back to Moses's homestead just as his dogs start to wake. We crank an ancient pump for water and light a glorious fire. My stomach is feeling sturdy, so I eat a hearty outdoor breakfast of gruel and butter cooked on wood and charcoal in an iron pot. Brian does most of the cooking with our driver Terence, the two of them ribbing each other constantly, while I sit on an empty beer crate by the fire watching the show.

With full stomachs, we wave farewell to Moses and head towards the town of Gobabis, planning to drive east along the Trans-Kalahari Highway into Botswana. But bureaucracy intervenes. The Botswanan government insists we cannot simply cross the border in the remote wilderness, but must pass through immigration channels in the capital Gaborone, hundreds of miles further along Capricorn. It will ruin the rhythm of our journey, but there is nothing we can do. We need to get there quickly, deal with the bureaucracy, and then hop backwards to resume our journey. One call later on our satellite phone, and a charter flight is booked taking us east to the Botswanan capital.

Outside Gobabis our two-car convoy turns on to a narrow dirt road leading to the airport. Gates to the field are shut and held together by a karabiner. I jump out of the lead car to open the gate, and slice my hand on a razor-sharp piece of metal. First blood of the trip. The airfield is empty save for five small corrugated iron hangars, just big enough for farmers' planes. We park next to them and ring the airline to check we are in the right place. 'Isn't the pilot there yet?' says the flight controller, reminding me of a mini-cab operator near my home. 'I'm sure he'll be there in a few minutes. He's just coming round the North Circular.'

2 · BOTSWANA

IN EVERY direction, the land is flat. Impossibly flat. So flat the horizon reveals the curve of our planet. As we fly low over Botswana, towards the capital Gaborone, the colour of the parched land below is a washed-out brown. Vast farms, thousands of acres in size but empty of water, have scattered herds of tiny guilty cattle slowly munching their way through arid bushes and dry grass.

First impressions of 'Gabs' are not positive. We search for its heart, but lose our way among glossy, glassy buildings and modern sky-rises. Roadside adverts smack of those in an accountant's monthly bulletin: 'Computerize your payroll!' bellows one. The capital seems functional and well-run, but also a little dull.

After we collect our filming permits we meet up with Letlhogile Lucas, a local journalist with a huge heart, a giant stomach and a great sense of humour, for dinner at the Buddha Bar, a new restaurant in a grotty Gabs shopping centre. Album covers line the walls and LPs double as place mats. We eat seswaa, a delicious porridge served with minced meat and veg. It is a noisy film night, with a packed crowd watching a screening of the Peter Sellers film *Revenge of the Pink Panther*. Around us, middle-class black couples mix freely with whites. Rare in Namibia, this is a common sight in Botswana.

Formerly the British protectorate of Bechuanaland, Botswana

became independent on 30 September 1966. Just a few years after the Brits left, the largest diamond reserves on the planet were discovered in the country. To its credit, Botswana did not collapse into chaos with different gangs battling over the stones, as has happened in so many parts of the world. 'We have remained secure and at peace, regularly beating the UK in polls which measure global stability,' says Lucas proudly.

The reason, ironically enough, is largely down to the fact that one tribe, the Tswana, dominates Botswana. Until the massacres in Rwanda, it wasn't politically correct to acknowledge the ongoing corrosive effects of tribalism in Africa. But even now, when a leader from one tribe takes a presidency, it is usually beholden on him to reward members of his tribe with plum jobs and lucrative contracts. Corruption flourishes and other tribes, feeling left out, then battle to take power so they can have their turn feeding at the trough. Of course in most of Africa the problems date back to colonial rule, when Europeans drew the borders of new invented states and deliberately included competing tribes in the same countries. Divide and rule. It was a useful way of controlling the locals. But, as the name confirms, Botswana is the land of the Tswana. So there has been no major inter-tribal friction.

Botswana today is a stable country and by far the largest producer of rough diamonds in the world. They provide half the government revenue and 80 per cent of exports. Botswana has extraordinary natural beauty and endless wilderness that draws the tourists, but its real wealth and power, like an iceberg, is below the surface. Lucas, who uses his surname as a first name, suggests I visit a diamond sorting centre and the Jwaneng diamond mine, the richest in the world, which many locals call simply 'the money pit'.

Only 24 tons of actual diamonds are mined around the world each year, but one-carat diamonds can sell for anything between £2,000 and £11,000 each, depending on cut, quality and colour. Under the gaze of guards and cameras at a sorting centre owned by Debswana, a partnership between diamond giant De Beers and the Botswanan government, I hold a small mound of 26 eight-carat uncut diamonds in my hand. I try to ignore the veil of slogans and advertising that surrounds diamonds. These are just transparent crystals of bonded carbon atoms. But it is no use. They are cold to the touch and ancient, formed when the planet was young. The rocks still inspire lust.

Locals see them in a more practical light. Dust, a Debswana executive with the voice of Louis Armstrong, who shows me around the sorting room, says: 'They have given us everything, roads, schools, hospitals.'

Later, I ask Lucas for confirmation.

'So where does the money from diamonds *really* go then?' I ask.

'Well, it's going on free education, free health services, free this and that.'

'In your own family, does everyone get to go to school?'

'Yes, they all go to school.'

'For free?'

'Definitely for free. You know, Botswana was the very first country in Africa to give free HIV tests, then one of the first countries to give free HIV/AIDS treatment in the terms of antiretroviral drugs. And it's all because of the money we earn from diamonds.'

The morning after that ringing endorsement Lucas takes us 120 kilometres from Gaborone and over the stubby Polokwe Hill towards the Jwaneng mine. 'Botswana's only mountain pass,' he says.

As I approach the mine, the sound of subterranean warriors fighting echoes in the air. In front of me is a vast pit more than a kilometre wide and 326 metres deep. At the bottom, tiny diggers hurl tons of rock into the back of tiny dumper trucks. Albert Milton, the mine's deputy boss, a relaxed Botswanan who studied at the Camborne School of Mines in Cornwall, grabs the yellow safety hand-rail surrounding the observation platform.

'This is the hole that makes Botswana sparkle,' he says with a booming laugh. 'At independence we were one of the poorest countries in Africa. Now we are one of the richest.'

Jwaneng means 'place of little stones'. Termites revealed the mine in 1973 by lugging minerals found among deep diamond deposits all the way to the surface. This is now the most valuable patch of land on Earth. In 2006 more than one billion pounds' worth of diamonds were mined from Jwaneng by owners Debswana.

Albert and I drive down into the pit on a road that circles lower around the edge. A colossus blocks the way, belching black smoke and dragging a long red tail. One of three giant electric excavator cranes at the mine, the scale of the 720-ton beast is remarkable. The creature snorts, its vast bulk begins to stir, and a hand at the front, armed with sharp, claw-like fingers, curls down to the ground. Albert and I climb into the bucket and I press my hand against its skin. Its sheer size makes it feel organic and alive.

'This is my baby,' says Albert, slapping the skin, 'this is what does the work.'

We jump through the teeth back to the ground and the hand rises smoothly into the air. The operator sits in a cab three-storeys high. With a simple, fluid action, he grabs 60 tons of broken rock and lifts it high into a waiting dumper truck. Down in the pit, everything is colossal. The size of the hole, the height of the hydraulic excavator, the scale of the dumper trucks waiting patiently to receive their load.

Security is tight. I am told not to touch the ground, or even try to tie my shoelaces. A security guard watches my every move.

'I would be happy to leave you down here for weeks, because you would never spot a diamond,' says Albert. The odds are a million to one, but we had better not take a chance.'

Four scoops of rock from the crane, and a truck is loaded. Its ten-foot tyres, £50,000 apiece, are threadbare. Industrial strikes in the US and demand from China have made it hard for Debswana to source tyres for their dumper trucks. Loaded with more than two hundred tons of rock, the truck makes slow progress out of the pit towards a crusher on the rim. For a stone imbued with such myth and romance, the extraction of diamonds is surprisingly industrial. Diamonds are only found in roughly one in 100 underground 'pipes' or deposits of kimberlite. Of those containing diamonds, only one in 100 has enough to make removal economically viable. Kimberlite rock is dug out of the ground, forced through crushers processing 3,000 tons an hour and then carried on belts through sorting machines that toss rock and send brilliant pebbles deeper into the plant for lasers and X-rays to select gems. Security at the mine is tight but not perfect. I find a stone stuck in my boot. I keep quiet. I rub it, I clean it. But the stone is just a stone.

We leave the mine and drive to the local Jwaneng Hospital, funded by money from Debswana. The sunny cottage hospital, a group of small, white-washed, low buildings with a lawn and sprinklers out the front, stands on the frontline of Botswana's battle with HIV/AIDS.

Botswana has the second-highest HIV rate on the planet after Swaziland, a pandemic driven in part by the role of migrant workers in the mines and lorry drivers thundering through Botswana heading for the Kazungula Ferry on the border with Zambia buying prostitutes and spreading the plague.

Migrant workers at sites like Jwaneng are among those hit hardest. Patients at the hospital cover their faces as we arrive. 'The stigma of AIDS is still a heavy burden,' says Dr Nzenza, who shows me around.

The Botswanan government believes at least 270,000 people out of a population of less than two million are carrying the HIV virus. The consequences have been catastrophic. Between 1990–95 life expectancy in Botswana was around 65 years. Then the dying began. Life expectancy has collapsed to less than 34 years. 'We are threatened with extinction,' Botswanan President Festus Mogae has said. 'People are dying in chillingly high numbers. It is a crisis of the first magnitude.'

Lucas tells me about a period a few years back when he was going to at least one funeral every single Saturday and Sunday for four months. 'Everyone was dying,' he says. 'I've lost neighbours, church mates, friends that I grew up with, workmates, colleagues, everybody you can think of, really.'

'All to HIV/AIDS?'

'Yes, I've seen a lot of people die, I've seen my friends die, I've seen almost everybody around me die because of HIV/AIDS. It's been incredibly traumatic.'

At Jwaneng miners were dying faster than new recruits could be trained. Others were off sick. Yet more were caring for ill relatives. So Debswana took a difficult decision and offered expensive antiretroviral therapy to its staff, and subsequently their families. The cost to the company has been enormous. But the cost of doing nothing would have been even higher.

Films such as *Blood Diamond* rightly show the dark side of the international diamond trade, which has created and fed appalling, bloody African conflicts in which millions have died. But diamonds have also bought benefits. In Botswana earnings from diamonds have enabled the government to provide antiretroviral therapy to anyone who needs it.

'A few years ago patients were crawling in here. People were dying on us all the time,' says Dr Nzenza as we walk the corridors. 'Now patients breeze in asking for their ARVs and tell us they can't wait because they need to get to work. They can be quite cheeky. But it is wonderful, because they are living normal lives.' We turn a corner and, as if on cue, a grinning patient appears waving a prescription at the doctor. 'Without the ARVs he would not have survived,' says the doc.

The availability of antiretroviral therapy in Botswana means AIDS is no longer a death sentence. The national funeral industry, once a huge growth market, is experiencing lean times. But HIV has already taken its toll. There are around 150,000 orphans in Botswana, nearly ten per cent of the entire population. Orphanages are opening across the country, a consequence of the steady collapse of the traditional African extended family. Orphanages simply should not exist in Africa. There should be a great-aunt who can look after a child orphaned by AIDS. But Auntie might also be a victim.

In Botswana the sexual behaviour that encourages transmission of AIDS is only now starting to change. 'What is now more understood is that when you are married you should only eat at home,' Lucas tells me with a gentle smile. I am a bit slow on the uptake. Finally I catch-on. 'This is a macho culture where taking numerous sexual partners has been perfectly normal. And we have had long traditions of polygamy. It has taken time to change that mindset.'

Eat at home. It is a simple phrase. But it is the issue at the heart of the AIDS epidemic in this continent.

Africans do not appear to be particularly promiscuous. Over a life-time they have roughly the same number of sexual partners as those in the rest of the world. The reason AIDS has blazed like a wildfire across the continent, the difference in Africa, is that Africans are more likely to have more simultaneous long-term partners.

In the south of the continent mining has long been one of the main forms of employment. Away from home for long periods, miners strike up relationships with prostitutes and locals, just as their wives, back home, liberated and cursed by a greater degree of sexual equality than in other developing world cultures, will often also take long-term lovers while their partners are away working. AIDS spreads faster and more efficiently in these long-term relationships than in one-night stands. In fact, the chances of contracting HIV from one sexual encounter are surprisingly low.

Too many African anti-AIDS projects are just focused on trying to get prostitutes to use condoms with clients, a campaign that has abjectly failed, as I have already seen in Namibia. Focusing on transmission by prostitutes stigmatizes carriers and discourages frank conversations about sex.

What works in Africa are open national discussions about the terrifying effects of AIDS and campaigns built around the simple concept of monogamy, what President Museveni in Uganda brilliantly termed 'zero grazing' and put at the core of his nation's ABC campaign: 'Abstain, Be Faithful and Use Condoms'. They are still coming to terms with the concept in Botswana, but it is the best hope for the country. Stigmatizing sex workers and saturating Botswana with condoms has not helped. But being faithful to a partner, what Lucas describes as eating at home, might just halt the plague.

JUDDERING ALONG at 2,000 feet, above a desiccated land, I suddenly glimpse water in the distance, shining like thin molten silver.

Lucas has sent us across Botswana towards the largest and most beautiful oasis in Africa, a lush and pristine wilderness home to one of the greatest concentrations of large game and wildlife on Earth: the Okavango Delta.

'On every side as far as the eye could see, lay stretched a sea of fresh water, in many places concealed from sight by a covering of reeds and rushes of every shade and hue; whilst numerous islands, spread over its whole surface, and adorned with rich vegetation, gave to the whole an indescribably beautiful appearance.' So wrote the Swedish explorer Charles John Andersson in his 1861 book *The Okavango River*. The delta is the end of the Okavango River, known as 'the river that never finds the sea'. Long ago it was part of a massive river system that flowed across Africa and out into the Indian Ocean. But tectonic shifts created a long natural dam that turned the Okavango into a shallow bathtub nearly the size of Wales.

Humans have been here since our beginning. Thousands of years ago this land was fed by an inland lake and early man hunted in a verdant paradise home to mega-fauna and gigantic animals such as enormous hippos. Some of the largest Stone Age weapons or tools found anywhere on the planet have been discovered to the east on the Makgadikgadi Pans.

The Botswanan town of Maun serves as the southern gateway to the delta. We land at the airport, after leaving Lucas back in Gaborone, in front of ranks of smart little planes standing ready to take wealthy tourists on sightseeing jaunts. Maun is becoming a tourist mecca, a growing town with hotels, ATMs, fast-food joints, a Bimbo's restaurant and a health centre (motto: 'We treat…God heals').

We have arrived just in time. Fresh water is coming to Maun. Creeping and crawling along the dry bed of the Thamalakane River on the edge of town, across thick, hard mud cracked into cubes, rain that fell more than six months earlier in southern Angola has trickled down a low gradient into northern Botswana.

Standing on the riverbed with Map Ives, a local wildlife guide, I watch the water soaking through the mud like a sponge. It fights its way past small mud islands that it surrounds, then inundates, and then, like a series of baths constantly overflowing, continues its rapacious progress. As it gobbles dry mud, air bubbles leap through the new water to the surface. Drowning insects crawl for safety and low-flying Hammerkop, known locally as the rain bird, swoop in. Four of them wade through the new water, feasting on insects and tiny fish flushed down the river. The rain water pushes dried donkey dung the same way, creating a fetid, stinking mess at the front of the new water, but cleaning the bed for fresh water that follows behind, already purified by reed-beds upstream. The pula, the currency of dry Botswana, means 'rain', a word people shout at weddings in celebration. Locals arrive to watch. 'We have been waiting for the water for months,' says one sightseer.

Map has a wispy light-grey beard, decades of experience, and a no-nonsense attitude. His excitement about the rain is intoxicating. I can see water on the surface, he tells me, but groundwater is creeping along a metre or two underground at an even faster rate, pushing and squeezing through tiny gaps left when round balls of sand are pressed together. This trickle is the beginning of everything. I can see that now, more than ever before. The ground, the insects, the birds, even a passing flock of goats, everything breathes a sigh of relief. Life has arrived.

Within a couple of hours, the creeping water becomes a steady stream, then a lazy river. Most of the liquid on the surface evaporates during the journey from Angola to the Okavango. But the dribble that survives the journey inches its way into the delta, gradually fills it up, then sits there nourishing an extraordinary array of wildlife that treks here from across the entire region.

'The Okavango is the biggest wetland, or protected wetland, on Earth,' says Map proudly. 'The biodiversity is enormous. Aquatic invertebrates, amphibians, reptiles, mammals, there are just thousands upon thousands upon thousands, if not millions, of creatures that live here because it is completely pristine. And all this, in the middle of the Kalahari! If you want to see African nature in the raw, this is the place.'

TIM RACE, who will be guiding and driving us back across Botswana to Lucas in Gabs, is waiting for us in Maun. Despite being a fourth-generation white southern African, he has an English accent, phrases like 'old chap' cross his lips and he arches one eyebrow with an insouciant air. Tim seems as English as Biggles. He should have a handlebar moustache, rather than his neat goatee. Crucially, he is calm and unflappable, vital attributes for the long journey ahead. Our plan is to explore the delta region before heading south overland towards the vast emptiness of the Central Kalahari Game Reserve. We will cross the Kalahari, or at least *try* to cross the Kalahari, then skirt along the Tropic of Capricorn and head back to the Botswanan capital Gaborone. Roads run east from there to the border with South Africa.

The distances are vast. Fortunately, Tim specializes in taking people off the beaten track. Waiting with him are two Land Rovers and driver Joe Letsebe. Painted a dark sandy colour, and with one pulling a cavernous empty trailer ready to swallow all our kit, the

20-year-old Landys reek of petrol, safaris and adventures in the spirit of the World War Two Long Range Desert Group.

On the downside, the windows are plastic sheets with stiff zips, and there are no seat belts in the back. Tim is an understanding sort, given to heeding the demands of long-distance travellers. A root around in a spare-parts box, coupled with some quick welding work, and he fits two straps to the chassis.

'I've been meaning to do that for a while,' he says. I gently suggest the vehicles might be a bit old for crossing the Kalahari.

'Don't worry, they'll be fine,' he says soothingly. 'They might look dated on the outside, but they're young on the inside. The parts never last more than a couple of years because they go through hell.'

First stop in Maun is a meeting with the army. The Botswana Defence Force (BDF), one of Africa's more respectable armies, helps protect wildlife in the area and has caught, arrested or shot dozens of poachers around the delta and across the country. But poachers are still active. Just days before I land in Maun, the last two white rhino in neighbouring Zambia's Mosi-oa-Tunya (Victoria Falls) National Park were shot by poachers travelling on speedboats. The gunmen are often former soldiers or guerrilla fighters and carry Kalashnikov assault rifles. They do not think twice about shooting guards or soldiers, let alone elephants. Between 1979 and 1990 at least 600,000 elephants, half the African population, were slaughtered. The commercial trade was banned in 1989, but ivory is still being smuggled to China to be used in jewellery and medicines, and to the Middle East to make handles for ceremonial daggers. A few weeks before our visit, 13 elephants were killed in northern Botswana for their tusks.

Tim drives us along sandy back roads out of Maun, past a prison where inmates, some of them poachers, wear orange Guantanamo

Bay fatigues. But this is no concentration camp. Inmates are playing football inside the barbed wire. A sign outside advertises the prison farm shop: 'Poultry and fresh farm produce'.

At the regional army base, an hour outside Maun, Captain Solomon Mamadi is gathering supplies for a journey into the Okavango Delta to check on an army anti-poaching patrol. There is anger at the latest elephant shootings. 'The order has come down from on high. We must hunt down the poachers and kill them,' he says. I climb into the back of a dark green army Land Rover with the Captain, and his driver takes us towards the buffalo fence marking the boundary of the Okavango Delta. It is a line stopping buffalo from spreading disease beyond Okavango. But it is also a clear line between a world of cattle and goats on one side and true wildlife on the other.

We cross into the delta and the world begins to change. We pass nervous giraffes with legs so gangly they appear to flee in slow motion. Another two hours of driving along impossibly bumpy tracks brings us to bushes concealing ten silent soldiers, invisible in their green jungle camouflage uniforms. Aged from 25 to 35 and loaded with assault rifles, knives, a global positioning system, field radio, binoculars and dozens of extra magazines for their guns, they are a potent force. Most African armies suffer from poor discipline, ancient equipment and corruption. By contrast, the BDF is well trained and well disciplined.

'Apparently we are the second best-paid army in Africa after Egypt,' says Captain Solomon, a tall, jolly 28-year-old who spent 18 months studying at the elite US military academy West Point.

The men report no contact with poachers. So the captain decides to show us what his soldiers are protecting. We head into the bush on foot with the squad, and go hunting for elephants, walking slowly behind an expert tracker at the front, a young lance-corporal with keen sight and a sharp mind.

'He will find them,' says the captain confidently. 'He reads the ground, the bushes, even the air.'

Within ten minutes the 'corp' finds a dry grass stalk broken by an elephant within the previous hour. The stalk has snapped under the giant foot, still just a shadow in the hard dust. The corp can tell the age of tracks by how long a spider takes to rebuild a web, or termites to repair a damaged mound. My brain needs a retune to understand this world. For the corp it comes naturally and immediately. There are three elephants, and he has their trail.

The corporal is so keen he is like a dog straining at a leash, pushing us forward and talking quickly about his hatred of the gunmen shooting 'our wildlife'. He leads our squad through the sweltering bush for half an hour. We hear our targets before we can see them. Three young adult bull elephants, fresh from a swim, tear at the undergrowth in search of food.

We approach quietly from downwind, but wary elephants can easily sense a squad of soldiers and a film crew. Two of them peel away and head deeper into the bush, leaving the biggest, most bolshie elephant staring at me staring at him. I keep my distance. Captain Solomon stands next to me.

'Don't make any sudden moves,' he says. 'You don't want to annoy him. If he charges, run in a zigzag and hide behind some thick scrub.'

Run in a zigzag? Hide? Where? The elephant flaps his ears, swings his trunk and glares at us. Fortunately, hunger wins over indignation. The bull is standing next to a tall ivory palm tree. At the top are bunches of ivory fruit, so hard they have long been used to make buttons. Elephants love them.

The bull squares up to the tree and then repeatedly head-butts the trunk, shaking and pushing it violently. I can feel the ground moving under my feet. Fruit starts to rain down. It bounces off his head, trunk and back, but he keeps shaking. After 30 seconds the earthquake stops, checks we aren't planning to steal his meal, and begins to graze, reaching down with his trunk and popping fruit into his mouth. The captain and I look on with wonder. Solomon beams the smile of a man eyeing his children at play. His men are watching for poachers from the undergrowth and this is one of their charges. Solomon turns to me.

'I have seen them many, many times, but they still fill me with wonder,' he says quietly. 'Now, Simon, you can see why we are under their spell.'

O N THE WAY back to Maun we stop in a filling station on the outskirts of the town and pull up next to a huge white four-wheel drive Toyota pickup. Behind the wheel sits a weather-beaten white man with a hard, flinty face. Two black workers sit on a green bench on the back of the truck dressed in camouflage fatigues. The vehicle has two spare tyres, a 1.5-metre-long jack strapped to the side, jerry cans, water tanks, an oil drum full of fuel, a snorkel lifting the air intake on to the roof, a huge winch, and a thick bull bar that appears to be made of scaffolding poles. It is a vehicle ready for hunting.

Some areas of the vast delta are parcelled off for photographic safaris, but others are run by firms that take rich Russians, Europeans or Americans out to stalk and shoot a trophy animal such as a buffalo or elephant. It strikes me as a fairly straightforward case of immorality, but when I ask for Tim's opinion he laughs.

'It's not as simple as you might think,' he says. 'Hunting contributes more to saving this place than tourism.'

I am amazed. According to Tim, hunters comprise five per cent of tourist numbers in Botswana, but provide 50 per cent of tourist revenue. 'That money is ploughed back into looking after the wildlife and the environment,' he tells me. 'It has a huge impact.'

There is much to protect. At 6.30 in the morning, the day after our patrol with the army, a Cessna Grand Caravan is waiting at Maun airport to take us to Lagoon Camp, a site Tim has recommended to the north of the Okavango. We fly low over the delta, across scrubby, shrubby land. Then the ambient light picks out trickling flood water. Small muddy lakes, hardly bigger than ponds, look up at me like winking eyes. The water is not contained, or even defined. Rivers have overflown their banks, pouring across the land, turning barren ground into swamp. Below me is one of the prime wetland sites and sights on the planet.

Height gives context. Everywhere there is water, there is greenery and life. And tracks – thousands upon thousands of game tracks, criss-crossing each other or joining together into motorways and heading towards water. Animals follow familiar paths and hippos leave the widest mark, powering their way through anything to get to a river. I can see them in the water, playful in the early morning light, just a stone's throw from the land and a herd of buffalo, their muscular bulk clear even from the air. I can see perhaps 300 of them.

'At least,' confirms Tim.

Finally there is magic. A red glint appears on the horizon. The sun rises, bathing the delta in a ruddy peach-pink light, and throwing decadent, evocative, willowy shadows. It is numbingly beautiful, nature showing off.

We land on the sandy airstrip near Lagoon Camp as an elephant is being shepherded off the runway and hop into a four-wheel drive

Land Cruiser, minus its entire top. No roof, no roll-bar, no windows or windscreen. Perfect for viewing game. The sides are battered and the suspension is knackered. It is only a few years old, but it has taken a beating out in the bush.

LT, a guide from the camp waiting for us at the narrow airstrip, tells us a pack of wild dogs are living just ten minutes from the strip.

'I prefer their older, more evocative name,' says Tim. 'Painted Wolves.'

We drive at speed through the bush then the car slows and crawls towards the den. We sit in the open car amid shrubbery just ten metres from the entrance, in the shade of a huge jackalberry tree that has grown above an old termite mound. The tree provides protection for the termites, which, in return, aerate the soil around the tree and avoid feasting on its roots and wood. Early morning light seeps through the trees like the waters of the delta. The sounds of hippo grunting and woodpecker tapping floats in the air. A large male Painted Wolf basks in dappled sunshine three metres away on my left. He is sleeping. With coloured fur and perfect camouflage, his name does him justice.

Tim leans towards me, points at the termite mound and whispers. 'Termites do more than just chomp through dead wood. They help to build the delta.'

By constructing vast earth mounds and tall air-conditioning stacks up to three metres high above the flood water, the termites provide a toe-hold and small island for acacia, ebony, palm, leadwood and merula trees. These in turn cleanse the Okavango waters of salt, a poison if spread across the delta, removing it from the water during transpiration and storing it around their roots. As the trees store salt, some 400,000 tons each year, their toe-hold grows and eventually becomes a small island, of which there are now 150,000 in the delta.

Termites start the process and build the ecosystem, one of the most beautiful places on Earth.

There is a squeal from the den. The male rises and stretches. He is lean, powerful, with huge ears and a coat of gold and brown flecked with white. He trots closer to the entrance and greets a female, her teats heavy with milk. They kiss, or at least raise their necks and lick tongues. There is more squealing, louder a second time. And then pups emerge. Nine bundles of yapping fur. Their parents, uncles and aunts, a group of six adults, yelp and nuzzle them lovingly.

In a viewing car next to us, an elderly American couple watch silently, blankets over their knees. A dog moves, they lift their cameras and click rhythmically. The dog disappears into the den, and they lower their expensive zoom lenses.

Painted Wolves are ferocious hunters and endlessly curious. Even adult male lions will run off when they see humans. Not wild dogs, says Tim. They might look cute, but the dogs can take down large animals, running next to them, snapping at their underbellies, taking chunks out of them even as the animals race for their lives. Brian leans forward to interject with a whisper.

'Their prey hits the ground dead,' he tells me with boyish admiration. Despite a bad reputation, the dogs have many fans.

'They're a wonderful pack animal and very good with their kids,' says Tim. 'Most hunters eat before their children, but these dogs will make sure their pups eat first.'

Younger dogs from the pack will even feed injured or older dogs that cannot keep up with a hunt. But there are probably less than 3,000 of the dogs running wild on the planet. It is a tiny number, spread thinly across African game parks and farmland, where these hunters have become hunted. Painted Wolves are the second most endangered carnivore in Africa. Despite the best work of conservationists, they face extinction.

We reverse away from the den noisily, but the basking dogs do not stir. Tim drives our car, while LT sits on a small chair positioned above the front bumper, from where he scans the bush for wildlife. Just 75 metres from the den, the clutch on the car fails, and no amount of tinkering by Tim under the bonnet with Brian's trusty Leatherman can fix it. LT calls the camp for backup, and produces a folding table from behind one of the seats. Then a chequered table-cloth appears. Time for a civilized breakfast. A hamper emerges from under the seats, along with mugs, flasks of tea and coffee, and a set of tiered steel bowls full of dried fruits and biscuits. We eat breakfast downwind from the dogs, occasionally scanning the bushes for hungry carnivores.

After a mechanic arrives with a spare car, we make slow progress towards Lagoon Camp. There is so much to see. Even among acres of bush turned black by a lightning fire just three weeks before, green shoots are appearing and zebra play among charred stumps. A lilac-breasted roller lands on a tree just metres from our car. It looks at us dismissively, then shoots into the air, rolls, and sunlight catches the electric-blue underneath its wings. It is exquisitely beautiful. The continent of Africa really does have the most extraordinary wildlife in the world. Majestic fish-eagles by the edge of the river, noisy blacksmith plover, and impala, which show us their backsides as they disappear at speed. Seen from behind, their fur forms the shape of an 'M'.

'Did you see the Golden Arches?' asks Tim. 'They're known as the McDonald's of the delta. Every carnivore's favourite fast food.'

WE FINALLY arrive at Lagoon Camp, a scattering of eight wooden lodges next to the Kwando River, a couple of hours later. I walk to a small river jetty, and watch, transfixed, as three huge elephants emerge from the reeds 150 metres upriver and begin to wade across. Some safaris can feel like rambles in glorified parks, but this truly is Wild Africa.

The afternoon is spent searching for more game. Elegant kudu are my favourite, their long spiralling horns, striped and spotted bodies, and dignified bearing giving them the regal air of a great stag. Kudu often stand stock still when scared, relying on their camouflage to blend into the background. When they take off, they do so literally, jumping more than two metres from standing. A large male kudu, startled by our car, leaps straight into a clearing in a thicket. We want to follow from a distance, but turning off well-worn tracks is difficult. Mopane trees, a dense hardwood that presents an impenetrable barrier, grow here as thick scrub just a couple of metres high. When David Livingstone came this way it took his men months to cut roads through the mopane for ox-carts. Even walking through it is a challenge, because branches are interlaced.

'There's an old story about the special connection between the mopane and the kudu,' says Tim as we pause to watch our quarry wandering off. 'Many years ago there was a hunter who liked to kill for pleasure, rather than for meat, and one day he pursued a young kudu doe into some thick mopane scrub. The trees saw she was upset and asked her what was wrong. She told them she was being chased by a hunter who didn't want to eat, just to kill. So the trees dropped their leaves all over the doe's tracks, and the hunter couldn't see where she had gone. He gave up and the kudu came back to thank the mopane trees for saving her life. And that's why the imprint of the mopane leaf is exactly the same as a kudu's hoof. And you'll never see a kudu eating the mopane tree, only sitting in its shadow.'

The mopane is certainly a special tree. To many, it symbolizes the tough, life-sapping heat of parched Botswana. It also harbours the mopane caterpillar, which appears during the summer, feeds on the leaves, and is then nabbed by locals and dry-roasted as a delicacy. Such a shame the caterpillars are out of season. Instead I make do with sun-downers back at Lagoon Camp, sipped under ancient, rambling knobthorn and jackalberry trees on a wooden deck overlooking the river. Just 20 metres away two hippos burble gently amid water lilies. An unseen hand lowers the sun slowly across the river, turning the water a dark silver as it drops below the horizon, painting the sky a broad spectrum from dark red, through orange, pink, into yellow, light blue, and then dark blue in the heavens above my head. It is quite the most picturesque sunset I have ever seen. The setting is serene and peaceful. For the first time on my crazy journey, I feel truly, deeply relaxed. I savour a few moments of quiet and calm, just sitting and watching hippos cracking the still water, their ripples fanning across the water, bumping into patches of grass drifting lazily down the river. 'There aren't many camp locations like this,' says Tim quietly behind me.

But for an extraordinary location you pay an exclusive price. I am here for just one night, but traditional Botswanan safaris can cost a few thousand pounds per week. Opposite me at dinner are a quiet American couple from San Francisco who are travelling with a private guide. Friends with Bill Gates, the wife plays bridge with Warren Buffett, the world's second richest man. Her next trip is taking an ice-breaker to see Emperor Penguins in Antarctica. Botswana makes a fortune from such wealthy tourists. The industry is the second-largest earner for the country after diamonds. And the Okavango Delta is the national jewel. If anything should happen to the delta, the consequences for both the natural environment and the Botswanan economy would be catastrophic. Worryingly, there are very real threats.

The Okavango River, which feeds the delta, rises in southern Angola and flows through Namibia before reaching Botswana. Namibia has said it wants to take more of the water from the Okavango, threatening the delta's very existence. The two governments claim they have resolved their differences and signed agreements establishing precisely how much water can be taken from the river. But dispute and possible conflict has been delayed rather than resolved. As Namibia gradually becomes wealthier, the government in Windhoek has said it might need to extract more water from the Okavango. But this could cut off the supply to the delta and destroy the oasis. In response, the Botswanan government has ordered its army to protect the delta by preparing for a possible future 'water war' with Namibia.

'There has also been talk of Namibia damming the Okavango for hydro-power, and that could have a terrible effect on the ecosystem of the delta,' says Tim as we sit nursing after-dinner beers by a small camp fire.

Conservationists believe the delta has already shrunk by half in the last decade. Some hydrologists think it is a cyclical problem linked to low flood volumes, and larger floods will return in the future. But many locals are unconvinced.

Fertilizer is also becoming a problem. Used by farmers upstream, it flows into the river and feeds the growth of papyrus and reeds. If too much fertilizer is used, plants will choke the panhandle entrance to the delta, cutting off the water supply.

'It would only take one minor change in one of the elements to significantly change this environment,' muses Tim. It seems extraordinary to think the delta could be at risk, but it is a uniquely fragile ecosystem. Subtle changes to the land around the delta, such as the use of fertilizer, could wreak havoc. It is a reminder, perhaps, of the fragility of our global environment. Small changes can have unexpected, disastrous consequences.

Mozzies buzz around our heads. They do not seem hungry, but I have suffered from their bites before. While travelling around the Equator I was diagnosed with malaria. So why take chances? I walk into darkness on the edge of the camp in search of my bag and insect repellent. My head-torch, pumping out a red beam to help me maintain my night vision, picks out two big eyes in the darkness staring directly at me. A huge hippo is loose in the camp, and I appear to be in his way.

Hippos kill more humans than any other animal in Africa. They might be two- or three-ton vegetarians, but the belligerent creatures can run faster than an Olympic medallist. Be you villager or tourist, if you stand between a hippo and a river or favourite waterhole, you risk being chomped into two by a hippo's huge teeth. I know this, and I feel very exposed. I glance at the pathetic, slender trees by the side of the path. They will not stop a trampling hippo. Then there is a crashing sound from the undergrowth behind me. The hippo turns to the side and bolts down a path towards the river. Tim appears beside me, flushed and worried. I start to breathe again.

'Didn't you hear the safety briefing earlier?' he asks, a tad peeved. I had been busily writing in my notebook. 'You're not allowed to walk anywhere in the camp after dark without an escort.'

I can hear the hippos chatting in the water. Their rumbling grunting makes them sound like fat men who have just enjoyed a great joke.

My room that night is a raised wooden riverside building enveloping a tented structure. The allure of a camp with the benefits of a lodge. Zips and mosquito nets keep out unwanted guests, both large and small, while a large bed and dark wooden furniture ensure a colonial feel. I am exhausted. Even noisy hippos cannot wake me in the night, but their droppings are scattered liberally in huge piles around the camp in the morning. There is even a large deposit on the bottom step leading to my room, as if one hippo had left me a special present for disturbing him the night before. Charming.

We only have a few more hours in the camp, so we set off along the Kwando River on a double-decker open boat. The scene is familiar. It is the Norfolk Broads. All the elements are there. But with sunshine, blue skies, hippos and crocodiles. Lurking by the water's edge, we spot one of the prehistoric creatures lying dead still.

'Crocs are perhaps the world's most efficient hunters,' says Tim. 'They can go for six to nine months on a good meal. They don't waste any body energy heating themselves. They don't waste energy chasing down prey. They just sit there, waiting for prey to come to them.'

Crocodiles are the only animal in the delta that will happily view humans as lunch. Lions rarely attack people. Other animals will only strike when threatened or angry. But crocs view us as just another slab of meat to be stored in their underwater larder.

We stop by a narrow bend of the river to watch a large hippo resting in the long grass on the other side. He sees us, stands, opens his vast jaws to yawn, then edges towards the water and pushes himself out towards the middle of the river. It is time for a game. The hippo faces us, looking straight in our direction, not 20 metres away, then slowly sinks below the water. I am standing on the low riverbank with Brian and Sophie. A few seconds pass, then a few moments more. The hippo does not appear. We start to back away, worried he is launching a sneak attack. Then air bubbles boil the surface off to the left, nostrils appear, and a great head rises out of the water, still staring right at us. The cheeky bugger is trying to scare us. I swear he is grinning.

TWO DAYS LATER. The sun has not risen and I am being driven along a long, straight, flat and dusty road. Out of the blackness in the opposite direction comes an ambulance travelling at speed with its lights flashing. The sign on the front says 'clinical waste'. 'Probably dumping bodies out in the desert,' says Tim from behind the wheel. I hope he is joking.

We left the delta the day before and drove south in Tim's Land Rovers, overnighting in the middle-of-nowhere town of Ghanzi, before rising early to head east, driving parallel with Capricorn towards the mighty Central Kalahari Game Reserve, the CKGR.

It is winter in Africa. The temperature before dawn is close to freezing and the wind tears through gaps around the flapping plastic windows of the Landy. I have my knees bunched up against the seat, trying to keep warm under a blanket. In the driving seat, Tim wears a fleece, gloves and a hat. In the back, assistant producer Simon Boazman is jolly in a T-shirt.

There is little to see on the drive and we chew biltong, local beef jerky, to keep our jaws moving and our brains awake. Headlights pick out a road-building crew sleeping around a fire on the verge. Then we come to a shuddering halt in the middle of the road. Tim pokes around under the hood, finds a loose wire and within moments we are back on the move. Tim is the southern Africa correspondent for *Land Rover Enthusiast* magazine. He can strip a Land Rover with his teeth then rebuild the entire car with tin foil. As he is taking us across the 52,800 square kilometres of the Central Kalahari Game Reserve, the second-largest game reserve in the world, naturally I find this rather reassuring.

A brisk morning's drive takes us to the edge of the CKGR and the tiny, pitiful settlement of New Xade. A donkey is standing in the middle of what passes for the main road. The ground around homesteads is muddy-coloured sand peppered with rubbish, piles of dung and animal pellets. There is a scattering of permanent single-storey buildings for local government officials, and then mud huts and small round wooden buildings, known as rondavels, with thatched roofs and circular outside walls made of long, roughly cut stakes of wood. They are the new homes of the San people, the fabled Bushmen, the legendary hunter-gatherers of the Kalahari.

The San are one of the oldest peoples on the planet. For tens of thousands of years they have lived an ancient way of life in southern Africa. New Xade is their resettlement camp, a place without hope, a place of despair, a place where 1,500 lives have been taken and souls removed. The San and other central Kalahari tribes were encouraged and forced to move there from the desert by the Botswanan government. They have been relocated, *transferred*.

I have arranged to meet Jumanda Gakelebone from the First People of the Kalahari organization, which campaigns for the rights of the San and their brother tribes. A quiet, intense, dark-skinned man a couple of years younger than me, he wears sunglasses, a baseball cap, a T-shirt that says 'I Love the CKGR' and speaks streetwise English.

There is some controversy about what to call the people Westerners used to know simply as Bushmen. 'We have been called lots of names,' says Jumanda. 'None of them are in our language.'

So what name do you use?

'Many prefer to be called San. If I talk to someone I say I am a Kua.' He spells it out for me in English. 'It means what you guys would call a Bushman. But in my language. Now we are naming ourselves.' Jumanda suggests I settle for San.

Outside the door to his hut, squatting next to a small, smoky fire, Roy Sesana, the de facto leader of the First People of the Kalahari, is drinking a mug of steaming tea. He is nearly 60, stocky, wearing a T-shirt and a thick fleece. He has deep, piercing eyes and a voice that rumbles and rolls with the clicks and trills that are the hallmark of the Khoisan language. It sounds like no language I have ever heard. Two toothbrushes poke from the brush roof of his hut. A green washing bowl sits by the fire containing a carton of milk and some toothpaste.

Roy and Jumanda are not living in New Xade by choice. They want to live on their ancestral lands in the CKGR, created in 1961 by British administrators to preserve the desert, the wildlife, and also the San. 'It is our home,' says Roy, 'not a game reserve.' But over the last decade, after a generation of harassment, the government of Botswana has moved or evicted the people of the Kalahari from their homes in the desert and destroyed many of their huts. In 2001 a census showed there were 689 people remaining in the CKGR. In 2002 the government sealed water boreholes, cut water pipes and used the police and 29 large trucks to move them out. Rangers and policemen attacked and beat some of the remaining San. Bullied and threatened, the San were moved to resettlement camps like New Xade.

The reasons for this are disputed. Many San and their foreign supporters believe they were moved because diamonds have been found in the Kalahari, and the San were in the way. Government ministers admit they will mine diamonds wherever they are found, perhaps not surprising given their worth. But diamonds have only been found in one place in the CKGR, and with current technology extracting them is not economically viable.

In fact, the transfer was for several reasons. The government wants the San to become part of the modern world. But providing them with services available to the rest of Botswana, like free health care and compulsory schooling for all children through primary school, is expensive if they are living in the middle of the Kalahari. Another reason is straightforward tribalism, still a curse on Africa. The Tswana, the tribe that dominates Botswana, look down on the San, and the Tswana-dominated government views their traditional lifestyle as an embarrassment. 'How can we continue to have Stone Age creatures in the age of computers?' the Botswanan president once asked.

Western conservationists are also to blame. They accused the San of endangering wildlife in the Kalahari by hunting and by introducing domestic cattle and livestock diseases. International pressure groups then made a difficult situation worse by weighing in on behalf of the San, making extravagant demands and infuriating the government.

So far, the government has had its way. Hunting has been forbidden and almost all of the San have been forced to leave the CKGR. The Botswanan government says the relocation is in the best interests of the majority of the San and of the nation as a whole, and that it has been carried out 'in the most sensitive and constructive manner possible'. The government also claims San who moved out of the Kalahari have been given homes, cattle and goats, and that nearly £3 million has been spent improving the facilities in New Xade and another settlement. There is indeed a decrepit school in New Xade, but there is no mains electricity. Unemployment in the village is nearly 100 per cent. HIV is attacking the community and some San have committed suicide, something unknown in the past.

'Is it progress when our people live shorter lives here than in the desert?' asks Roy. Like aboriginal people the world over, many seek escape in alcohol. Men sit around drinking. Empty bottles and Castle Lager cans litter the streets of New Xade.

'Our people are dying here,' says Roy, his proud eyes almost pleading. 'They want to go home to the Kalahari.'

The people of the Kalahari are mentally and emotionally equipped for the desert. It provides them with life and purpose. Living in tiny isolated communities ensured the wildlife and fauna in any one area was never over-used. But there is no life-giving desert for the hundreds now living in the resettlement camps. Around them is empty scrub that has been grazed and exploited. Food in the resettlement camps needs to be paid for. Likewise, water is available from pipes, but for a price. The people of the Kalahari must earn money to pay for necessities they previously harvested or hunted for free. Against their will, the people of the Kalahari have been forced to enter our modern, grasping, consumer-driven world. They are trying to live a way of life most do not understand.

In the dust outside Roy's small house I spot a four-week-old British Airways airline baggage sticker, the type airlines attach to bags as they pass through airports. This one bears the name 'Sesana' and is for a flight Roy took home to Botswana from London, where he had been meeting politicians and campaigning for the Kalahari people. The Botswanan government perceive them as innocent, even simple, but Roy and the Bushmen are no fools. They have fought their battle around the globe. At the end of 2006 the San won a landmark victory when the Botswanan appeals court said they should be allowed to return to the CKGR. But the government still keeps them out.

'We have won our fight against the government. They should let us return,' Roy says defiantly.

Jumanda takes me up the road from Roy's home to meet Khumanege Lentodi and his wife Sesodo. With their two kids, Batshabi (which means 'refugee') and Obuile ('returning back'), they are going to attempt to return to the Kalahari. We arrive just as Sesodo is packing and finishing the laundry, using a hose connected to a stand-pipe at the edge of their small homestead, which consists of two round rondavel huts, a small concrete building supplied by the government, and a couple of underfed donkeys surrounded by a basic brush fence.

I ask Sesodo if she will miss the easy access to water in the dry desert.

'No,' she says quickly. 'It's not the most important thing. What I really need is to be back in the Kalahari, on my land, close to my ancestors.'

Sesodo empties the family rondavel and begins packing their worldly goods into the back of a flat-bed blue pickup truck. Out come blankets, an ancient blue cool-box, a ten kilogram bag of maize, a black cast-iron cooking pot, clothes, shoes, a box of Sunlight washing powder, a large multicoloured striped bag, two axes and a large bag of potatoes.

As Sesodo packs and dries her laundry in the sun, I talk to Smith, an earnest San youngster who has sidled up nervously to chat. Smith is studying to become a teacher. He plans to take his education back into the Kalahari and teach his people about their culture.

'We have been held down for so long my people now believe they are a lower caste,' he says. 'We have to teach them about our culture and awaken their pride.'

He has a mobile phone. Does he want to live in the CKGR?

'I want the right to live there, the right to be with my people.'

Khumanege appears. He plans to drive his wife, children and some cousins to Metsiamanong, a remote, isolated village deep in the Kalahari and then return for more supplies, chickens and a few goats. But he worries his borrowed car will not survive the trip into the CKGR. To avoid problems at the entrance to the reserve, we plan to drive ahead and meet them at the village. But there is no road, only a sandy track, and no guarantee either of us will make it. After tearful farewells, Khumanege and Sesodo pile their family and belongings into the car and set off with us following. When they stop for more goodbyes, we have to keep going. We only have limited supplies and need to keep to a tight schedule if we are to get to our designated camping sites each night and then make it out the other side.

We reach the edge of the reserve after driving for a few more hours along a bumpy, narrow track. The warden's office is empty. Five minutes later he appears in his car, surprised to see us. Few cars pass this way. The last entry in the register for a vehicle entering the CKGR at the same gate, heading west to east, is two years before. The warden wishes us luck. Our plan is simply to bump our way across the Kalahari on narrow, sandy tracks cut by prospectors in the 1950s until we reach the remote San settlement. We will camp at night in tents under the stars.

The journey starts well. We push our way along a track of deep sand, bouncing between low, shrubby and thorny bushes that screech against the paintwork of the Landys.

The Kalahari is said to be the largest basin of sand in the world, sinking 1,000 metres deep in some places. It is hot, harsh and desperately dry. The word Kalahari is itself a corruption of 'the great thirsty land', but it is not a typical desert. The surface has only occasional rainfall, but a mixture of hardy trees, bushes and grassland somehow manage to survive. The Kalahari looks like an overgrown orchard hit by drought. Silver clusterleaf, Camelthorn acacia and trees, some of them ten metres high, dot the landscape. They are green, thanks to light rain just two weeks earlier. And hardy enough to survive in the Kalahari. Everywhere around us is Kalahari appleleaf, a bushy plant growing a few metres high with delicate green and yellow speckled leaves. Appleleaf survives in the desert by pushing a long tap-root system tens of metres down into the sand to where water lurks, sitting on calcrete, a white clay-like substrate, nicknamed Kalahari concrete and used to strengthen roads. When life can reach the water, life survives.

Wildlife is thin on the ground. But over a low hill a huge kori bustard, the heaviest flying bird in the world, waddles down the road away from us. Males can weigh 20 kilos and spend most of the day shuffling around on the ground for seeds and lizards. We give this one a shock and it soars into the sky, its eight foot wing-span giving it a prehistoric size.

I am hoping to see a honey badger in the Kalahari, perhaps the most fearless animal on the planet. 'Pound for pound it's also the most belligerent animal in southern Africa,' says Tim. Despite its diminutive size, the honey badger has been known to attack and kill venomous cobras, leopards and even, according to some reports, elephants. Knifelike claws are backed by sharp teeth and tough, thick, loose skin which enables it to wriggle around and bite, even when an attacker has its teeth in the back of its neck. Against larger animals such as elephants, the honey badger's favourite tactic appears to be biting and ripping genitals, resulting in the victim haemorrhaging blood.

The fighting spirit of the honey badger is legendary. Other animals show it due respect. 'Conservationists in Namibia saw a honey badger plodding in the direction of a pride of lions resting under a tree,' says

Tim, doing a remarkable impression of a plodding badger, 'and the lions spotted it coming and began to perk up, thinking an easy meal was on the way.' As the honey badger drew closer the lions picked up its scent and realized what it was. 'The lions shuffled out of the way, the badger plodded on, straight across where they had been sitting, and the lions sat back down looking slightly embarrassed.'

What a fantastic creature. Scared of nothing.

We barrel along the tracks, making slow progress across the desert, and the constant slow-rolling motion of our car reminds me of a trotting horse. My body cannot decide if it is soporific or induces nausea. The soft sand starts to suck at our tyres. We are tugging a trailer loaded with heavy tents and camera equipment, and even Tim's Land Rover struggles. Suddenly the engine roars. We have hit soft sand and the Landy grinds to a halt. We all climb out to give it a push, and the second Land Rover, carrying a lighter load, helps pull us out using a bright blue nylon tow rope. Another few minutes and we've stopped again. This time it takes 15 minutes of pushing to get the Landy moving. We drive for another five miles and stop again. It becomes a routine. After the first dozen stops I lose count. I feel tired and irritable. Pushing the Landy through sand for 30 or 50 metres in the hot sun is exhausting. And if we hit a patch of sand we cannot pass we will have to turn back, and all the pushing will have been for nothing.

On the first day we are aiming for a waterhole eight hours into the Kalahari, a mecca for animals in the dry desert. But progress is painfully slow and the darkness beats us. We stop by a large tree on a bend on the only track heading towards the settlement and wait for Khumanege and his family to catch us up. As the sun goes down, Jumanda takes me to gather firewood. Normally a quiet and contemplative soul, he comes alive in the bush.

'Look, this is the monkey orange tree,' he says, pointing at green fruits high in a bushy shrub. 'They'll be ready in a few months.'

Jumanda grew up in the CKGR. His parents would set off into the desert in the morning to find food, just as a British couple might commute to work. When he discovered his parents had been transferred out of the reserve to a resettlement camp he was angry with them for leaving without a fight.

Dropping to his haunches, Jumanda shows me how to make a rope from barbed three-foot-long mother-in-law's tongue. The plant thrives on neglect, surviving the dry season long after everything else turns brown. Scraping the plant exposes strong fibres that run the length of the leaf and can be rolled together on a thigh to form a tough string. Women find it an effective way of shaving their legs, says Jumanda with a wink. With the twine, the San build delicate traps that can strangle an ostrich or catch steenbuck, a small antelope that finds shelter from lions and other prey among thorny plants.

Jumanda tells me the Kalahari appleleaf is used for treating cuts and bruises. That a San hunter, left alone in the desert, can cook an ostrich egg without water, and dig out roots for moisture. I accidentally crush a devil's claw seed pod under my boot. Whole, it looks like a small explosion turned it inside out, thrusting out sharp spikes that catch on a hide and propagate the plant.

'When crushed like that it's very good for pain, kidney and stomach ailments,' says Jumanda. Then, of course, there is the art of lighting a fire. 'Find and mould a small ball of dry grass. Then take two special sticks. Sharpen one and twirl and rub it quickly between your palms against a flat edge of the other stick. Patience and time will produce smoke, then ash. Tip the ash into the grass and blow gently.' He pauses. 'It can take a while,' Jumanda admits. 'Matches are faster.'

We walk on. Jumanda points at shrubs that yield tubers and wild carrots. I begin to worry about the great predators of the Kalahari, the black-maned lions that roam the desert scrub.

'There are none around. They are my cousins. When they are near the hair on the back of my head stands up and my forehead begins to itch.' Jumanda says this with such sincerity I find myself trusting my life to his itchy head.

'We live together with our cousins. We even feed each other. So if the lions have killed something, if I'm really very hungry, I will just walk straight to the lion and shout at it, and it will run away, and I will get the food, I get the meat. Neither side can afford the other going hungry.' But sometimes one side breaks the rules. One time Jumanda was hunting an eland, and just as he was about to spear it a lion appeared from the side and jumped on the antelope.

'I shouted at the lion and he was very rude to me. I was very angry. But the lion was more hungry than me.'

'So there's a relationship between you then, between the community here and lions?' I say. 'I had no idea.'

'Yes, a big relationship. Even though,' and now he smiles, 'it often seems that we hate each other.'

We drag our firewood back to camp, where Tim has produced tents, camp-beds and blankets from his tardis-like trailer and is cooking a small bush feast. The tents are a heavy, thick canvas.

'They'll keep out the lions,' says Tim. 'Even if they slash the fabric it's cross-stitched so it won't tear.'

Hyenas, jackals, leopards and wild dogs are also out there, but less of a threat. So if a lion comes into the camp, what should we do? Stay in the tent and keep quiet. But what if we're outside the tent? Get inside quickly and zip it up. As I glance nervously at the shadows around the camp, Tim begins cooking baked potatoes, cauliflower cheese and thinly cut steaks. Old wooden trunks in his tardis hold juices and a welcome crate of beer. With the fire toasting our toes, we sit on camp chairs around a dining table, raise a can to the stars and the cooking, and listen to Jumanda's tales of life in the bush.

As the night wears on, his stories of ferocious lions and man-hunting hyenas became ever more outlandish. It is difficult to know how much is teasing. Jumanda cocks his head towards the darkness, his alert ears hearing predators in the darkness. Or so he says. Hyena appear at the edge of the camp, their darting bodies just visible in shadows thrown by our torches. There is no sign of Khumanege and his family. As the low sliver of cold, hard moon drops closer to the horizon, turning a deep, dark orange, we carefully zip ourselves into our tents, and leave the fire to smoulder.

IT TAKES another day of solid driving and another night under the stars before we arrive in the tiny village of Metsiamanong. Homes in the village consist of at least one round rondavel inside a fence made of vertical thorny branches laced tightly together. There are no tracks, just gaps between the homesteads. We arrive early in the morning and drive slowly along the outside of one fence, letting two concerned villagers see Jumanda sitting in the back of our car. 'Jumanda! Jumanda!' they holler, throwing their arms up with joy. Slowly other villagers begin to emerge.

We stop the car and Jumanda greets his uncle Mongwegi Gaoberekwe, a village elder. Mongwegi is delighted to see his nephew, and we are all swept along and into Mongwegi's homestead as the two hug repeatedly. I feel ridiculously tall, ludicrously overfed and embarrassed to intrude, but Jumanda wants his uncle to show us around.

Uncle Mongwegi is a small, warm, wizened man in his fifties who has lived in the Kalahari his entire life. He is wearing a purple hat, a cast-off from the West, to shield his eyes from the bright morning sun, and has a tiny frame swallowed by an oversized, thick, dirty greatcoat. His homestead is roughly 40 metres long by 20 metres wide, surrounded by a rudimentary fence made from spiky branches placed in heaps. Normally they protect a small field of crops from small antelopes and desert foxes. This year the frost had taken much of the harvest. Mongwegi gestures to pathetic patches of withered plants.

'It has been a hard winter,' he says, his voice clicking away in the ancient language of the Kalahari. Some of the food eaten out here is grown around the homesteads, but most is gathered in the bush.

'Have you been able to gather all the food you've needed this winter?' I ask Uncle Mongwegi. Jumanda translates.

'Yes, we've collected blackberries and wild beans.'

A youngster appears with some of the beans, which look a little like dried peas.

'What will you do with them?' I ask. 'Will you cook them?'

'Either you roast them or you cook them with water and eat them.'

'Do they taste good?'

'I don't know from your side, but we...' he laughs, 'to us, they are very tasty.'

We all chuckle together. With the help of Jumanda interpreting, it is like having a chat with a friend in a pub.

Mongwegi used to have a few goats and a donkey, but the government took them away. I ask how he has coped without them.

'My life has been difficult since my goats were taken. It's very, very bad, because I used to get milk from those goats, and sometimes

I kill them for meat to eat, because we are not even allowed to hunt the antelope [in the Kalahari].'

Until recently Mongwegi used to hunt animals in the reserve with bows and arrows, or by setting traps and snares.

'Before 2002, they used to give us a special hunting licence, even though they were troubling us, but in 2002, after the relocations, hunting was stopped.'

Life has changed dramatically for Mongwegi. 'What would happen if you were caught hunting?' I ask. 'What would be the punishment?'

Mongwegi looks me straight in the eye. His gaze is piercing.

'I'm afraid they might kill me,' he says.

I am taken aback. 'They might kill you? Who would kill you?'

'The Officers of the Department of Wildlife and National Parks.'

Some outsiders have claimed the people of the Kalahari cannot grasp the concept of ownership. So I ask Mongwegi who owns the Kalahari. 'Does it belong to the government, or does it belong to your people?'

Again, he holds my gaze. He knows exactly what I mean.

'I *know* the land belongs to me. It doesn't belong to the government. Even the British colonial government, when they declared this as a game reserve, we were here. We were using this land, we owned this land even then.'

'It sounds to me as though you now want the government to leave you alone.'

'The government is troubling us; it's so troubling,' he says with a weary, pained expression. 'With all of our heart, I want them to move away from us, and just leave us alone.'

JUMANADA AND Mongwegi start chatting about family business, so Brian and I wander off, nosing around the homestead.

I poke my head inside Mongwegi's rondavel hut and gasp. It is a masterpiece. A tinderbox forest of dead branches harvested to make a circular structure perhaps five metres in diameter. Branches, layered thickly and tied tightly together, snake and weave upwards to the apex, which stands four metres high. There is no hole for smoke. Fires are kept outside. The branches meet at the top, drawn snugly to their point. The effect is fluid and hypnotic. Branches worked like this are natural sculptures. For a few moments I feel a sense of awe. Then I return to reality. It is a home, not an art installation. The thick branches are to keep out hungry hyenas and the lions of the Kalahari. Around the edges, pushed to the sides, are red, white, blue and black plastic barrels, containers and buckets. Two goat skins are drying by the entrance, narrow so it can be barred for easy protection. On the sand in the middle of the rondavel is just thin bedding and an even thinner blanket. The previous night I slept in my clothes under a thick sleeping bag and blankets, and was still chilled. It will be bitterly cold in here during the long winter nights.

Outside the hut, families are gathering around a warming, smoky fire for a meagre breakfast of seeds and weak tea. There are 20 thin adults and 20 children, wearing ragged and discoloured Western cast-offs. Some huddle under cheap blankets. Others just shiver. Several feet have car-tyre sandals, a few have old trainers, most are bare. The villagers tell us more San are roaming the Kalahari, searching for food while avoiding government patrols. Jumanda is wearing a white towel around his neck to keep warm, like a boxing trainer. He leans down to grab berries from the outstretched palm of a young woman sitting by the fire. He flicks her ear and she thumps him in the stomach.

'Is she another of your cousins?' I tease Jumanda. 'Or is there a bit more history there?'

Jumanda laughs. 'There's a bit more history,' he says.

I stretch my hands towards the warmth. The women are sitting in a circle, passing around metal pipes stuffed with bark. An elderly woman with a wrinkled face like a gnarled walnut, a black chequered blanket around her shoulders, pushes black animal pellets into the end of her pipe and takes a drag. She passes it to my neighbour, who sucks deeply, then hands it to me. As I inhale, gently, the old woman laughs and the few remaining teeth in her mouth stand proud like tombstones. My lungs fill with a foul-tasting acrid smoke. It is a struggle to avoid retching. I pass the pipe to my left, and a group of watching mucky children are convulsed with giggles.

The faces and colours of the villagers around the fire are a mix, from the tea-coloured skin of the old San through to the darker tones of Jumanda and Uncle Mongwegi. Tribalism still holds Africa back. But there is none out here. They have very little. But the people of the Kalahari have each other.

'The government says it wants us out of here because of the animals, but we do not harm them,' says Uncle Mongwegi quietly as he passes me an old clay pot containing a steaming brew of bitter tea. 'This is our land, this is my home. This is where I have been since a boy. They have forbidden us from hunting. It is very hard to survive, but I will not leave. Even if they come with guns, I will not go in their cars. They treat us very badly. It has always been this way. When people discover we are peaceful, they walk all over us.'

Khumanege and Sesodo, the returnees from New Xade, have still not arrived at Metsiamanong. 'Either they were not allowed into the reserve or they simply broke down,' says Jumanda. Uncle Mongwegi points towards a quiet, stocky man with high cheekbones, light skin and the narrowed eyes typical of the San. Mosedane Belesa and his wife Qwiko Owa were taken out of the Kalahari and moved to New Xade a few years ago.

'I was not even told where I was being taken and where I'm going. I just found myself on a truck,' said Mosedane softly. He has gentle features and an innocent manner.

Life in New Xade was clearly not easy. They returned to this area from the resettlement camp just a couple of months ago.

'So why did you come back from New Xade?' I ask.

'I didn't have a house. I did not find a job, and I really did not like it there. So I came home. Life here is better. Life here is what made me a man.'

To Mosedane the decision to return was simple. 'Life is miserable there,' says Mosedane solemnly. 'This is home. If you want to find food in the [resettlement] camp you have to find money. Here, if I want something to eat, I can just go out into the bush and find food for free.'

I turn to Jumanda. 'This is the crucial point, isn't it?' I say. 'That here, you can live an existence that's not dependent on having to have money. You can just go out and find food in the bush.'

'Yes. Absolutely,' he says, nodding vigorously. 'If you take some-body into an area where their survival is [based] on money – it's like if you take me and dump me in the middle of London, how do you expect me to live? I need to have a lot of money to live in the UK. And if you take an old man to New Xade who is used to setting snares and surviving from catching food in the bush…Well, you make his life very difficult.'

I wondered if life could really be better in the desert.

'Would you be happier if there was electricity here?' I ask Mosedane.

'Yes, I might be happy. We would like electricity.' It could keep lights burning at night and power basic fridges for food and medicines.

'But if electricity comes,' I warn him, 'then so do officials.'

'Yes,' he responds slowly, 'there you are telling the truth. That might give me a big, big problem. Perhaps we should manage without.'

I recall a parallel in South America on my Equator journey. The Waimiri tribe fought back when the Brazilian government built a road across the Amazon and through their land. They were virtually anni-hilated. But when democracy came to Brazil the government declared them a national treasure and gave the Waimiri certain controls over their land. They live today in careful isolation. So they have medi-cines, computers and Internet access. But they roam and hunt on their own land, shadows in the bushes by a road on which drivers are forbidden from stopping. Jumanda listens carefully.

'Yes,' he says. 'That is what we want.'

At my feet kids are tugging at my trousers, wanting to play. I make a monster face and they leap backwards with shrieks and laughs. The bravest two have another go. I crouch and make a slow chopping movement with my hand while my face goes into exaggerated karate mode. My attackers drop into an identical stance, pull more expres-sive faces, and begin chopping with legs and arms.

'Jackie Chan!' says a boy, a slip of six years in brown shorts and a T-shirt. 'Bruce Lee!' says a seven-year-old girl, visibly malnourished in a dirty black and red check skirt.

Am I hearing things? After each punch comes the same names. Perhaps they watched videos while relocated outside the CKGR. Perhaps they have fought one of the many foreign anthropologists and journalists of all colours and hues who have passed this way taking stories and pictures. I am being beaten-up by Jackie Chan and Bruce Lee in the middle of the Kalahari. What a way to go.

The people of the Kalahari have been bullied by everyone. The Tswana originally called them the 'Basarwa', the 'people with nothing', and enslaved them. European settlers shot them like vermin. Victorians paraded them in freak shows. Anthropologists thought they were sub-human, with tonal clicks similar to animals. The modern Western view of the hunter-gatherer Bushman was shaped by the great explorer and author Sir Laurens van der Post, who travelled through the area in 1955. But even in the 1950s, Van Der Post struggled to find any true hunter-gatherers. Their way of life had already changed. Not an impression you would get from reading his book *The Lost World of the Kalahari*. He declared the San hunter-gatherers to be the 'lost soul' of all mankind. 'He completely romanticized their way of life,' says Tim.

Bushman life changed over centuries. Different groups had radically different skills and lifestyles. In the modern era change started with the arrival of Europeans, who recruited San as trackers and soldiers. Perhaps the biggest change came in the 1940s and 50s when prospectors arrived in the Kalahari, pushed roads through the desert and, crucially, sank water boreholes deep below the thick Kalahari sand. The San settled in homesteads near the boreholes, planted a few crops and kept chickens and goats. Clothes replaced animal-skins. The true hunter-gatherer Bushman began to disappear. Now, after the Botswanan government has stopped the older generation from hunting and put many of the younger generation through schools, the hunter-gatherer no longer exists.

There are roughly 85,000 San left and they have become one of the most disadvantaged groups in southern Africa. Destitute and marginalized, they live in resettlement areas or the slum outskirts of villages and towns across Angola, Botswana, Namibia, South Africa, Zambia and Zimbabwe. The traditional Bushman way of life has gone, perhaps for ever.

IN THE EVENING we camp just south of the Metsiamanong settlement in the closest designated camping site in the reserve. Jumanda and I both want to stay with Uncle Mongwegi, but we cannot risk sleeping in the settlement in case late-night government patrols catch us. It is not worth putting Mongwegi at risk.

Yanked back from my dreams, I am woken in the early hours of the morning by my rumbling guts. I grab my torch, toilet roll, a spade to bury ablutions and matches to burn the paper, and try to leave the tent quietly, without disturbing my neighbours. Then I trip over the tent flap and sprawl in the dust. It is all most undignified.

I walk into the bush, dig a small hole a respectable distance from the camp and squat down. As business proceeds, I shine my torch into the inky black scrub, idly scanning for animals. I see a flash of movement off to my left, just beyond the limit of my beam. My heart thumps. From the darkness, a pair of eyes stare back at me. A wave of nausea flushes my body. The eyes move rapidly around me towards my front, keeping their distance. Another pair of eyes appears back to the left. A terrified voice inside my head tells me they are lions. Another, calmer, says they are probably hyenas. I feel supremely vulnerable, squatting in the desert with my trousers around my ankles, my bare bum exposed to the world. But for some reason I do not leap to my feet and sprint to the camp. Perhaps my brain will not countenance such indignity; perhaps I am just petrified. The dark creatures move around me in a circle. The lead one stops. I steady my torch. I think it is a hyena. My fingers reach for the spade. Silently, I lift it above my head, then bring it thudding down, whacking the ground and then a branch, once, twice, three times. The eyes vanish. I hold the torch between my teeth and finish my business with feverish speed, then stumble back to the camp, glancing over my shoulder, expecting to see the pearly whites of Jumanda's black-maned cousins. I zip the tent tight and fall into a fitful sleep.

N EXT MORNING, emboldened by daylight, I walk into the shrub to burn my waste paper. Breakfast for me is just a sip of water and a banana. I need to kill the bug inside. By mid-morning we have packed our tents and readied ourselves for another long drive. We head southeast for seven hours, leaving the reserve through an open gate and overnighting at a remote lodge. My diarrhoea rumbles on, but the lodge has locking doors and flushing toilets. Finally, I sleep soundly.

Back towards the Tropic of Capricorn the next day, which we cross on an empty red-dust road. We are returning to the capital, Gaborone, where we are due to meet up with jolly journalist Lucas again. Main roads in Botswana are generally wide, flat and straight. But suddenly we find ourselves on long stretches, frayed at the edges, which are just wide enough for two vehicles if both drivers are sober. After the emptiness of the Kalahari the experience is a shock similar to rocketing through width restrictions at high speed. Our Land Rover shakes with the vibration as we pass each car and I grip the edge of my seat.

At a police checkpoint smart, polite and earnest young officers check vehicles and IDs. Would they ever ask for a bribe? 'No, it's extremely rare,' says Tim. 'It's happened to me once in the last ten years.' When corruption started to become a problem, the government established an independent anti-corruption unit headed by an outsider, with an open public hotline. Posters and billboards across the country broadcast the same clear message: 'Botswana has ZERO tolerance for corruption. It is illegal to offer or ask for a bribe.' It was a simple strategy that worked. Transparency International, the international corruption watchdog, now ranks Botswana as the least corrupt country on the continent, and less corrupt than several EU states.

Botswanans are proud of their incorruptible police, and their well-run, forward-looking country, a fact Lucas confirms that night when we finally arrive back in Gaborone, share a well-earned beer, and recount tales from our travels. 'Of course there are still lots of problems and issues for us to resolve.' he says. 'But in many ways we are becoming a very modern country.' Yet one of the many things I find wonderful about Botswana is how the old ways still lurk close to the surface. When Lucas married, he paid a 'bride price' of six cows to his wife's parents for the right to marry their daughter.

'I know it sounds very old-fashioned, but I wanted to keep my wife's family happy, and also my mother and father. They respect the traditions. My wife was very pleased with the bride price I paid. Six cows meant I valued her highly.'

Lucas personally bought the cows and herded them to the home of his in-laws. The image brings a smile to my face. 'I know, I know,' he says, 'but many people are still not ready to give up these traditions. They can be a good thing. They can still exist in modern Botswana.'

As if to prove his point, Lucas takes me to see a traditional healer, the sort of person who used to be called a witchdoctor, to seek her advice on my rumbling guts, and to check whether my journey around Capricorn will be a success.

In her tiny corrugated iron shack in the village of Otse, just outside Gaborone, Tsemaletsile Maswabi, a slightly built woman, carefully places a hat made from jackal fur on her head, wraps a printed shawl around her waist, and begins her diagnosis.

Tsemaletsile is a traditional healer of local repute. She is a proud woman, used to commanding respect. On the floor against one wall in her shack is a two-foot-deep jungle of scores of glass bottles, small plastic containers, old Coca Cola bottles and Crosse & Blackwell jars, all containing mysterious powders, potions and lotions.

A small bag made of rodent skin and fur is produced and Tsemaletsile asks me to blow inside. She holds the bag tightly, mutters for a few moments, then casts the contents on to a crumpled white cloth on the floor. An assortment of shells, dice, coins, plastic discs and cubes of bone are spread across the floor. Lucas and I sit on the ground, waiting expectantly. My healer breathes deeply, studying the bones intently. She points at my right ankle. You are suffering pain at the back of your foot, she tells me. It hurts when you walk. It is true. I have long had a problem with my right heel and a bone growing backwards out of my foot. It had been playing up, but I had not limped into her shack. I am impressed. I nod vigorously.

This is a green light. Tsemaletsile responds with enthusiasm, working her way up my body. Next are my knees. Apparently they are loose. Then my legs are troubling me. As is my groin, hips, stomach, back and neck. And I have a mystery illness that will reveal itself in time. Lovely.

Rather than giving me a sleepless night, what I really want is some potions for my stomach. And perhaps a charm or spell that will help me on my journey. Tsemaletsile looks back at her bones. 'Your journey will be free of problems,' she says confidently. I turn to Lucas. 'Does she understand I'm going all the way around the world?' He translates. Tsemaletsile glances down again. This time she is less certain. 'There will be few problems on your journey.'

For my stomach, Tsemaletsile examines her jars, picks out a

couple to check their contents, then pours termite soil, a reddy-brown powder, on to a piece of plastic bag. Then brown and white powders are mixed together. 'Take this and you will have good fortune,' she says.

Traditional healers like Tsemaletsile still have enormous power in Botswana, as they do across the continent. In sub-Saharan Africa there is roughly one traditional healer per 500 people, compared to one doctor per 40,000 people. Even in Gaborone, one of the wealthiest cities on the continent, there are ten times more healers than doctors. A sizeable number are complete quacks, promising to heal AIDS or cancer with vegetables. So the Botswanan government plans to register and regulate the healers. It already uses them to spread a safe sex message, distribute condoms, and encourage people to have HIV tests.

On one wall of Tsemaletsile's shack is a laminated certificate from the local Bamalete Lutheran Hospital confirming her completion of an HIV/AIDS training course. She refers to it proudly. On another wall is a family planning flip-chart, with diagrams on the internal workings of male and female bodies, and a pictorial guide to wearing a condom.

'When people first started dying from HIV/AIDS we thought it was witchcraft,' she says, 'then we thought it was just foreigners who would be infected.'

'Can you treat patients with HIV/AIDS?' I ask. The clarity of her answer surprises me.

'If I think they might be HIV positive I refer them immediately to a hospital,' she says. 'And I am always pushing people to go for tests so they can know their HIV status. I have had one. It would not be right to encourage others if I had not had one myself.'

I feel guilty, but encouraged. Part of me had judged Tsemaletsile by her surroundings. And perhaps by her jackal-fur hat. Yet many Western medicines are derived from African herbs and plants. The termite soil she prescribes for my stomach is high in iron and folic acid. She takes many of her treatments directly from nature.

'I just get a small axe, cut the herbs and dig out the roots. I even walk on small bushes or rocks looking for herbs. After finding them, I wash them, grind them and use a sieve to make finer particles from the herbs.'

Recruiting Tsemaletsile and other traditional healers to the anti-AIDS campaign is essential. Locals will listen to her when she describes the devastating horror of AIDS. Getting her involved will save lives.

To the side of the shack, a mould and sacks of concrete reveal that Tsemaletsile has been working with her teenage daughter to make foundation blocks for a new home. Perhaps in a few years she might have a shop selling herbal medicines.

Lucas and I drive along bumpy tracks around Tsemaletsile's village to a small cemetery. Many of the graves are covered by low green shading, a new burial tradition. I look across a sea of green netting. There have been scores of deaths here in just the last few years, dramatic evidence of the ongoing toll of HIV/AIDS. Amid the plague, many Botswanans still believe in the dark arts. The Otse village chief, a powerful and influential man in a position salaried by the government, had died the previous year. Many of his family are convinced he was killed by witchcraft. It can be used to explain the unexplainable, but it can also involve juju and ritual sacrifices.

'Around election times, problems with witchcraft become more serious,' says Lucas. 'Politicians want to use the most powerful *muti* [traditional medicine] and magic to win their campaigns. Human flesh is the most powerful *muti*. And the most powerful human flesh is that of a young child.' There have been cases where even educated entrepreneurs have buried the genitalia of children at the site of their new business to ensure good fortune.

The next morning, back in a hotel in Gaborone, the headline on the front page of a local paper catches my eye: 'Fear grips village as threats delivered by an owl shock local businessman'. Surely this is a case for Precious Ramotswe, the traditionally built, matronly star of Botswana's great literary advert, *The No. 1 Ladies' Detective Agency* series of bestselling books?

I only have a day or so left in Botswana, but it seems a good time to meet Professor Sheila Tsou, the Minister for Health, who is battling HIV/AIDS and trying to regulate traditional healers. Many think she is the model for Mma Ramotswe. She has played her twice on the stage in Gaborone, and is the author's choice for the role in a Hollywood version of the book.

I meet the minister for tea at the Gaborone Sun, a hotel featured in the books. Noisy refurbishment work and a crowd watching a televized rugby match prevented us meeting at The President hotel, where the detective usually takes coffee on the terrace and considers her cases. The minister, an amply proportioned, ebullient woman, wears a power-suit and a scarf wound tight around her head and tied with care and precision. 'The way I tie my scarf is a family secret,' she says with an infectious laugh. 'One company offered my daughter a job if she would tell them how I tie it, but she refused, saying I would kill her!'

We talk about AIDS and about traditional healers, who the minister is determined to regulate. But she says they can still teach conventional doctors a thing or two. The minister leans forward conspiratorially.

'Before I became a minister,' she says, 'I was working in a hospital where we had a man who came in with constant hiccups. The doctors tried to treat him but his hiccups continued for days and days. Then a traditional healer was brought in, and he burned a feather in front of the man and wafted the smoke up his nostrils and he was immediately cured. Incredible!'

She straightens and gives me a well-what-do-you-think-of-that look. I nod meaningfully.

'We must not lose these skills. But we must also make sure we know what works. Who knows, perhaps there is a plant or a herb out there, somewhere in Botswana even, that can be used to treat *serious* diseases.'

Botswana is an extraordinary country. A place of computers and mobiles, wild carnivores and fragile wilderness, friendly politicians and traditional healers. A country without grasping officials or greedy cops. It is a much-needed reminder that Africa is not just one suffering continent, but many countries. Some are ruled well, many are ruled badly, but a broad brush should not tar them all. Botswana is a country that works. Without ignoring the appalling treatment of the San, this is a country visitors can enjoy without a gnawing feeling they are voyeurs at a sideshow of suffering and disaster. Botswana is not an Africa of fear and horror. After years of travelling in states ridden by conflict, it is Africa, but not as I know it.

SAFARI AND SAPPHIRES

3 · SOUTH AFRICA

I AM STANDING at the main crossroads in the market town of Louis Trichardt, a former Afrikaaner stronghold in the Limpopo region of northern South Africa, watching the world pass me by.

The Tropic of Capricorn cuts through an area known as a Boer heartland, farmed by generations of white settlers, and I expected this town, my first stop as I travel east through the country, to be stuffed with Afrikaaners.

Sure enough, a white farmer with a porcine face drives past alone in the front of a pickup truck with three spare seats in his twin cab. Two of his black workers are left standing on the back, buffeted by the wind. Another family pickup drives past with two blond, crew-cut boys in the back. They look like extras from the movie *The Boys from Brazil*.

Louis Trichardt was named after a Boer general who led whites to the region in the 1830s. But most faces on the streets today are black. According to my guide Nhlanhla Mthethwa, a burly Zulu born in the apartheid township of Soweto, it is a reversal of the days when only whites were seen in the town centre.

Reconciliation has been slow and painful in South Africa, but since the end of apartheid this hick white farming town has gradually become more representative of the new democracy. Although Louis

Trichardt now has a refreshing, uniquely African feel, on this second leg of my Capricorn journey I'm planning to explore ongoing tensions between blacks and whites in Limpopo, the sunny province buttressed against the borders of Botswana and collapsing Zimbabwe. Brian is back behind the camera on this journey, with Chris Martin directing. Chris normally makes award-winning documentaries with John Pilger, but has agreed to lower himself to my level for this trip. Joining me for the first time on one of these work trips is my fiancée Anya, who will be filming on a second camera and working as assistant producer. We are weeks away from our wedding, so we both hope everything goes smoothly. From here we'll head east together, through the great game parks of South Africa, across Mozambique and over the sea to Madagascar.

Nhlanhla leads us along the main street in Louis Trichardt. Outside one supermarket, a young woman dances and sings gospel karaoke on a loudspeaker to attract customers. Further up the road, a new arrival from Zimbabwe, just an hour north of the town, is standing outside a shop selling a basket of what appear to be dried slugs. We stop to chat. Love, as her name translates to, tells me life across the border is going from bad to worse. 'There is no work and no food in the shops, nothing. The country is being bled dry.'

Her slugs are dried mopane worms, the caterpillars that feed on the mopane tree. I came across these in Botswana, but managed to avoid eating them. A crowd gathers around us. I ask Nhlanhla if he has eaten them before.

'I tried them once under duress,' he says with a distinct lack of enthusiasm. 'They were crunchy, very crunchy.'

Love has a beaming smile and a winning sales patter. I buy a bag and Nhlanhla and I agree to take a worm each. They are small, black and hard, with little caterpillar heads and feet. I have a perverse desire to see how bad they are. We take bites and chomp on crispy bodies. They are disappointingly bland, a bit like eating dried wax. But mopane worms are touted as a new superfood and farmers in southern Africa are trying to produce them commercially. Acre for acre, they can provide twice as much protein as cattle. I fear they will need some serious marketing help before people start asking for bags of salt and vinegar caterpillars.

But where are the Boers? Shoppers on the high street tell us most Afrikaaners are gathering at a local sports field, where a country fair is underway. There are the usual bumper cars, vomit-inducing spinning rides, and terrifying tower rides that leave your stomach in the sky as they drop you to the ground. But there are other indications this is still the land of the Afrikaaners. Alongside stalls selling candyfloss and ice-cream, there are others selling music by Boer pop stars and biltong, a salty, smoky meat with an almost spiritual significance for Afrikaaners, dried in a process invented by the Voortrekkers, who colonized the interior of South Africa during the Great Trek from the British-controlled Cape. Air-dried and seasoned with vinegar, salt and coriander, and high in protein, biltong tastes a damn sight better than mopane worms.

As I wander around the fair, the Afrikaaner national dress of khaki shirts and shorts is everywhere. You'd think someone would want to be a bit different. There's not a Hawaiian shirt in sight. Instead I find a stall offering powerful stun-guns that can zap burglars or muggers with a lethal buzz of blue electricity. Whites in Louis Trichardt, who own the best farmland around the town, no longer have the comforting feeling of superiority that comes with minority rule. Many feel isolated in this new black land and as the crime rate in South Africa rockets, farmers are being targeted. So whites are organizing themselves into groups, societies and unions. Above tents on the edge of the fair, a group of Boer farmers fly the Vierkleur four-colour flag, a symbol of the apartheid-era Transvaal region, and a relic of the past that makes both Brian and Nhlanhla shudder.

Gideon Meiring is a tall, barrel-chested man in his fifties with thick ears and a don't-mess-with-me manner. He used to be an intelligence officer in the apartheid-era army. Now wealthy hunters travel from Europe to shoot game on his farm north of Louis Trichardt. He also heads the local farmers' union, which runs 'Townwatch' security patrols. Like Neighbourhood Watch, but with guns.

Gideon shows me around the farmers' stall at the fair. 'The Boer are here to stay,' reads a defiant banner in front of their tents. Next to the CB radios and walkie-talkies is an example of their 'battle dress', a mesh jacket with pockets for a pistol, stun-gun and torch, worn by many union members on patrol. The union also runs self-defence courses for whites fearing attack. One woman on the stall is introduced as a specialist in defence against 'home invasion'. Two girls in their late teens, one with blonde Heidi tresses, are rifle instructors, and Gideon drives us all to a house on the outskirts of the town so he can show me an AK-47 assault rifle.

'We train the people to handle an AK-47 because the people who attack farmers on their farms from time to time make use of AK-47s,' he tells me. 'You must be in a position to handle that weapon. And to return fire accurately.'

One of the girl instructors slaps in a magazine and opens up on a bush in the back garden. The noise is extraordinary. She passes the gun to me. It is sturdy and heavy. I bring it to my shoulder and fire off a couple of bursts. To my surprise, I get the shots on target. The bush disintegrates. I feel a surge of adrenalin and a worrying rush of power. Afrikaaners may have lost control of the national government, but up here on Capricorn, it seems, they still have money, farms and guns.

THE LAND around Louis Trichardt is green and lush, with bright trees covering packed valleys. The mythic red-rock Soutpansberg Mountains, just north of the town, trap clouds and ensure rain falls to the south.

We drive through road tunnels underneath the mountains, heading 50 miles north towards the Zimbabwe border and the humanitarian catastrophe that is Robert Mugabe's blighted land. On the northern side of the mountains, barren plains are home to the first ancient-looking baobab trees we have seen on the journey. Swollen with stores of water, their trunks and texture remind me of elephants. A hole gapes wide on the body of one, like a mouth. Those just metres from the tarmac look like guardians of the road. Gathered in gangs on the hillsides, with their limbs splaying like demented ravers, the baobabs have the appearance of invading triffids.

Within an hour we are in Musina, a northern market town, busy with shoppers and frightened, camera-shy refugees fleeing the chaos of neighbouring Zimbabwe. Across the border, inflation is now running at roughly 10,000 per cent and unemployment at more than 80 per cent. More than four million Zimbabweans have fled their country in search of food and jobs. Between one and three million have crossed into South Africa illegally. Thousands are crossing every week in Africa's largest exodus outside a war. Even blind and handicapped Zimbabweans have crossed the border and can now be found begging in Johannesburg, Africa's El Dorado.

On the edge of Musina we meet a local film-maker, formerly from Zimbabwe, who knows men involved in the people-smuggling trade, and can take us to a section of the border where desperate souls cross into South Africa. His name is Godknows.

'Zimbabweans have such interesting names,' Nhlanhla Mthethwa tells me with a chuckle.

'You can talk,' I say.

The main border crossing between Zimbabwe and South Africa is just to the north of Musina, at Beitbridge. The road is narrow and the scene is chaotic. Cars and lorries coming south from Zimbabwe are empty, belching smoke from dirty engines. Those heading back drop low on their rear axles, loaded with bags of vegetables, drums of oil, petrol and containers of paraffin, taking home supplies unavailable in empty Zimbabwean shops. By the bridge, women in long, colourful dresses walk across balancing suitcases and huge bags on their heads. We have neglected to get permits for filming, and are detained for several hours by angry South African customs officers who threaten to confiscate our camera. This is the legal border, but there are also illegal crossings.

With Godknows guiding, we take dusty back roads from Beitbridge out to the border fence. It is an old-fashioned divide, spanning 15 metres, of a type marking tense frontiers around the world. A two-metre wire fence topped by barbed wire is followed by a gap of flat earth, then roll after roll of razor wire stacked on top of each other, another flat gap, and another tall fence made from razor wire. A formidable barrier between wealthy South Africa, the richest country in the region, and Zimbabwe, which Robert Mugabe has turned into his own private catastrophe.

We drive along the road that tracks the border for just five minutes, over a hill, and five or six black figures dart away from the wire and across the road. When they see us they sprint deeper into South Africa and along the dry bed of a narrow, twisting river. We pull level and through the undergrowth I see glimpses of panic-stricken faces glancing back. By the time we come to a stop, they are gone. I can see their crossing point: a junction between different sections of razor wire where the fence is lower. The wire has been flattened. Footprints in the sand on the other side suggest this is a popular spot to cross.

We hear a roar of engines and turn to run back to our cars. We are not supposed to be on this private road. Four South African border patrol four-wheel drives rocket over the hill. The guards box us in with their vehicles and demand to know what we are doing. We are unprepared. At the back of our cars, Nhlanhla tells them we are filming monkeys by the road. At the front of the cars, Chris tells them the truth. They tell us to leave before dark, when armed robbers prey on the wretched border jumpers.

We drive on. Over another hill and we can see a snaking bend of the Limpopo River, 'great, grey-green and greasy' to Kipling. Not at the moment. The bed is parched and beaten by the sun. During the wet season it is wide, powerful, and busy with crocodiles. But still people cross, swimming the river, going over or under the razor-wire fences, and then taking their chances on private farms and game reserves stocked with hungry lions.

Fifteen minutes later. We summit the peak of another hill and speed down the other side. Suddenly there are more shadowy shapes emerging from the trees and bushes on the Zimbabwean side of the border, some already crossing the first of the three fences. We brake hard. Brian and I run towards the wire. In front of us ten men and two women are now over the first fence and struggling feverishly with the middle rolls of razor wire. They are frantic. Two lift the rolls with their bare hands so others can scramble underneath. Three more grab at posts spaced apart in the middle of the razor rolls. The stakes hold wires that used to carry a lethal electric current during the time of apartheid. Two men swing themselves over the rolls using the posts, but the stake closest to us snaps under the weight of the third man. He falls forwards into rolls of razor wire that cut into his flesh. Hands pull him free and he staggers to his feet, blood spurting from a slash on his lower leg. The men at the front of the group are now at the wire just a few feet in front of us. I can see the sweat on their faces and fear in their eyes. They tear at the ground with their hands, digging out the bottom of the fence as if the devil himself is snapping at their heels.

My heart is pumping. I am desperate to cheer them on, to help them under the wire, but my brain tells me to keep back. They are doing just fine. They lift the fence just enough to scramble underneath and run past us across the road into the bushes.

The injured man hobbles behind. The side of his left shoe is red with blood gushing out over the dirt. He picks up speed and we all run deeper into the bush, shouting for our drivers to get their cars off the road and out of sight. Forty metres into the bushes, the group pauses, exhausted, sweating, panting, gulping for air. I urge them deeper into the bush. South African patrols are everywhere. And the blood is leaving a trail.

We run between bushes and stumble over boulders for another hundred metres. Four of the group race ahead. Eight pause again and sit on the ground. We can snatch a few words before they must disappear.

The injured man is still bleeding badly but wants to talk. Sweat is pouring off his face. He uses a piece of paper to stem the pumping blood while Anya runs back to the cars to get our medical kit. I check his wound and realize the paper he is using is a Zimbabwean 5,000 dollar note. Once it would have been worth around £350, but now it is rendered worthless by Mugabe's hyper-inflation. The border-jumper tells me the situation in Zimbabwe has reached breaking point. There is no food in the shops. Life is disintegrating.

The people-smuggler sits on the edge of the group, great beads forming on his brow and rolling down his cheeks. He has brought them across the border. Now he must lead them across a private farm to a road where cars will collect them and drive them south towards Johannesburg. We do not have long to talk. The police could be along any moment. The people-smuggler makes the journey on Tuesdays and Thursdays and brings roughly 60 people across each month.

'We watch the army patrols and come over now when they have gone to lunch,' he says. He is a lowly link in a chain often taking less than £4 from each smuggled soul.

I ask if others in the group are prepared to talk. Three lads in their late teens and early twenties mumble that their English is poor and shake their heads. Another man in his early thirties, tall, muscular, with flip-flops and muddy toes, says his English is not great but he will try to say a few words. I squat beside him and ask what he would like to tell us. He pauses, searching for the words that might help me understand the enormity of the suffering across the border.

'There is no work, no hope and no food in Zimbabwe,' he says slowly. 'We are starving in Zimbabwe, so I jumped the border. I've got no passport.' He pauses, trying to distil his feelings. 'I want to be a man like you. So I jumped the border to get money in South Africa.'

His few words convey a world of suffering. He is a mechanic, now prepared to do anything for a few pounds. His father died of AIDS a few years before and he has younger brothers and sisters to care for. He wants a job, he wants to put food on their table. He wants freedom, a family, education for his kids. Everything that comes to most of us lucky enough to be born in the West. I find his quiet dignity overwhelming and my eyes moisten with tears. We pass Nhlanhla some money and food to give the group, and watch as they leave, slipping between the trees and bushes, and disappear into the afternoon shadows.

That night we stay in a quiet hillside hotel overlooking the main road between Johannesburg and Zimbabwe. Afrikaaners and white Zimbabweans keep the underground bar busy, snapping drinks orders at the black barman. The previous night, one of the hotel guests had been Robert Mugabe's personal shopper, returning to Zimbabwe with a mini-bus loaded with food, wine, supplies and the finest cuts of meat. Even as the country disintegrates around him, the crazed old dictator has a well-stocked larder. So he's all right then.

NOON THE next day finds us waiting for Gideon in a petrol station on the main road from Johannesburg to Zimbabwe. His group runs patrols looking for Zimbabwean illegal immigrants. Five pickup trucks arrive and a selection of Afrikaaner stereotypes leap out. There are thickset young blond men wearing the Boer uniform of khaki shirts and shorts. A couple have pistols on their hips. There is a chubby chap with a sweaty, piglety face, a high-pitched voice, clipped moustache and a *bop-pens*, a belly built by beer. He has an air of menace. Gideon himself wears dark wraparound sunglasses. His patrol has already caught two Zimbabweans, who now sit in the back of a pickup sipping Coke and eating slices of bread, their hands shackled with black cable ties. I ask one of them a few questions about Zimbabwe. Before he can answer, Gideon orders him to sit up straight.

The men repeat the tragic tales we heard yesterday. The situation in Zimbabwe sounds utterly abysmal. A vast human tragedy is being played out across the border. The farmers turn the refugees, who they call Zimbabwean illegals, over to a police patrol that arrives in the petrol station. Both men will be deported to Zimbabwe. Nobody doubts they will be back.

We head out on patrol with Gideon in a pickup, cruising along tracks through the veldt, a green light flashing on the roof and two other vehicles flanking our car. It all feels faintly ridiculous. Macho games. Gideon says refugees trespass on white farms, cutting fences and setting traps for animals. He says some border-jumpers have attacked farmers and when they reach towns they claim benefits and become a drain on the country. The police are useless, says Gideon, so his men are protecting the area, flooding it with patrols and adopting a policy of 'domination'.

'Just like the old days,' he says in a telling moment of reflection.

Fear of immigrant invaders is not confined to Afrikaaners. South Africans of all colours are notoriously xenophobic about new arrivals nabbing jobs and housing. We drive north by the side of a railway line, heading towards Zimbabwe. Many jumpers follow the line south. After an hour, the guys in the patrol car in front spot two fleeing refugees, leap from their cab and run into bushes beside the road. Brian and I scale a barbed-wire fence and follow for a few minutes until we meet Rudolf, one of the patrolmen, his face flushed, returning to the cars. The Zimbabweans have escaped.

It is only when I see Rudolf's face and watch jokey back-slapping as the men commiserate after losing their prey, that I realize this is all about the thrill of the hunt. Afrikaaners have lost control over South Africa. Vigilante patrols hunting for destitute refugees are a way for the whites to discharge testosterone, protect their pack and reassert power, just like the good old days.

We drive back towards the petrol station where we left our cars. The sun is setting over the African bush. It is a hypnotically beautiful land, unchanged for thousands of years. The final rays of light fall on the spindly branches of a vast baobab tree with a trunk the size of a small house.

At dusk we reach a railway crossing and another car from the patrol joins with us, catching two small black figures between the two cars.

'Don't try to run,' screeches one of the patrolmen and nine Afrikaaners converge on two frightened Zimbabwean lads in ragged clothing carrying their worldly possessions in tiny bags. I am appalled and lost for words. They are just boys.

The patrolmen are not violent with the lads, but there are no kid gloves, not even for our benefit. They put cable ties around their thumbs and bundle them into the back of a pickup. The wide-eyed boys say they are 15 and 16, but look younger. The farmers profess sympathy for their captives, but they will still hand them over to the police.

'On the one hand, you feel very sorry for them,' Gideon says, 'because they're helpless, hungry people, because of a certain political situation, but on the other hand, they threaten our safety and security, our well-being, our property, even our lives, so it sounds like a contradiction but that is the situation.'

The boys look confused and scared. It's impossible to be unmoved by their plight.

Radios crackle and another pickup races up with two more prisoners. The farmers patrol during light and dark, catching scores of people every day. Around 5,000 Zimbabweans are deported from South Africa each week, and the numbers are increasing all the time. The farmers may have genuine security concerns, because a handful of Zimbabweans have crossed with weapons, but they pursue border-jumpers with unseemly zeal. And their actions are short-sighted. Expat Zimbabweans are keeping their country afloat by sending money home. Without money from abroad – 'remittances' – Zimbabwe would completely collapse, destabilizing the region and flooding precious Afrikaaner farmland with hundreds of thousands of refugees.

I've seen enough. We head back to our cars and drive south for an hour to Louis Trichardt, where the Afrikaaners also run a town patrol. We meet outside a petrol station just after one of the group has had his car stolen. I thought they were the ones supposed to be providing the security.

Squashed into the cab of one patrol pickup, we drive around a black township just beyond the suburbs. The farmers have green strobe lights flashing on their vehicles. The townies go for flashing white. Our driver, one of the patrol organizers, is a thoughtful sort who accepts that part of the reason the Afrikaaners patrol, might be a feeling that they have lost their empire. The patrols give them back a sense of power and influence over a community they no longer control. Car theft is a major issue in the town. Three patrolmen recently had their cars stolen in a single day. But when the organizer and I get out to chat by the road, he leaves his keys in the ignition. Given the recent misfortune of his group, I wonder if this is wise.

I FEEL no pang of regret at our departure from Louis Trichardt. It is a pleasure to leave. We head east across the country and south towards Capricorn.

Our route takes us across the former black Bantustan of Gazankulu, home to the Shangaan people. It is still an almost exclusively black region. We pass a jolly school with whitewashed walls and hundreds of kids playing outside, all of them black. The outside world might think the new South Africa is a land where blacks and whites live together happily, but integration is still a long way off.

'There are still two countries, two peoples here,' says Nhlanhla with a note of sadness.

By the road I buy bananas from a wooden shack with produce neatly stacked outside under the shade of a sagging yellow Sol beer umbrella. The stallholder leaps around wearing a pretty red dress and carrying a tiny baby boy on her lower back wrapped in a bright red towel. He sleeps silently.

A minute further along the road and three Rasta barbers are squatting on the verge by the roadside, touting for business from passing drivers. Their salon is four wooden stakes topped by a piece of corrugated iron. Electrical cables have been jerry-rigged to power their clippers.

'Look at those entrepreneurs,' laughs Nhlanhla.

Rastafarians aren't supposed to cut their own hair and this group has an impressive collection of dreadlocks. But they still gesture to and harass passing drivers and villagers who have hair longer than an inch, shaming them into a cut. It's a bit of a cheek. Thirty metres away on the other side of the road, two more Rasta barbers are pulling in the customers thanks to one major competitive advantage. Their salon shack has a chair.

We cruise on, approaching the outer reaches of north-east South Africa. It is an area where the threat of HIV/AIDS, itself exacerbated by President Thabo Mbeki's involvement with health quackery and disastrous mishandling of the crisis, is matched by the threat of malaria.

Throughout history, malaria has been our greatest enemy. Perhaps half of all the humans who have ever lived have died of malaria. Millions of Africans are infected each year and around 3,000 African children die of malaria every day, one every 30 seconds. Malaria is the curse of the tropics, a disease almost entirely found between Capricorn and Cancer. We might have forgotten about it in the temperate West, but the South African government is still waging war on this scourge, battling the mosquitoes that slip the malaria parasite into our bodies as they feed on our blood. Their weapon of choice is DDT, an old insecticide used by much of the world and then banned when toxic side effects were revealed. In Latin America DDT has been shown to shrink the penises of otters until they cannot mate. It thins eggshells and gives alligators both male and female organs. Used incorrectly, DDT can be wickedly dangerous.

We stop in the town of Giyani to meet Zactly Sekgobela from the Department of Health, who is in charge of battling malaria in the Mopani District right next to the Tropic of Capricorn. He has 27 teams of sprayers and aims to treat 400,000 homes with DDT and a pyrethroid pesticide each year. 'This year I want to beat my target,' he says.

Zactly takes me to a temporary camp for his spraying teams. A concrete wall has been marked ready for training. DDT needs to be sprayed in just the right quantities. Too little and mozzies will survive and acquire resistance. Too much and it will pollute homes, the environment and fragile human bodies.

Europeans and Americans used DDT after the Second World War to help eradicate malaria in the West. Then Rachel Carson's 1962 book *Silent Spring* warned that DDT harmed wildlife reproduction. The book encouraged many countries to ban the chemical and helped to launch the modern environmental movement.

South Africa only stopped using DDT in 1996. Malaria cases rose sharply, hitting more than 64,000 in the year 2000 with at least 458 deaths. So the government started spraying again, and by 2005 malaria cases had dropped to 7,754, with deaths falling to 64. According to Zactly malarial mozzies are being steadily eradicated, pushed ever further towards the outer reaches of the country.

Zactly takes us to watch a spraying unit working in the village of Thomo, a pretty but poor settlement of a few hundred small huts and thatched rondavels sitting on rich red soil. Women from the Zion Christian Church (ZCC), a southern African church with four million members, are gathered in the open on the outskirts of the village for choir practice wearing green and yellow blouses and skirts. Their rich voices provide a serenade as we go in search of Zactly's malaria control teams.

Between a bungalow and a couple of rondavels, a dozen sprayers are pouring a milky liquid into pressurized spraying containers. Wearing wellies, gloves, hats and masks, the sprayers hoist the containers on to their backs and move en masse towards the dwellings, ready to exterminate.

These control teams may already be paying the price for using DDT. Studies have shown the sperm count of sprayers has dropped dramatically. I ask the men if they worry about their health. They laugh or shrug. Zactly says many of them have been doing it for 25 years, and their health is fine. But I am not convinced. Nobody really knows the long-term effects of exposure to the chemical.

Outside one of the rondavels, a jolly, middle-aged woman is waiting for her kitchen to be sprayed. A thin shaft of bright sunlight shines into the blackened interior. We carry her pots and pans outside. Not because contamination is risky, according to Zactly, but to make it easier for the sprayers to move around inside. One pot is so heavy it takes three of us to lift it. I ask the owner whether she objects to the spraying. She tells me her relatives have had malaria and she worries about her three children contracting the disease, so she doesn't mind the DDT. I glance into the hut where the family sleeps. They have one bed-net for protection, but it is old, the mesh holes are starting to open, and the net is not large enough to shelter the entire family.

I find it extraordinary that the wealthy South African government has not managed to ensure everyone has a net. After the Kenyan Health Ministry gave out 13.5 million insecticide-treated nets to protect children in 2003, child mortality fell in some areas by more than 40 per cent and hospital admissions went down nearly 60 per cent. Nets are lifesavers.

Zactly admits nets are important for prevention, but South Africa still wants to use chemicals to eradicate the problem.

'Why do you think conservationists and the developed world want South Africa to stop using DDT?' I ask him.

'The Europeans and Americans have used it, but now they are telling us to stop,' he complains. 'I think it is because they want us to buy alternative expensive chemicals from their firms. But they aren't as effective. DDT works for us.'

Zactly has been working with spraying teams since 1975. He goes fishing overnight by mozzie-infested lakes, almost daring them to infect him. They bite him regularly, but he has never developed the dreaded fever.

'Maybe I have DDT inside me,' he says as a joke.

It's a chemical that hangs around. He might just be right.

WE TAKE the road south and east. The land starts flat but soon we are speeding between distant hills. The temperature today, in late July, is 30 degrees Celsius. Not bad for winter. It's dry here, but many of the trees are still green with leaves, and heading towards Tzaneen in the south-east of Limpopo province we pass beds of bright flowers, then plantations and forest after forest of slender trees, many as tall as 25 metres high.

We decide not to stop in Tzaneen, a market town where Boer farmers are stocking pickups with sacks of veg, but a group of Shangaan men in dirty clothes and smart ZCC caps give us a cheery wave as we brake to let them cross the road.

The road takes us across a wide plain at the side of which the Drakensberg mountains, the highest in South Africa, rise to form a solid wall of craggy rock that spans the horizon like the stubbly back of a giant crocodile. The mountains, known as uKhahlamba in Zulu, or 'barrier of spears', push us further south and east and the land starts to open as we approach the east of South Africa and the vast beauty of the Kruger National Park, one of the most famous wildlife reserves on the planet. We are getting closer to the border with Mozambique. But our progress is slowed by a leisurely roadside lunch, so we decide to overnight near the town of Hoedspruit.

As the sun drops we head to a simple lodge on a large wildlife reserve outside Hoedspruit. We pull up round the side of wooden buildings in front of a few strands of electrified fence that hold back the darkness of the wild bush beyond. Anya and I are unloading our bags from the back of the car when huge shadows move in the blackness. As I draw my torch, two massive rhinos snort and wave their heads.

'They wander around in front of my house,' says the manager. 'They're fantastic guard dogs.'

Waking after an excellent night's sleep, I check the weather. The light is utterly dazzling and the air impossibly clean. We are in the Valley of the Olifants on the western edge of the Kruger National Park.

This is the land of the classic safari. Kruger is one of the top destinations for Europeans or Americans arriving in Africa for their honeymoons, loaded with bottles of hand-sanitizer and preconceptions about the Dark Continent, and wanting to see the Big Five: lion, black rhino, leopard, buffalo, and elephants, the biggest of them all.

Elephants are extraordinary consumers, eating between 150 and 250 kilograms of food a day. They are also destructive, knocking over trees to get at the succulent leaves. Can there ever be too many elephants? Apparently so. There are now at least 14,000 in Kruger. Herds can annihilate vegetation, pushing other species in the park towards extinction. Many conservationists and Kruger officials believe the only way of controlling their numbers is to cull them. Plans have been drawn up to separate and shoot thousands of the elephants in Kruger, perhaps half the number. It is hugely controversial, with respected conservationists lining up on both sides. In a bid to understand the issues involved, we drive from our lodge to the Kapama Game Reserve, still on the western edge of Kruger, where a game guide takes us out to look for ellies, as most locals lovingly call them, in an open-top Land Rover.

We bump past warthogs and impala, looking for scat and tracks on the ground. A giraffe is slurping the leaves off a tall tree. It has evolved to perfectly fit with its environment. But so has the tree, our guide tells us. After a few moments of attack, the tree starts to release tannic acid, pumping it into its leaves to create a revolting taste. Other trees downwind sense the tannin and start releasing their own. We see it happen. Or, at least, we see the giraffe's mouth turn. He stops eating and moves upwind in search of more breakfast.

Then all of a sudden, a herd of elephants is munching the bushes on our right. My eyes widen. There are at least ten, brilliantly camouflaged against the bush. They are huge, majestic, imperial. Tiny ellies at the middle are protected by mothers, with flashing white tusks mounting guard at the edge. They are moving at walking pace through the bush, but our presence spooks them, and they pick up speed, crossing the track behind us. Two little 'uns cross quickly, while Mum stares at us menacingly, daring us to threaten her family. They lumber off into the bush, their great backsides swaying through the trees. Within 15 seconds these huge creatures vanish completely, melting into the bush.

Surely there must be alternatives to culling these graceful giants.

The longer scientists study elephants, the more we realize how special they are. These are creatures that live for around 65 years. Females teach younger elephants about the geography and food of their world, and offer advice on how to raise young. Elephants display many of the emotions we associate with humans. They love, play and sympathize with each other. Elephants will smell the bones of a dead friend or relative, mourning them with sounds too low for humans to even hear. New discoveries of elephant behaviour are made all the time. Scientists now think elephants can sense the movement of other herds, particularly those fleeing danger, up to 20 kilometres away. They detect sonic vibrations through their feet.

Even claims they are simple destroyers of vegetation are not entirely accurate. Yes, they have large diets and a tendency to knock over trees and bushes. But by snapping the trees, ellies allow sunlight to hit the ground, opening up grasslands that are crucial for herbivores such as zebra and wildebeest, which in turn provide food for the big cats.

As the ellies move silently through the bush we try to follow, but the vegetation is too dense for our vehicle and apparently it is too dangerous to walk. We re-trace our steps through beautiful Kapama in search of lunch, but the outside world interrupts: we pass under electricity pylons carrying high-voltage wires across the bush. Apparently this disappoints some guests. But then many American tourists arrive at Johannesburg airport expecting to see lions shooed from the runway.

By the road outside Kapama are more high voltage sentinels carrying power across the country, along with telephone poles and a railway line. We pass a huge billboard advertising a new housing development complete with private landing strip. There are few areas of pristine, untouched land left on the planet, a fact that often comes as a huge shock to tourists who come to this region of South Africa expecting a natural wilderness. They pay vast sums for a safari and often discover they are actually on a small parcel of land resembling a glorified park. Wildlife documentary-makers, even the greatest, have a lot to answer for. They offer us visions of untouched worlds and intimate shots of glorious creatures, simultaneously feeding the myth that wild paradise still exists and encouraging expectations that a safari or nature ramble will afford close-up encounters with wildlife.

THEY ARE against elephant culling at the Kapama lodge. But not everyone agrees. We drive ten miles down the road to meet Brian Jones, a local wildlife guru who runs the Moholoholo Wildlife

Rehabilitation Centre, a veritable haven for abandoned, injured and poisoned animals and birds.

We find Brian sitting behind a cluttered desk. He is a grizzled, angry, passionate man in his sixties with a rapid-fire delivery and a reputation for straight-talking. In an area of South Africa relentlessly marketed as wild 'Big Five country', he is quick to point out there is actually very little wild habitat left anywhere.

'White farmers and businessmen have parcelled up the land,' he says bluntly. 'They build fences that protect their patch, but they prevent natural migrations and interfere with the ecosystem.'

Brian explains that after buying a reserve, an owner will spend millions putting a good fence around it and building the infrastructure. 'Now he's got to get tourists to get the money back, and now he's got to have animals there to show the tourists,' he says. And because tourists watch African wildlife documentaries that always show an abundance of impressive animals, as opposed to the reality where small numbers of animals are scattered over huge areas, reserve owners overstock their land with large game, creating completely artificial worlds.

But animals and birds in this region do not respect borders or barriers and they need vast amounts of space to be wild. Elephants, for example, like to migrate along rivers, which run east to west across Kruger. But the park is a narrow strip running north to south: a spectacular piece of bad planning. Kruger may be a flagship African park, but as Brian Jones tells me, along with most other wildlife parks in Africa and around the world, it is an environment completely created by humans.

Brian is the wisest conservationist I have met on my journey. I ask what he thinks about culling elephants in Kruger. He tells me he wishes there was an alternative. But nothing else will work effectively, or quickly enough.

'Elephants are having a devastating impact in Kruger,' he says. 'We have to be willing to take the tough decisions necessary to protect the whole reserve.' Humans have interfered with nature and created these man-made environments, setting themselves up as gods. So now humans must take responsibility for their actions and take tough, some-times painful decisions about the animals in the reserves and parks.

'We're not looking at saving just an elephant. Don't we want to save the leopard, the lion, the cheetah, the trees, the grass, the birds, the stoats, the rabbits?' he asks. 'We've got to be simple, put our human emotion aside and look at the whole picture.'

To illustrate his point, Brian takes us to see one of the youngest Moholoholo residents. Tom, a six-month-old rhino, is trotting around his enclosure. He is only small, about the size of a Shetland pony, but he has power and weight. I slap his thick hide.

'He can't feel that. He needs something a bit stronger.'

Brian produces a closed folding knife and rubs it across Tom's hide, then lowers his hand underneath and uses the knife stock to tickle his belly. After a few moments of seduction, Tom's knees start to wobble. His pupils dilate and his eyes roll back. A look of bliss spreads across his armoured face and he topples on to his side.

Tom was found by Kruger rangers stuck in mud around a water-ing hole. In the past he would have been left to die, because rangers were forbidden from interfering with nature. But humans created the watering hole, says Brian, 'so they should not shirk responsibility when deciding what lives or dies.' Tom was allowed to live. He was rescued and taken to Moholoholo. At our feet, he is still trembling with pleasure.

In a small concrete enclosure next to Tom, there are two small beasts resembling a cross between a skunk and a British badger. Finally, after spending hours scanning the bush for them while crossing Botswana and the Kalahari, I am able to see honey badgers for the first time.

Stu Robertson, a 21-year-old from just outside Brighton, is caring for the badgers, carnivores, rhino and hippo. Quite a responsibility.

'I love it here,' he tells me conspiratorially when Brian is out of earshot. He has the smile of a man who cannot quite believe his luck. 'I applied to lots of conservation centres and they said they wouldn't consider me without a PhD. But here Brian has taught me so much about wildlife and Africa.'

One of the honey badgers lived in Stu's room until it started shredding his clothes. Now both are kept in a roofless concrete enclosure and watched carefully. Honey badgers are incredibly smart and cunning. They were spotted widening a crack in the wall of their enclosure, but when they realized a trainer had seen them, they play-acted innocence. What, us? Only a chance conversation between staff uncovered the escape bid.

'Another time they stole a feeding bowl and started to bury it in the dirt,' says Stu. 'They wanted to put it flat against the wall so they had enough height to climb out.'

We move on. Brian takes me to see his old friend Big Boy. The giant male lion is kept among trees and bushes behind reassuringly high fences. As we approach, Brian starts calling to the lion with a whooping growl. Big Boy responds, prowling along on the other side of the fence parallel with us and growling back at Brian, greeting his human friend. We stop either side of a large gate. Brian and Big Boy swap roars. 'We used to go on walks together, hang out together,' says Brian with a smile. It is like watching Dr Dolittle working the animals. Chunks of meat are produced and passed through the fence to Big Boy, who growls with gratitude. It is a fantasy scene. Everyone wants a lion as a friend.

The road south from Moholoholo finally takes us to the entrance to Kruger. It is time to cross the reserve. Row after row of signs greet us near the Phalaborwa gate. Madsafari tours, Matomani Lodge, 79 Bush Lodge – sites now selling! An office to the right of the road is painted in zebra stripes. This small town is right at the edge of Kruger. We pay the park entrance fee, and drive into Kruger.

Not ten minutes inside and we have stopped by the side of the road. A herd of at least 25 elephants are moving across a narrow river bed, spraying each other with water and wallowing in the mud. Further on, another herd, then another. The ellies are everywhere and the damage they have done to trees and shrubs is obvious. There are endless flattened, twisted and broken bushes and trees. Other visitors pull up. Within a few minutes there are eight cars and a small tour bus, all cluttered around the road, watching the ellies. A South African couple stand on the roof of their car, taking photos of the elephants on their mobile phones.

Kruger is a glorified safari park attracting a million visitors a year. But it is packed with elephants and an abundance of game. It will not be like this in Mozambique, where civil war and poachers have devastated the wildlife. There is a border crossing at Giriyondo on the eastern edge of the Kruger, but it closes at 3 p.m. The time is now 2.28, and we need to hurry if we are to meet our new fixer on the other side.

4 · MOZAMBIQUE

MICKEY FONSECA, who will be guiding us across Mozambique, is waiting at the tiny Giriyondo border post with two new drivers and two old, dusty twin-cab 4WDs with cracked windows and stiff doors. I swapped emails with him as we planned our Capricorn journey, but this is the first time we have met. He is 31, mixed-race, with toffee-coloured skin, a green and yellow T-shirt, shaved head and a small goatee.

'Welcome to Latin Africa,' he says with an outstretched hand and a relaxed smile.

I like him immediately.

Mozambique still has a bad reputation. War, famine, floods. But beautiful beaches, fresh seafood and the laid-back Latin vibe befitting a former Portuguese colony once attracted more visitors than neighbouring South Africa and Zimbabwe combined. This is a country with spicy food and a spicy way of life. Neighbouring countries can seem a little staid next to Mozambique. It is Cuba in Africa.

We drive through an arch and out into Mozambique. I am genuinely excited. We have not landed in a major airport or hopped off a train in a capital city. We are out in the bush in the remote west of the country. Ahead of us is a completely new Capricorn nation, and we are going from one of the richest countries in Africa to one of the poorest. Or, as Mickey puts it, from the first world to the third.

Mickey's cousin Pino, a young Castro lookalike, is behind the wheel of the first car as we drive down a track around which shrubs and trees scatter dappled sunlight. We are close to Capricorn in the Parque Nacional do Limpopo, the Kruger's smaller brother, one million hectares bounded by the mighty Limpopo and Olifants rivers, with the Shingwedzi flowing through its heart.

During Mozambique's devastating 16-year civil conflict, when South African-backed Renamo fighters battled the Marxist Frelimo government, at least a million people died and wildlife in this area was massacred. Poachers and fighters roamed the border with AK-47s, shooting anything that moved. Elephants that crossed into Mozambique, perhaps when a section of fence was washed away, learned to return to South Africa before nightfall or poachers would kill them off. But since the end of the war in 1992, things have slowly improved. More than 600 elephants now live in this park, and most crossed the border from Kruger on their own. Some experts think the elephants are communicating over huge distances, telling other herds in South Africa it is safe on the Mozambique side.

Because there is still less wildlife on this side of the border, trees are taller, broader, untouched. The land is richer, more attractive to elephants. I can see their dung on the road ahead. Gazelles and impala scatter, two female kudu and a giant male, with its extraordinary twisting horns, take off into the bushes. There have been few large carnivores here since the war. Antelope numbers have had a chance to recover.

As darkness gathers, we arrive at the remote and secluded Machampane tented forest camp, a former secret Renamo riverine hold-out. It is our first night in Mozambique. The camp manager, Pieter Retief, a towering white South African with the demeanour of a man wedded to the outdoors, crushes my fingers with his meaty handshake and shows us to tents overlooking the Machampane River. There is no electricity and no phone. Baboons are hooting in the trees across the water. It is idyllic. Compared to this pristine piece of nature, Kruger was a theme park. A full moon rises and I make notes on my laptop until the battery fades. Then I light a candle and revert to trusty paper and pen. They never run out of juice.

It is 4.30 a.m. I am woken from deep sleep by a low roar. I drift off, only to be roused again by a sound like a dragon panting. Lions are close to the camp.

At 5.30 a.m. I hear a scuffling noise outside the tent. Something is heading straight for us. Then a strong South African accent pierces the night.

'Good morning,' hisses Pieter. 'I'm sure you're sleeping well. But this is the best time to go for a bush walk.'

Within ten minutes Anya, Brian and I are up and injected with scorching coffee that bubbles on the camp fire. As we snake out of the camp in single file, a yellow moon, full and luminous, hangs low in the night sky.

We walk briskly and silently behind Pieter and Julius, a young Mozambican park ranger who is providing back-up security with an ageing AK-47. Up ahead the lions are on the move, marking their territory with short roars. I start to have doubts about the wisdom of this walk.

'They sound close,' I whisper to Pieter as I stumble along. 'We seem to be heading in their direction. Isn't this a bit dangerous?'

Pieter waves his hand dismissively. He assures me a bush walk is fairly safe. Lions out here normally run away from humans, he says.

'*Fairly* safe?' I query. 'And what do you mean, *normally* run away? What happens the rest of the time?'

Anya looks at me askance. She is supposed to be marrying this wimp.

'Ach, it'll be fine,' says Pieter. 'They're just big pussycats. They hardly ever attack humans.'

A trickle of sunlight glares from the horizon. Pieter checks the ground, searching for distinctive lion prints in the grey dust. He spots marks in the dirt. Pieter pauses, bends down to the ground. He looks excited.

'This is a fresh lion print,' he says quickly. 'Not 15 minutes old.'

We are out in a true wilderness. Lions are ahead of us. We are tracking them, chasing them, *hunting* them. It is thrilling, frightening, and perhaps a little stupid.

As the dawn sun begins its journey across the heavens, we walk faster, trotting quietly through thick bush on a bank that tapers down on our right to a thin stream of a river, checking patches of open ground for more prints.

Pieter leads us down the riverbank towards long grass. He crouches down and whispers: 'We need to be careful here. There could be lions ahead and this grass is the perfect spot for an ambush.'

'What do you mean, an ambush?' I hiss back. 'I thought we were supposed to be tracking the lions. Who's the hunter and who's the prey?'

Pieter just smiles. His face is flushed with excitement. And then to my surprise I smile back. For all my innate sense of self-preservation I have become completely involved in this primitive chase.

'Oh come on then,' I say, almost in spite of myself. 'Let's get closer.'

We creep through the grass, our senses on full alert. In Africa, the cradle of our species, this feels right. This was human life for tens of thousands of years. I feel like a Maasai warrior.

Above: Simon with a beautiful cheetah called Anya, a Jack Russell called Anyway, and Olivier Houalet, better known as Catman, who is trying to protect the big cats at his sanctuary near the Namibian capital Windhoek.

Left: Catholic priest Herman Klein-Hitpass with women from his Stand Together centre on the outskirts of Windhoek. Nearly 1,300 prostitutes attend the centre and 75 per cent of them have HIV. Tessa Peri is at the back in a hat and red top.

Below: We stopped for a call of nature by the road taking us east towards the Kalahari. In the tree is the communal nest of the black-chinned social weaver bird.

Left: Batseba Ndukireepo, the daughter of the Ondagare, or keeper of the holy flame, at Otjongombe, a tiny Herero settlement close to the Botswanan border. Batseba wears the traditional Herero dress, introduced by German missionaries, comprising around 12 metres of material and six to eight petticoats.

Below: The extraordinary Okavango Delta in Botswana, a lush and pristine wilderness home to one of the greatest concentrations of large game and wildlife on Earth. Everywhere there is green and life. And tracks – thousands upon thousands of game tracks, criss-crossing each other or joining together into motorways and heading towards water.

Above: A child plays on the bumper of our Land Rover in the tiny settlement of New Xade, to where the people of the Kalahari desert, the San bushmen, have been resettled – many against their wishes – by the Botswanan government.

Below: Children of the Kalahari playing around the tiny village of Metsiamanong inside the Kalahari Desert, Botswana. The young girl in the middle called herself 'Bruce Lee' when she started play-fighting. Homes in the village consist of at least one round rondavel inside a fence made of vertical thorny branches laced tightly together as protection against their 'cousins', the lions of the Kalahari.

Above: Tsemaletsile Maswabi, a traditional healer in the village of Otse near Capricorn. In sub-Saharan Africa there is roughly one traditional healer per 500 people, compared to one doctor per 40,000 people. The Botswanan government uses healers to spread a safe-sex message, distribute condoms and encourage people to have HIV tests.

Below: Brian Jones, a wildlife guru angry about the lack of wild habitat for animals, cares for Tom, a six-month-old rhino, at the Moholoholo rehabilitation and awareness centre in the east of South Africa near the Mozambique border.

Right: The team at the border between
South Africa and Mozambique (l–r) –
Brian Green, drivers Khumblani (back) and
Mashodane (front), Chris Martin, Anya,
fixer Nhlanhla Mthethwa and Simon.

Below: Food comes to the windows on
a train crossing Madagascar. The line
connects impoverished and remote
farmers growing coffee, bananas and
vanilla with markets on the coast.
Thousands of tons of produce are shifted
each year. Without the line the farmers
would need to slash and burn more
forest to grow rice.

Left: In Mozambique, practising the ancient
sport of Bokdrol Spoeg, or kudu dung spitting.
South African hunters who fail to catch an
antelope take their sun-dried pellets and spit
them as far as possible in the direction of their
departing meal. Simon won.

Left: Nelson, a giant Gambian pouched rat, with Jared Mkumbo from the charity APOPO, which is using rats to detect landmines in Mozambique. There are still 100 million land mines buried in 60 countries around the world, killing around 50 people a day and rendering land unusable. At current rates, land-mine removal will take at least another century. More than 170 million square metres of land in Mozambique are still waiting to be cleared.

Below: The streets of the old town area of Fianarantsoa in Madagascar. Part fairy tale, part old France: uniquely Madagascan.

Below: The giant baobab's spindly branches look like roots. Legends suggest God pulled the tree out of the ground and stuck it back the wrong way up. These extraordinary trees, one of the great symbols of Madagascar, are being destroyed as forests across the island are chopped and burned.

Above: Travelling across Madagascar the dramatic landscape changes from grassy plains to forests of thorns, plains of baobabs and, eventually, high plateaux. Despite deforestation and desperate poverty, it is an amazing island.

Below: Ilakaka, Madagascar – Jean Chrisostome, seated front, a carpenter turned farmer, prepares to descend 18 metres down a thin hole into airless darkness in search of precious gems. He has no idea why foreigners want sapphires, but he knows if he finds one he can buy a farm and cattle. His oxygen is supplied down the white plastic funnel. Dozens of men have died underground in this area. Often their families cannot afford to recover their bodies.

Above: An impressive penis that once belonged to a zebu in Madagascar. Now on the menu at a café in the capital. It tastes as bad as it looks.

And then, from the other side of the river, comes a low roar, much closer and much louder than before. It is a spine-tingling, soul-quaking sound. No matter how urban your ears, the roar of a lion awakens ancient fears. We stop, rooted to the spot, and Julius fingers the stock of his AK-47. Across the stream, a male and female lion appear from behind shrubs and pad majestically along the other bank. The female has her nose to the ground as if following a scent. The male has his head high. They move slowly, proudly. I can see their rippling muscles and powerful frames. There is just a thin strip of water between the lions and us. A quick bound and they would be across. They are terrifyingly close.

Suddenly, they pause. We are downwind and behind them. But they sense our presence. Slowly the male turns his head. He takes in his world. Then he stares at us. Time stops. I feel completely alert, completely alive. It is the single most exhilarating moment of my journey. Movement among large bushes 50 metres further along the river distracts us all. Both lions turn their heads sharply and the pair skulk off towards the sound, vanishing behind thick bushes.

We walk on, trying to spot them. For a minute there is silence. Then rustling, snarling, roaring, the sound of crashing movement among the river bushes, followed by the piercing trumpet of a star-tled elephant.

With a crack and a clatter, the huge grey shape of an old bull elephant emerges from the bushes, his ears flapping, his trunk stiff, his tusks flashing, and flanks still glistening with water. He is just 30 metres in front of us. He looks directly at us, his vast ears flare, he trumpets again, turns around and heads off away from the lions and the river.

Well, I could not be more thrilled if I'd seen duelling dinosaurs. My mouth gapes open.

'Xisivene, a big old tusker,' says Pieter. 'He's been around here for a while. The lions have spooked him. That's probably why they roared. A bit of macho posturing to claim the territory.'

The river widens and meanders around ancient rocks and we clamber across to the opposite bank. We scan the bushes, the shrubs and the horizon. There is no trace of the lions. Pieter thinks we have frightened them away.

'Ach, I think they've slunk away from the river,' he says.

He sounds disappointed. But I could not be happier. Being out in the wilderness with lions and elephants is a dream. Anya, Brian and I beam at each other. We all know this is an incredible privilege.

Instead of the animals we find piles of new elephant dung. But how fresh? And how many elephants? Pieter crouches next to them, turns to me and smiles a wicked grin.

'So, Simon, for temperature you have a thermometer, for atmospheric pressure you have a barometer, and for elephant dung...you have a fingerometer.' And with that he thrusts his index finger deep into the elephant dung and urges me to do the same.

'Come on,' he says, laughing. 'This is how we do it out in the bush. Get your finger in there.'

I follow his lead, reluctantly. The dung feels like cold, muddy grass. I wait for Pieter's judgement.

'Hmmmm,' he says thoughtfully, looking up to the sky. 'So you have a feel around to check for moisture, and then, to test the warmth, you give ... it a lick!' And with that he whips his finger out of the dung and thrusts it into his mouth. 'Yum, yum. Come on, Simon, give it a go!'

Not bloody likely. I think he's been out in the bush for too long. I recoil, but the mischievous glint in Pieter's eye gives the game away. He switched fingers.

Our walk develops a scatological theme. To cope with the disappointment of losing our prey, Pieter suggests we try the ancient sport of *Bokdrol Spoeg*, or kudu dung spitting. South African hunters who fail to catch a kudu or gazelle instead take their pellets, dried and supposedly sterilized by the sun, and spit them as far as possible in the direction of their departing meal. I suspect this is another attempt to get me to put poo in my mouth. But Pieter finds some pellets and we square up. The best of three.

He manages about three metres, but curses his own technique. 'Ach, too much top-spin.'

'Normally we follow each round with a shot of Schnapps,' says Pieter enthusiastically. 'But I didn't think to bring the drinks cabinet.'

I curl my tongue lengthways around the pellet, lean back and let rip. At least four metres. I win the first round, and the second. We find some giraffe dung on the ground, larger and with a slight tang. More force this time. More velocity. My arc and aim are good. More than five metres. A small victory. I walk back to camp with the swagger of a champion dung-spitter.

THE LIMPOPO Park may be a wilderness, but it is also a home to thousands of Mozambicans living in villages scattered around the middle of the park and riverbanks to the north and south. As we leave the Machampane camp and head east to the edge of the park, we pass through the village of Macavene. Only an hour or so from the Machampane lions, there are mud and stick huts for several hundred people and thorny corrals for cows. Herds of suicidal goats wait until we are nearly on them, then race across the track in front of our cars. A new South African Land Cruiser overtakes us. It is sleek, white, with tinted windows and thick tyres. The villagers in Macavene make no money from the tourists who pass by their land in air-conditioned four-wheel drives.

Instead the Mozambican government and many foreign conservationists think the villagers, with their livestock and human diseases, should be moved out so the Limpopo Park can be expanded and left as a natural wilderness.

The people of Macavene and seven other villages are inside the new Great Limpopo Transfrontier Park, a colossal reserve being formed by merging Kruger and Gonarezhou Park in Zimbabwe with Limpopo in Mozambique. More than 55 kilometres of the 400 kilometres of silver cable fencing between South Afrida and Mozambique has already been removed, creating a 35,000-square kilometre 'peace park' nearly twice the size of Wales. More than 6,000 animals have moved across on to the Mozambique side. It is a valiant attempt to expand the land available for wildlife at a time when humans are encroaching on reserves across the continent. Nelson Mandela is a patron of the Peace Parks Foundation, which also hopes to bring down barriers between parks in Botswana, Zambia, Zimbabwe, South Africa, Malawi and across southern Africa.

But while wildlife will benefit, humans could suffer. Outside her tiny mud rondavel, Nomsa Mbonbe, aged 22, sits barefoot on the red soil stripping corn into a bowl from dry and rotten cobs. Four goats loiter close by. Every few moments one sneaks closer to grab at corn lying on the ground. Nomsa shoos it away with a length of branch.

Nomsa has been told the government wants villagers to move out of the park, but says the reasons have not been explained. With Mickey translating, Nomsa says many of the villagers were born here, but they are forbidden from hunting on park land. There are few jobs and Nomsa's husband has travelled to South Africa in search of work.

She says life is becoming tougher, because elephants trample their crops, lions kill their livestock, and they are not allowed to fight back. The wildlife must be protected. But what about the humans?

I have heard this story in several forms already on my travels. Across sub-Saharan Africa, populations are expanding but natural resources are scarce. Humans and animals compete for land, food and water. Villagers find themselves on land governments or conservation groups want to earmark for animals and exploit for tourist dollars. Ultimately, there are just too many of us on the planet. Conflict is inevitable.

Deeper into the village, a drunken party is underway to celebrate a dowry payment. There are scores of babies, men and women, young and old, and millions of children, who crowd around us giggling, laughing, squealing and shouting a few words in English. 'How are YOU?! How are YOU?!' Mickey and I cannot move for small children.

Amid the colour and chaos, Simião Mafumo, 49, a headman in the village, confirms locals have been promised new houses if they leave.

'They said we were going to move, they promised to do everything, to replace the things we have here, the houses and animal shelters,' he says. 'We accepted it because we respect the government but we're not moving.' The buildings they have been offered are smaller than their homes in the village.

'All the promises are just lies,' he says with disgust.

'But has the government explained why they want you to leave?'

'No. Not at all.'

I turn to Mickey. 'It's incredible the government hasn't said "these are the reasons why we feel you need to move out of the park". Do you find that surprising?'

'Yeah,' says Mickey, nodding. 'I find it very surprising.'

Everyone knows that evil corporations push native peoples off their lands for oil or timber. But across the world, respected conservation groups also do much the same, wrecking lives and cultures to create national parks. It has been this way since the birth of the conservation movement. Bernhard Grzimek, who helped create the Serengeti National Park, and Joy Adamson of *Born Free* fame were both accused of expelling locals from land they wanted for animals.

I want to know how the villagers survive out here in the park.

'Are you allowed to hunt around here?' I ask Simião.

'If we hunt we get arrested,' he tells me. 'It's a big problem for us. We used to hunt but now it's forbidden and we have lions and leopards that are hunting our cattle. Elephants eat our crops. If we do anything about it we get into trouble with the authorities.'

'What will you do,' I ask, 'if the park rangers insist that you have to leave?'

'If they come and try to force us out of here without giving us anywhere else to live we will go to war,' says Simião. A dozen male heads are gathered around listening. They nod vigorously. Perhaps it is the booze talking. A tin cup of Mal Cuado, a local hooch made from maize, is pressed into my hand. I take a few swigs. It does not challenge lager, but it is strong and cheap. I have another couple of gulps, just to be polite, hand it back, and let the villagers get on with their party.

We leave the park and drive over a dam, behind which laps the waters of the Limpopo River. In 2000 this area and much of Mozambique was inundated during floods. Seven hundred were killed, nearly half a million forced from their homes. Dramatic television footage showed tens of thousands fleeing, thousands of square kilometres under water, and a woman giving birth to a child in a tree.

Mozambique is much poorer than the other Capricorn countries I have visited on this journey. After the end of the civil war it was thought to be the poorest country in the world. A booming economy has helped the country rise a notch up the rankings, but it is still in the bottom ten.

As we speed along a road heading south-east towards the town of Xai-Xai there is no electricity and few cars. Bags of charcoal are sold by the side of the road and small fires twinkle in the dusk light outside tiny reed shacks. Soon it is dark, but life goes on. Our headlights pick out women of all ages and sizes balancing extraordinary loads on their heads, moving through the night with perfect postures. It is a medieval scene. Then a lorry, loaded almost to collapsing point with charcoal, coats our car in dust and muck.

Mickey tells me that ten years ago he used to drive a similar truck out here with his uncle to buy charcoal to sell in the Mozambican capital, Maputo. Now he's a producer for Mozambique TV and works on Hollywood films such as *Blood Diamond*. That's education for you.

We cross a flat plain next to the mouth of the Limpopo. Farming has restarted since the floods. Irrigation systems quietly circle vast fields of tomatoes. By midnight we have reached the town of Xai-Xai, pronounced shy-shy. Outside a Portuguese restaurant, an impromptu party is underway. Bare lightbulbs reveal tiny shops, street kids waving cans of soft drinks at passing cars, and a group of local men swigging beer outside a store with thick metal grilles.

And then we are through the town, driving along a dark, sandy road next to small dunes beyond which there is a thunder of crashing waves. To my right, the dunes part and I can see white surf by moonlight. Weeks into the journey and I have lost track of time. I have no idea what day it is. Instead I measure progress by how far we have travelled. Ironically, although I am following the Capricorn latitude, it is the longitude of our position that now marks our trip around the world. The water to my right is a glorious sight. We have crossed the African mainland and reached the Indian Ocean. This is a milestone in our Capricorn journey.

We arrive, tired and hungry after the endless drive, at a group of self-catering log cabins and lug our bags up a steep coastal hill looking out over the sea. It appears Anya and I will be sharing with a troop of hungry mice, who scuttle across the floor. The only working light is in our bathroom, but the moon across the sea illuminates the room. It is too late to go hunting for food, so I unpack my small stove and boil water for packets of freeze-dried Norwegian meals. After the long day, the mushy beef stew is a feast. Dessert is dried fruit, with flapjacks for an extra rush of calories.

After feasting, Anya and I try to shower off the dust and dirt accumulated from days of travel. Pipes clunk and groan, then spew brown sludge over my bare feet. I curse the Soviet-era plumbing. The hard, stained, lumpy bedding is no better and the pillows are padded with rocks. Tiny feet patter around during the night, weeing on the floor and pooing pellets into our bags. But the next day we are out early on the wide, empty beach below our creaking wooden room. Apart from a group of local kids, who run along through the surf as if training for a marathon, there is nobody around. The coastline of Mozambique, stretching 2,500 kilometres north to south, feels like one long, stunning beach.

Beauty masks the battering this area of Mozambique took during the war. Landmines still litter the countryside, taking limbs and lives. Minefields have been identified and marked. But although de-mining operations have been running for years, the 2000 floods disrupted work. Many mines floated and moved in the water. In some areas the de-mining has had to start again from scratch.

There are still 100 million land mines buried in 60 countries around the world, killing perhaps 50 people a day. A mine can sit in the ground for 20 years until it takes a victim. Some have delayed action, so they will take the second or third person that walks across them. They render vast areas of land unusable.

Traditional methods of de-mining, such as using humans with metal detectors, are costly and time-consuming, with every bottle cap or can requiring hours of patient probing and extraction. At current rates, land mine removal will take at least another century. More than 170 million square metres of land are still waiting to be cleared in Mozambique alone.

But an hour west from Xai-Xai, I go to see a Belgian project taking an innovative new tack.

The grassy area of training land in front of me is divided into squares with sides ten metres wide. Two men standing either side of the square wear body armour and a curved Perspex screen over their faces, designed to deflect a deadly blast if a mine they are clearing explodes. They are linked by a rope attached to their ankles.

Between them, three-year-old Nelson is crawling through the grass harnessed to the rope. His pink nose twitches as he sniffs and snuffles for the telltale smell of explosives under the ground. He finds a mine, turns a full circle above it, then starts scratching at the ground. His trainers are delighted.

Nelson is a rat. But not just any rat. Nelson is a Gambian giant pouched rat, the size of a small cat, with a thick, long tail and a huge pair of testicles that he drags behind as he strains at the leash, desperate to find a mine and earn a small piece of banana as a reward. I'm not mad on rodents, particularly the army of mice that kept me awake last night. But Nelson is special; he's a cute, cuddly lifesaver.

Jared Mkumbo is the man in charge of a local team of de-miners from the charity APOPO, which first had the revolutionary idea of using rats to detect landmines. You can imagine the response they received when they suggested the scheme to foreign donors. Rats? To detect landmines? Are you mad? But rats make great detectors. One can clear 100 square metres in 30 minutes. When three of them work the same field they have a 100 per cent success rate.

'They have a fantastic sense of smell, are light enough to tread on a mine without setting it off, they are easy to transport, and they work for peanuts...or perhaps a few bananas,' says Jared with a smile.

Dogs have also been used to detect mines, but they cost a fortune to train, are tied to one handler, and can detonate mines with their weight. Nelson should live for six to eight years, offering, in purely financial terms, a healthy lifetime of work on ten months of training.

Why stop at landmines? APOPO is training Rescue Rats to crawl into collapsed buildings after earthquakes and search for human survivors. The charity also uses them to detect tuberculosis, which kills at least two million a year, many times more than die from landmines, and infects another eight million. The rats sniff human saliva samples for TB. A skilled lab technician can check 20 samples a day. A rat can test 150 in 20 minutes.

Nobody knows what molecules the rats are able to sniff out, but dogs have been known to detect cancers and tumours in humans. Some human diseases cause tiny changes in our body smells. Our noses cannot detect the change and technology does not yet have the required sensitivity. But rats might be up to the job. So go on, have a look at www.herorat.org and adopt a rat.

WE TAKE the Estrada Nacional Numero Um road north from Xai-Xai towards the Tropic of Capricorn. The EN1 is the main highway connecting the country together, running like a backbone from the south of Mozambique to the Rovuma River in the north and on into Tanzania. Long stretches are more like country tracks. The tarmac is worn and frayed, like the edges of an old scarf. Deep craters swallow our wheels. In front of us, a tiny pickup truck hums along, swerving between holes. A man wearing mirrored sunglasses and a dirty black T-shirt lounges in the back on a fat pile of firewood.

During the war, most of the fighting was along the roads. Renamo rebels targeted all of the roads leading to and from the cities to spread terror and destabilize the government, so people could not travel from one city to the next without travelling in convoys guarded by Frelimo forces.

'But people still needed to make a buck, goods still had to be moved around the country,' says Mickey. 'A lot of people died on this road.'

Frelimo was a huge threat to the apartheid regime in South Africa. ANC guerrillas were trained in Mozambique and then crossed the border to battle the apartheid regime. So the South Africans backed Renamo. Mickey was a schoolboy in Maputo during the fighting. 'It wasn't too bad in the capital. But we were still taught how to drill and duck bullets.'

The countryside rolls and turns around us. Palm trees, cashew trees, mango trees, marula trees, massala trees, a tropical bush fruit. There are corn fields, cassava trees and even, according to Mickey, the odd marijuana plantation. It is countryside with a sleepy, tropical feel, broken by small villages and market stalls selling fruit, vegetables and huge quantities of second-hand clothes.

We break our journey near the coastal town of Inhambane, arriving late at night and dozily moving our bags into a small seaside house rented from friends of Mickey. Dinner is fresh fish in a restaurant owned by a dreadlocked Mozambican Rasta. The punters are other Westerners: surf dudes and beach bums. The area around Inhambane, the first truly touristy town we have visited on Capricorn, has a world-class reputation for surf and relaxation. Cold beers are thrust into our hands. We submit willingly.

We wake to glorious sunshine. Close to the beach, the Waterworks surf café has a thatched roof over a bar run by Avi from Haifa, who has shades on top of sun-bleached hair pulled back into a short ponytail. A line of surfboards is stacked to the side. 'Surf, eat, drink, shop, chill out & relax,' says a sign. There are more dreadlocks, this time worn by Westerners reading in the sunshine, preparing for another hard day by the beach. This is still a destination off the beaten track. The first few who made it here have a proud, pioneering air. But backpackers are now joining them. 'During the holiday season it's horrible here,' says Mickey. 'You can't move for tourists.'

Mickey and I take a small wooden ferry, crewed by men wearing Popeye uniforms, across a huge azure bay surrounded by palm trees from Inhambane to the town of Maxixe. It is more like a large canoe than a boat. I am crammed up against two stroppy plain-clothes policemen who demand to see our permits and insist on sitting at the front of the canoe. How we laugh when they are soaked by spray.

Dust blows a storm in Maxixe. We have arranged to visit a clothing wholesaler who sells second-hand clothes in tightly compressed 45-kilogram bundles to the market traders who work by the road in local villages across the region. The stalls are everywhere in Mozambique. Labels on bundles stacked in the dark warehouse mark blouses, denims, trousers, jackets and rugby shirts. The clothes are donated by well-meaning Westerners keen to help Africa and Africans. But some experts now question whether Africa should accept such charity.

I walk around the warehouse. Among the coats and skirts there are bundles of second-hand underwear. Yellow and brown stains are clearly visible. B. Wright is written in indelible ink on one pair of flowery panties. The manager of the warehouse, a smart Indian woman, says she does not like selling the underwear. She thinks it's demeaning for Africans to be wearing soiled Western cast-offs.

'Of course it's demeaning,' Mickey responds with a shrug, 'but these are cheap. This is Africa. People can't afford the new clothes.'

Mickey sees the second-hand clothes as a necessary evil, a solution for poverty-stricken families desperate to clothe their kids. I am not convinced. These bundles of clothes strike me as part of the problem, part of the reason Africa is still held back and still held down.

Charitable Westerners donating their cheap clothes to Africa have undercut the local clothing industry. No Mozambican firm could ever make a T-shirt cheaper than a Western T-shirt donated for free. Combined with the double-whammy of imports of cheap clothing from the Far East, this form of Western charity prevents Africans from starting their own local textile businesses, a vital first step on the road towards industrialization and the creation of a real economy.

Mozambique used to have textile and cotton factories, but they've closed, undercut by cheap cloth from Asia and B. Wright donating her knickers. So there are no Mozambican firms able to buy the output of local cotton farmers, who also cannot sell their cotton internationally because Western governments subsidize their own cotton producers.

There is a similar situation with cashews, which grow on trees across Mozambique. Cashews were sorted and processed mechanically in huge factories until the World Bank decided the country needed to lower export tariffs on the nuts. Indian firms now buy the cashews raw and ship them out. Cashew factories in Mozambique have closed and thousands have lost their jobs.

Although Africa has made some progress in recent years, in other areas it is sliding backwards, forced to become a supplier of raw materials but unable to establish the industry required to give people jobs and lift them out of poverty. Around 400 million people around the world have been lifted above the $1 a day poverty threshold during the 20 years to 2001, but many Africans are getting poorer. Mozambique is supposed to have a developing economy. Everyone here is a budding entrepreneur. Skinny barefoot hawkers sell clothes, drinks, food, sunglasses, toys, trinkets, water. Everyone hustles. But the country is still hidebound by rules created by the West, which ensure easy access to local markets for our multinationals, but discourages the development of Mozambican industry. The West and now the East stack the odds, holding Africa back, and keeping Africans down.

The hypocrisy is sickening. Travel in this continent with your eyes open and as a Westerner you soon realize you should not only be ashamed of the colonial past, but the colonial present as well.

We drive north from Maxixe and stop right on the Tropic of Capricorn. The surrounding land is lush and green. Palm trees drip with coconuts. Two men are walking slowly along the road, one on thin metal crutches. They have been harvesting coconuts all day, and are crossing Capricorn to get their daily wages from their boss. They earn two metical for each tree they clear, roughly four pence, and can climb 25 trees a day. So they earn around one pound for a hard day's work. One pound. The disparity in our incomes, the gulf between us, is simply gobsmacking.

The younger of the two has been crippled since he was five years old. His lower left leg hangs uselessly, the foot wasted and twisted. He thinks it was rheumatism, but it sounds more like polio. He has a shy smile, a delicate laugh, broad, strong shoulders and thickly calloused hands. He climbs with his arms and his one good leg.

'Can you imagine how strong he must be to climb a palm tree like that?' says Mickey.

I ask if they know much about the Tropic of Capricorn. Inácio, the older of the two, brightens. He remembers seeing Capricorn on an atlas. 'It is a line,' he says, 'but I don't think it is just in Mozambique. I have heard it goes through *other* countries as well.' He says these final words with wide-eyed wonder. I smile and inwardly thank my luck. What an honour to be making this journey.

We wave them goodbye and they potter off along the road. We are still a few hours away from our new target, the town of Vilanculos, the gateway to the Bazaruto Archipelago, a sprinkling of Indian Ocean islands just off the African mainland which Mickey says have a developing reputation for top-end tourism. Stretches of road on the way to the town are wide with smooth tarmac. But much of it is a narrow obstacle course with deep, sandy craters marking the surface. Lorries and cars, loaded with people or goods, weave around the holes. Perhaps someone in the local transport department has been pocketing the maintenance budget. Corruption is more of a problem in Mozambique than in almost any other Capricorn country.

The sun sets to our left as we drive. Yet again, our headlights become the only lights on the road. Out of the darkness come women carrying pots, clothes and buckets of water. Then a few men pedal through the night on Chinese-made single-speed bicycles, one with half a small tree strapped to the frame. Just before midnight, we arrive in the quiet coastal town of Vilanculos and check into a hotel on the edge of the town overlooking the sea.

After a few days of hard driving we have a lie-in the next morning. At 8 a.m., as Anya and I are about to slope off to find breakfast, I remember we have not yet seen the islands of Bazaruto, and I flick a curtain to see what lies outside the window. The view is stunning. Shaded by palm trees, the wide beach below our hotel is a scene of early activity. A small man in ragged shorts hammers at the skeleton of a new dhow as fishermen tow a huge net into the water. Small red, green and blue fishing boats bob on the ocean, and across azure water shafts of sunlight filter through blankets of fluffy clouds to illuminate the sandy islands of the Bazaruto Archipelago on the distant horizon.

A 1,400-square-kilometre national park, the archipelago is home to hotels and the full spectrum of marine treasures: sharks, dolphins, Nemo fish, whales, huge manta rays, whale sharks and elusive dugongs. A torpedo-shaped mammal related to the elephant, a dugong is a strange and mysterious creature with the bulk and blubber of a legless hippo.

Bazaruto has lapping turquoise waters, pristine beaches, beautiful reef, and some of the finest diving on Africa's east coast. I would love to have spent time snorkelling with dugongs, but they are endangered and elusive animals that tend to hide when boats are near. I am also visiting at the wrong time of year, when dugongs prefer to hang at least ten metres below sea level among seaweed. So spotting them could take a while, and our Capricorn budget does not cover swimming around for a week in the sunshine. This isn't a holiday, you know.

But perhaps there is a faster way of finding them. Mickey introduces me to his friend Almeida Guissamulo from the Eduardo Mondlane

University, Mozambique's foremost expert on the dugongs. He is 38, black, studious, quiet, with a face that radiates gentle goodness. And he has studied dugongs for nearly a decade. Surely he can help.

We take an afternoon walk on Vilanculos beach. Almeida tells me sharks and humans both find dugong tasty. The creature, the saltwater cousin of the manatee, has few defences. It lives in an area of the ocean busy with sharks, and it is not even a nifty swimmer. It sounds like one of nature's crueller gags. When trapped in nets, dugongs do not surface to escape, but dive deeper, and drown. Not surprisingly, fishing is decimating the global population of dugongs. The colony around Bazaruto is the largest on the coast of East Africa, and one of the last remaining viable populations of the animal in the world.

The tide is out and two dozen fishermen, women and kids are reeling in the vast net they have spread perhaps 30 metres out into the sea and 200 metres along the coast. Working in pairs, they are sliding oars through holes in long ropes that snake out into the sea, putting their backs to the wooden poles, tugging the net free of the surf and singing as they work. It takes them an age to pull the net closer to the shore. I wait and watch, expecting fish to pour on to the beach. But the huge net is gathered into a small circle, around which the fishing family gather, squabbling noisily. They pick out a tiny number of fish and carry bright pufferfish off in their T-shirts.

The reason for their small catch lies over the horizon. Giant Chinese, Japanese and Spanish factory trawlers are vacuuming up the contents of the deep ocean and threatening life in the dugong's national park. We look out over the water to the archipelago.

'The dugongs are out there, somewhere,' says Almeida, 'but you could look for days and see nothing. Your best chance of spotting them is to take a flight over the bay.'

Almeida is right. Just minutes after taking off in a tiny four-seater chartered plane, we reach the main channel between the coast and the archipelago. A few moments later, we spot a grey torpedo shape 100 metres below us. I can see one solitary dugong hanging motionless in the water, and another mother and calf, then another, then two more. We head over Bazaruto island, turning right to head back to the mainland, and two humpback whales breach the surface. It is a glimpse into a secret marine world, and a chance to see why this marine park is proving to be such a draw for wealthy foreigners. They come for sun, sand and snorkelling around the stunning islands of the archipelago below me. I decide to take a closer look.

THE NEXT morning the tide is out and Captain Ben, a local boat-man, has anchored his small fibreglass fishing boat 20 metres out to sea. We all carry our bags and supplies out into the surf, clamber aboard and race across the water. After nearly an hour we pass the resort of Indigo Bay, which we glimpsed from the air the day before. Huge chalets stretch along a pristine beach. These islands are marketed as a high-end tourist destination, their reputation sealed with visits by Prince Harry and Sting. From the boat I can see a liveried black waiter carrying a drink to pink flesh sheltering under a thatched umbrella. Rooms at hotels and resorts on the islands can cost more than £1,000 a night.

From the comfort of the boat, I cannot quite see the attraction.

The islands are not what I was expecting. Often on these journeys I find myself completely overwhelmed by the beauty, the scale, the sheer inventiveness of nature. From the air yesterday, the islands of the Bazaruto Archipelago were tropical beauties with palm-fringed beaches straight from a Bounty bar advert. But from our boat they have the appearance of huge sand dunes sprinkled with thorny bushes.

Just ten minutes around the island from Indigo Bay and the luxury lodges give way to tiny local huts. A few small wooden dhows bob in the water. Tourists are not alone on these islands. Mickey has arranged for us to meet Paulino Zibane, who waits for us on a long, wide beach and greets us as we land. A fisherman in his mid-40s, he heads a local community association and represents many of the 3,500 islanders, and tells me life on the islands is becoming harder.

'Fishing is not difficult,' says Paulino. 'But the fish are disappearing. In the olden days, there were not as many fishing nets [out there] as now. There's a lot of fishing activity. Lots of boats come and fish in our waters. Even the lodges have many boats and they are always out fishing.'

These islands used to be famous for pearl diving, but now a dozen boys and men are weighing and selling small, pathetic catches of fish outside three tiny huts on the edge of the beach. There are no other homes or buildings in sight. The Bazaruto hotels say they have paid for a borehole and a community centre, but it is hard to believe we are just around the corner from a luxury resort.

We walk together back into the interior of the island, through the shallow waters of a small mangrove swamp and up a hilly dune towards Paulino's home, emerging into a clearing with a few basic huts. In early 2007 Cyclone Favio damaged Paulino's main hut, and countless other homes across Mozambique. Paulino now lives with his pretty wife Helena, 28 years old to his 46, in a small reed and thatched rondavel. The lock on his door suggests jealousy and petty thieving. Clearly not everyone on the islands is profiting from the arrival of wealthy foreigners.

Ten metres from his rondavel, Paulino is repairing another small hut, which will be our home for the night. It has two rooms, a bare concrete floor, a corrugated iron roof, and walls made from bundles of reeds and white sheeting stamped with the blue logo of UNICEF. A howling wind whistles through empty windows. I do not mind the basic accommodation, but my heart sinks when I spot cockerels strutting around. I know what they will be doing at three in the morning.

Paulino says a storm is coming. All of us wonder whether we have chosen a good night to arrive on an isolated low-lying island. There are gags about Indigo Bay and jokey suggestions I might like to stay with Paulino while the crew decamp to the resort.

But then we all pitch in. We bale sand out of the huts, seal windows with our gaffer tape and UNICEF sheeting, tie our mosquito nets to wood beams, gather wood and light a fire on the sand outside. Paulino produces a small torn tent, which we pitch in the open for Mickey and Chris.

Helena is starting dinner. Mickey muscles his way into the outdoor kitchen. He has bought squid, vegetables, peppers, garlic, loaves of bread and five fish. Helena produces a yellow plastic bucket and Mickey marinates the fish in lemon and garlic, then grills it over the fire on chicken wire. We eat a feast and I make a mental note to always travel with a chef. Paulino, sitting quietly in the long shadows thrown by the fire, gives us a double thumbs-up as the food is served with a couple of beers. Discussion follows later.

Paulino was born on Bazaruto. His father was born here. He has a football team of kids to support, and is upset the government is not allowing him to start a community-based tourism project that would let foreigners stay among locals. When hotels and resorts began opening in the archipelago, government officials promised islanders that they would receive a cut of the fee tourists pay to enter the national park. The money was supposed to be spent on schools and health care. But the islanders claim that they have only seen a fraction of the promised funds.

Islanders were also guaranteed jobs, but out of 3,500 only a few dozen have been given menial work in the resorts. Most of the staff are mainland Mozambicans or Zimbabweans, who speak good English and have a history of working in top-end safari camps.

For more than a decade Paulino battled Renamo as a government soldier. He left the army as a captain, a senior officer. Now he earns less in a year than many hotel rooms on Bazaruto cost per night.

'I sometimes get a bit shocked because I wasted time fighting, defending our land, but now I can tell you that I live in very poor conditions. The salary I make is very small. I can't adequately support my children. But what am I to do? Mozambique is the place where I was born. I have nowhere else to go.'

He pauses, and sighs. He looks exhausted.

'If I had had a better education then maybe I would be earning more cash,' he tells me. 'But I didn't get that. Instead I spent eleven years fighting a war. I came back. There was no time for education. I started a family and this is what I earn…this is my reality.'

I ask if he minds foreigners holidaying on the island.

'I don't object to foreigners having their holidays here, but we were promised there would be more benefits for us.'

My hackles rise at the sheer injustice. Such stories get no easier to hear.

A FTER DINNER Paulino and Helena are in bed by 9 p.m. Life on the islands is timed by daylight. The crew and I sit around the fire for another couple of hours, then slope off to bed. Anya and I sleep in Paulino's guest hut on a thin Therm-a-Rest blow-up mattress. The strip of bedding does not soften the concrete, but we doze off, at least for a few hours.

At 2 a.m. it starts to rain. My dreams are pierced by the sound of a waterfall crackling on the tin can above our heads. The noise is incredible. As I wake, groggy and confused, Chris and Mickey burst into the room, soaking wet, swearing, cursing, and dragging their bags and dripping bedding. Their tent has blown over. A tropical storm is breaking overhead. Water is pouring into our hut.

We try to squash into the room together, but the rain is relentless. I make space for Chris and Mickey, and tip a bed-frame, which has most of its wooden slats missing, on to one side. One by one the remaining slats clatter to the ground, making an almighty racket. I am exhausted, but I start laughing, almost hysterically. Then Chris starts laughing, but with an edge. He is soaked.

I lie back on the ground listening to the downpour. Rain seeps through the reed walls and forms small puddles on the concrete. The wind picks up, shaking our roof. Buffeted by wind and rain, the hut begins to shake. Despite the chaos I doze until rhythmic snoring jolts me awake. I can sleep through most noises. But snoring and cockerels defeat my defences. The latter start crowing at 3 a.m. Not at dawn. Not when they are contracted to start working. But 3 a.m. In a tropical storm, in harmony with rhythmic snoring. That's just not fair. Cockerels 3, Reeve 0.

The rains have stopped by the morning, but Bazaruto looks even less attractive under ominous low, grey clouds. Our backs ache and our kit is soaked. We wander down to the beach to check if the boat and Captain Ben survived the storm. Ben slept onboard, tossed around on the waves and drenched with water.

'Don't worry,' he says in broken English. 'I have sailed here since I was a child. My feet are webbed.'

Ben says a bigger storm is coming. It is Sunday and nobody is fishing. There are no village gatherings, no colourful weddings, parties or ceremonies. There is an air of poverty, depression and lethargy, and if we stay another night we will be trapped on the island for a couple of days, missing expensive flights and connections taking us east along Capricorn to Madagascar. We decide to leave.

The journey back to the mainland starts smoothly enough. The island dunes shield our boat from the wind. But then we turn into the open channel between the islands and mainland Africa and the waves swell. We become a cork thrown around by merciless waves. Water deluges the boat and soaks our clothes.

At the wheel, Ben turns and shouts. It is time for lifejackets. We tie them around our chests and hold tight. The sea develops the colour and fury of the North Sea. Buckets of salty spray fill the air like clouds, lashing faces and stinging eyes.

Although she is quite capable of looking after herself, I stand with my arms around each side of Anya, clinging to a metal rail. It would be very unfortunate if she drowned just before our wedding. We crash against waves that lift us off our feet and slam us back down into the trough. The force threatens to snap both our spines and the boat.

Because of the direction of the waves, we take a route that arcs back to the coast, conveniently skirting away from the darkest patch of cloud, half a mile or so off to our right. The weather and waves are still atrocious. Ben turns around to check we are still onboard. When an air-stewardess looks nervous on a tricky flight, I always take that as a sign to pray. Ben looks worried. Then, off to our right, the furious grey cloud turns in our direction. I can't believe this. The weather worsens. The trip becomes quite the most unpleasant boat journey of my life. And it goes on, and on, and on, until my arms and legs ache from the battle to stay onboard.

For two terrible hours Ben battles with the raging ocean until the coast appears through thick mist. I have never been so happy to see land. We bump against sand just off a beach and sit there for a moment collecting our stomachs.

'Never again,' groans Mickey. 'I am never going on another boat.'

Ben looks at his passengers with pity. We are dishevelled and green. He tells me it is the second-worst crossing he has had in more than 30 years.

'Sorry,' he says with a shrug.

'No. Thank you. I think you saved us,' I manage to say.

Then, in a complete daze, we all slide over the edge of the boat into knee-deep waves. As I wade back to the beach I kick a brick under the water. I am so woozy the pain does not reach my brain for a full minute. Then I sit on the beach, rubbing my toes, and I say a prayer of gratitude. Before this trip I expected the main threats to be from car crashes and nasty bugs. Yet here we nearly drowned. We are lucky to survive.

Despite the stormy sea, the coast is impossibly peaceful and gloriously steady. We treat ourselves to a night at a quiet hotel, and that evening sip bottles of cold beer and regale anyone who will listen with tales of our hellish journey.

At Vilanculos airport the next morning I discover an open-roof terrace and a café offering stuffed crabs with a spicy sauce for a single dollar. Now this is the way to travel. We are leaving Mickey and heading east to Madagascar. It is a single word evoking images, at least for me, of a magical island of forest and fauna, packed with bizarre and unusual animals.

5 · MADAGASCAR

WE ARE SITTING on rusty steel trolleys in the small baggage hall at the main airport in Antananarivo, the capital of Madagascar, known by all as Tana. Five of our 20 bags and cases have not appeared and we have time to kill as we wait for them to arrive. We weigh ourselves on the baggage scales. I am 83 kilos. Brian tips the scales at 88. Or 86 if he stands on the side. He frowns, shakes his head and starts doing press-ups on the ground.

The baggage belt stops turning. Still our bags have not appeared. A bored airport official says they were removed from the plane as we transited through Johannesburg from Vilanculos. Madagascar is a former French colony, long ignored by Paris. The official gives us a classic Gallic shrug. Maybe they will come tomorrow, maybe not.

We were not planning to stop in the capital. It is a long way north of Capricorn. But without our kit and clothes we cannot risk heading south to the town of Tulear, close to the line. So we meet up with Batsola Andrianjaka, our young, attractive and lively Malagasy fixer, check into a hotel in Tana, and head out to explore.

Tana is unlike any other city I have visited on Capricorn. In fact Tana is unlike almost anywhere I have ever been. Let's start with the architecture, a mix of dilapidated French colonial buildings and clay houses with steep sloping roofs. There are hills sprinkled with church steeples and ramshackle brown huts, surrounded by a jigsaw of green and muddy paddy fields, even within the city.

The influences here appear to be a mixture of French, Nepalese, Vietnamese, with a bit of added Lima. The gendarmes wear kepis. The taxis are exquisitely battered, four-decade-old, cream Citroen 2CVs and Renault 4s. There are biblical wheeled wooden carts pulled by zebu, the horned cattle ubiquitous on the island. Cheeky barefoot urchins pull broken rickshaws. Life is lived on the streets: welding, chopping, cleaning, selling, buying, butchering, washing and dominoes, all in the dirt by the side of the road. There is no attempt to disguise or hide the poverty.

And the people? The people are the richest mix of South Asian, African and Oriental colours and creeds I have seen on this journey. Gnarled old African women, their faces the colour of mahogany, squat and gossip with discoloured Latin shawls wrapped around their shoulders. Tiny feral children, descendants of Indonesian settlers, run semi-naked, their clothes in tatters, their hair matted with dirt. Batsola herself is a compact, curvaceous woman straight out of a Gauguin South Seas painting. Tana is one of the most overwhelming and visually surprising cities I have visited.

But then Madagascar itself is out of the ordinary.

This island, at 560 kilometres wide and 1,600 kilometres long, is the fourth largest in the world, more than twice the size of Britain. It split from mainland Africa 165 million years ago. Plants and animals have had time to evolve into uniquely Madagascan creatures.

Isolation has fostered eccentricity. There are devilish aye-ayes, (primates with sharp teeth, the face of a rodent and a long, slender middle finger), and endangered lemurs ranging from mysterious shadows with heads the size of my thumb, right up to the 13-kilogram giant howling indri, which can leap up to ten metres from tree to tree. More than 95 per cent of the reptiles and amphibians on Madagascar are unique to the island, along with countless creatures, absurd and magnificent, that crawl, slither, walk, swim and fly. On this island are more than half the world's chameleon species and 200,000 species of flora and fauna, more than 90 per cent of which are endemic. They all help make Madagascar the second most biologically diverse country on the planet after Brazil. It is a shining jewel in the Indian Ocean. Or at least it should be.

Humans arrived more than 2,000 years ago, not from East Africa, but sailing between 6,000 and 10,000 kilometres from Malaysia and Indonesia in one of the great feats of human exploration. The first Malagasy encountered three-metre tall elephant birds and giant jumping rats, and promptly set about exterminating them. Trees were chopped across the island so rice could be planted. Hundreds of years of deforestation followed, a catastrophe for Madagascan wildlife. Massive lemurs the size of gorillas are now extinct. Their smaller cousins are still found only on Madagascar and the neighbouring Comoros islands. But logging of their forests has decimated lemur numbers.

Just as seclusion has encouraged nature to evolve in weird and wonderful ways, so centuries of isolation from the outside world have allowed human imaginations to run riot on the island, creating the exuberant and complex taboo beliefs of *fady*. In some parts of the country *fady* suggests chores must be performed on a Wednesday while standing. And while kneeling on a Thursday. Other *fady* relate to food, warning against passing eggs from hand to hand, or eating bread from a red plate. Harmless enough.

Slightly more unusual, at least to my ears, is the extent to which Madagascans still worship the dead, in beliefs matched by few other cultures. This is a place where ancestors are regularly disinterred from tombs and their bodies re-dressed in new shrouds and paraded around a village. Even many of those who consider themselves Christians will at least turn the bones of their dead relatives. Madagascans do not fear death the way we do in the West.

'This is a country where death is more important than life,' explains Batsola, as we sip coffee in a roadside café in Tana. 'Death is the chance for a humble human to become a powerful ancestor, someone respected and consulted by the living.'

People like Batsola and even young teenagers will spend time thinking about where they will be buried. Not fearfully. For them it is just another stage of life's adventure. You have to admire their sangfroid. But other beliefs are less benign. Twins in one region are considered evil and abandoned in the forest to die. In another, deceased nobles are left out under a burning sun, and the juices that drip from their corpses are gathered in a cup, which is then passed around among the relatives.

The next day our bags have still not arrived. Batsola offers to take me to the local market. It is noisy and frenetically busy. A crowd gathers trying to flog moist, fragrant sticks of vanilla, deftly swapped for dry, lifeless sticks when I agree to buy a bundle. There are stalls selling pants, clothes, pots, herbs, amusingly-shaped vegetables, and even skinned frogs.

'Well, we *were* a French colony,' says Batsola, almost apologetically.

Batsola tells me that locals eat zebu penis soup. I try to keep her quiet, but the rest of the crew overhears. We stop at a filthy café just outside the market. It is a shack with dark rooms at the back and a few chairs out the front. One of the women from the kitchen displays a penis nearly a metre long. It looks revolting and I'm served a watery soup with pieces of gristly willy. The taste is rancid and tipping salt into the broth does not make it more palatable. But I am rewarded later with a meal in our hotel, and a mug of decent red wine Brian and Chris managed to procure during our stopover in Jo'burg. We have a ration of six bottles to see us across the island.

A NOTHER DAY and the airline finally relents and sends our bags to the island. We head to Tulear, on the south-west coast, on a quiet flight that reveals a devastated landscape. Below us are scarred and barren rusty-red hills. This is not the natural Madagascan paradise of my childhood imagination. For hundreds of years poor Madagascan farmers have practised *tavy*, the simple form of slash and burn farming used to clear land to grow rice, feed cattle and make charcoal.

Wood is used as the main source of fuel and ash from chopped trees and shrubs is mixed in with the soil. But it is not destruction for the sake of long-term creation. It is a cheap form of fertilizer that only works for a couple of years, and then the land must be left for pasture and burned each year to ensure the growth of the grass shoots zebu love to eat. It is a simple and unsustainable form of agriculture that pays no heed to the long-term needs of the land or the next generation. But people worry about feeding their kids before they worry about feeding unborn grandchildren. Since independence in 1960, the population has trebled and the rate of destruction has increased dramatically.

Between 1984 and 1996, 600,000 hectares (or 1.5 million acres), an area bigger than Norfolk, was burned each year. The result has been the loss of around 90 per cent of the Madagascan rainforest. Only a fraction remains and each year rains wash away more topsoil, turning the rivers red with dirt.

The world was warned. I remember environmentalists telling us 10 and 20 years ago that we were losing the forests of Madagascar, just as they warned us about the great trees of Borneo, Africa, Asia and Latin America. Now the forests have gone. Much of Madagascar's unique wildlife, its ferocious fossas, chameleons, lemurs and geckos, are only found in national parks and a few scattered and isolated pockets of natural wilderness.

'Sixty years ago, 100 years ago, this was all forest,' says Batsola wistfully as we look out of the plane windows. Batsola is a cosmopolitan woman, a member of the Madagascan royal family even. She studied for a Masters in France, and speaks English learned in Brighton with a husky and impossibly sexy French accent. She knows what her country has lost.

'This island has changed so much, even since my parents were kids. It used to be known as the green island, now it is the red.'

As we descend towards Tulear, fire and smoke marks the remote horizon. There is a haze around us from slash and burn.

Tulear is a flat seaside town with heat that saps energy. A town of hammocks, sand, palm trees and sunshine. We arrive on a weekend and nobody moves at speed. Nobody, that is, except for barefoot rickshaw drivers, who seem to comprise most of the population and run their passengers around town, competing aggressively for custom.

The next morning we meet Coca Rakotomalaza from the World Wildlife Federation, a biologist originally from Tana, and drive two hours north from the town along the west coast of Madagascar and through fifteenth-century villages to the Ifaty forest. A track takes us into a wilderness of primary forest packed with plant species of completely alien shapes and sizes. There are octopus trees that reach for the heavens with arms loaded with two-inch needle-sharp thorns, giant baobabs, giant delonix, the pachypodium (fat feet) tree, which looks like a baobab with added thorns, and the giant givotia, which locals along the coast use for making heavy pirogues, or canoes. This is not just another country, but another planet.

It is the baobab that really impresses with its spindly branches that look like roots. 'Locals say the baobab was too proud, and God lifted it out of the ground and put it back the wrong way up,' says Coca. The upside-down baobab. It is the best description of this crazy tree.

The Ifaty forest is one of the few remaining patches of primary forest on Madagascar. This is what has been lost across the rest of the country.

On the way back down the coast to Tulear there is evidence of slash and burn all around us. We pass through a medieval village of tiny thatched huts and stop by a new field perhaps 100 by 80 metres. It is not the season for *tavy*, but I can still see ash mixed in with the red, sandy soil. Stumps litter the ground. A thin woman wrapped in a sarong is bent double, hacking at one stump with a blunt machete. Behind her a metre-tall spike of a stump, its branches cut, is still burning. A giant baobab in the centre of the field, its two-metre-diameter trunk scorched but defiant, stands amid the destruction. But to the side, at the edge of the burn, another baobab has been snapped and broken. There is a giant tear and the top half has toppled to the ground. Three tiny kids are using the smooth surface as a slide. The size, age and girth of this tree gives it the feel of a creature, a rare and precious animal that has been killed. It is a desperate sight, a scene replicated across the island.

Blame is hard to apportion. *Tavy* is a technique the rural poor use to scratch a living from the soil, but it has not made them rich. There are 20 million Madagascans with an average earning of a few hundred pounds a year. This country is poor. Dirt poor. Probably one of the

20 poorest countries in the world. The reasons can be summarized as climate, colonialism and corruption.

The French, attracted to the island by natural riches bestowed by the climate, left their Madagascan colony in 1960 having failed to create an educated class who could run the huge country. A brief spell of independence was followed by the leadership of Admiral Didier Ratsiraka, who drove the country downhill. He deliberately made the country poorer so he could secure more foreign aid and pocket the cash. Ratsiraka actually destroyed bridges and roads while looting the treasury, and kept the country as a basket case until a protracted revolution in 2002 brought Marc Ravalomanana, a yoghurt tycoon and former mayor of Tana, into power. The French, who despite criticizing American foreign policy still happily support African dictators and tend to treat Francophone Africa as a cow they can milk till its teats shrivel, welcomed the fleeing Ratsiraka to Paris, where he settled with his corrupt millions. In his place, new President Marc built roads and set about trying to modernize Madagascar. Now a personality cult is building around him and he shows no sign of wanting to relinquish office.

There are a few bright signs. Madagascar is the greatest conservation priority in the world and the new yoghurt president has promised to triple the size of the island's national parks. The rural poor are being given fuel-efficient stoves and educated about the dangers of *tavy*. But the damage has been done.

We stop by the road next to the sea and a final patch of mangrove forest, a type of vegetation, hard as nails and termite resistant, that can survive in salt and fresh water. Somewhere out there across the quiet sea is the coast of Mozambique. The sun is setting and a red blaze fills the sky.

'What are you doing?' a young Malagasy woman asks Anya as she films. When we tell her we are filming the sunset her response is bafflement. 'Why?' she asks. Locals are using the beach as a latrine. For them it is just a resource. To our Western eyes it is a visual paradise.

TIME TO head east across the island. Roads are rare and none track Capricorn. We will be travelling across Madagascar a degree or so to the north, parallel with the line, driving to the town of Fianarantsoa in the central highlands, then taking a train to the east coast. Along the way we hope to stop in the Wild West town of Ilakaka, where thousands of Malagasy miners are clawing gems out of the ground.

The road east is newly tarmaced, thanks to President Marc, but narrow, unmarked and largely empty. It takes us through tiny listless villages with thatch and reed houses the size of chicken coops, women grilling cassava and selling charcoal made from the few remaining trees, and mini wooden shack shops selling mangos. We pass an ancient, wheezing car, a blue Renault 4 in an earlier stage of its extraordinary life cycle, and count eight people crammed inside. There are bags and sacks stuck to the roof, on top of which are two trussed goats. The driver smiles and waves. He is sitting in the lap of a passenger.

The black road carves across a sandy plain, through a low forest of thorns, a plain of octopus trees, then a plain of baobabs, some with high carved caves where herdsmen can shelter, over a rolling hill and across a vast plain of golden yellow grassland with just one solitary, lonely tree standing defiantly off to our left in the harsh midday sun. Again and again, we are all left gasping at the beauty.

'I've never seen a landscape change so dramatically, in such a short space of time,' says Brian. And he's been about a bit.

Batsola tells me there are several distinct ecosystems in Madagascar. In the east there are rainforests, cooler high plateaux in the centre, spiny deserts in the south and dry savannah to the west. This grassland is African savannah, but without the lumbering elephants who shape so much of the mainland. Here man is the maker, the destroyer. Over centuries of *tavy*, humans created the landscape, but not the mountains. Nothing on four legs or two could build the tabletop hills and mountains greeting the clouds on the edge of the plains to my right.

We race on and reach a small forest. A narrow bridge slows our car. A dozen children aged from five to ten emerge from bushes and ambush us wielding plump green chameleons on long sticks and shouting '*Bonjour Vazaha*!' (foreigners – pronounced 'vazz-ar'). One tries to claim they let travellers pose for photos with chameleons for fifty pence, and that they let them go back into the forest at the end of the day. Another tells Batsola we can buy them, eat them, do whatever we like with them.

We pass through their village. It is another medieval affair. But the modern world stakes a claim. A thickset man by the side of the road has a pistol strapped to his bulging waist. We are drawing closer to the lawless town of Ilakaka and a region of Madagascar with some of the greatest deposits of gems left on the planet.

Then we cross another extraordinary plain under a vast sky. It is classic Americana, familiar from a thousand Westerns, with a herd of zebu doubling for buffalo. Cowboys should appear over the horizon.

We chug over a low hill and there across a plain, perhaps eight miles away, nestles Ilakaka, smoke rising gently from dozens of small cooking fires. It is distinct, compact and, from this distance, peaceful. Ten years ago this town did not exist. But in 1998 locals found pink sapphires lying on the ground, and within two years at least 100,000 Malagasy descended on the area. Ilakaka is the scene of the most intense gem rush in modern history.

Locals still have the fever. On the outskirts of the town dirty miners are walking towards the smoke, shovels and picks slung over their shoulders. One wears a headlamp. The land around the town is drilled with more holes than Swiss cheese. Around here there are rubies, sapphires, garnets, amethysts and aquamarine. We pass a road-block of spikes laid across the road by three soldiers armed with assault rifles and drive down the main street. The buildings are cobbled together from corrugated iron and weathered grey wood. There is no pavement and the road is busy with people. Our cars weave through the crowd past shacks and offices with Thai and Sri Lankan gem deal-ers sitting on plastic chairs, loupes ready to check gems thrust in front of them by muddy miners. 'Big boss buys big stones for big money,' reads one sign. There are bars, barbers, men sitting by the road play-ing cards, with fags hanging from their mouths, and open shops selling shovels, digging bars, buckets and spades. Chubby prostitutes stand in doorways. It is brazen and lawless, the Klondike, circa 1897.

Batsola has arranged for us to meet the local mayor, who lives along a rutted track 17 kilometres outside this new settlement, in the original village of Ilakaka. Despite all the mining, the landscape retains an obvious, striking beauty. Beyond the town, rugged rocks soar hundreds of metres out of the ground, Madagascar's own Isalo Massif.

The original Ilakaka village is a sleepy backwater compared to the bustling, new town. As we arrive, a young girl runs off to find the mayor, but after 20 minutes he still has not appeared, so we set out to find him with a local character who smokes a pipe made from car parts. He takes us through a dirt-poor village with mud houses nestling cheek and jowl, so close there is no room for sunshine to hit the ground between their roofs. Cobs of corn dry under eaves. There are scores of people milling around and children scream or laugh as my lanky head appears outside their windows and over their fences. Some have never seen a white man. One child looks at me and immediately starts bawling.

After a five-minute walk through narrow passages, we arrive at the two-storey mud home of the mayor. In his tiny courtyard there is a blue Citroen. Curiously, there is no space for the car to drive in or out between the houses. Perhaps it has been reassembled from spare parts.

Abdoul Anzizy appears wearing a baggy grey suit and clean shirt, and stroking a new red tie. He is one month younger than me, but groomed, composed and carrying a thin black faux-leather briefcase, spectacularly incongruous in this dusty village.

Abdoul is largely responsible for the gem rush in this region. Back in 1998, while looking for semi-precious stones, he found the original, very precious, pink sapphires. The locals were so happy they elected him mayor.

'I'm very popular here,' he says modestly. In one year during the height of the gem rush the mayor says he found 20 kilograms of sapphires, but sold them cheaply and wasted the money, like all of the locals. Some spent their new wealth washing their cars in beer.

'Can you believe how stupid we were?' asks Abdoul.

Then experienced Thais, Sri Lankans and West Africans arrived and became the dealers. The Malagasy became the miners.

The mayor takes me back into Ilakaka to a deep pit on the edge of town, the biggest mine, a source of rubies, and blue and pink sapphires. Locals call it the Swiss Bank.

The land is scarred and fissured. Scores of men are working as a human conveyor belt, moving earth from the side of the Bank so it can be extended and lowered another ten metres. They are wiry, muscular men wielding long spades and wrecking bars, and they earn just over one pound a day. Closer to the town and the land is loose and dotted with round holes. I slide towards a black circle with the diameter of a manhole cover, then regain my footing.

'Be careful,' says the mayor, grabbing at my arm, 'someone dies around here every few days. Many are buried alive. Often their families cannot afford to get them out of the holes. So they just stay down there.'

What a way to go. I look at Batsola and we both shudder at the thought.

Above one of the holes a simple wooden winch holds a thin cheap rope and a sack that will take Jean Chrisostome 18 metres down into the airless darkness. A husband and father of five, his short muscular frame caked in yellow dirt, he was a carpenter before the lure of gems brought him to Ilakaka. Now he sits next to the hole, picking at his huge white teeth with a twig wielded by calloused hands. Mud is in his hair, his eyelashes, not just under the ends of his finger and toenails, but actually underneath his nails. At the bottom of his hole, dark 10- and 20-metre ratty tunnels stretch out sideways in each direction, taking him closer towards Heaven or Hades, depending on whether he finds a gem or dies in the darkness.

I gaze down the hole and darkness grabs me. I can imagine myself at the bottom of the hole, looking upwards to the sky. But trapped. Squashed on all sides. My entire body suddenly convulses. Even a projection of such intense claustrophobia is enough to make my insides curdle.

'Do you worry about working down the hole?' I ask. Batsola translates.

'The main worry is, "Will I survive today?"' he replies. 'People die doing this, especially here in Ilakaka. At least 20 per year, but that's the risk of the job. In the end, you just get used to it. You need to survive. There's nothing else to do.'

Dozens of men have died in this area. Jean tells me he worries about the rope snapping, the ground caving in, and his oxygen supply failing. It is a wonder the supply works at all. A 30-metre-long piece of thin plastic sheeting is taped into a roll, with a large plastic bag secured to one end. Wind pushes air into the bag, which is then squashed by a friend to squeeze oxygen down the sheeting and down into the pit. It is the most primitive form of mining. Only a desperate man, a miner with the half-crazed belief that a beautiful gem is waiting for him below, would take such risks.

Jean is lowered down into the darkness. He looks back up at me. His wife prays for him when he goes below.

'We can only pray and rely on God,' he says.

And then the winch creaks and turns and I watch from above as his smile fades and the inky blackness takes him. We produce a huge filming reflector, like a circular sheet of shiny gold, very appropriate in this mining setting, and use it to direct the sun down the hole. There is a shout from the bottom. Jean has never seen his darkness in light.

Aided by a useless torch, he crawls around gathering sandy gravel which is brought back to the surface in buckets and bags. He works quickly and the winch turns and he comes back to the light with a bag that is tipped on to the ground. The miners start working through the soil. One reaches for a stone, brushes off the dirt, and holds it up to the burning sun. It is just a stone. He tosses it to one side.

'We're going to wash all this with water and then look for a sapphire,' Jean tells me. 'If we find any, then we thank God. If not then I'll have to come back and go down the hole again.'

Each time he goes below, Jean wonders if he will find a gem that will buy him a farm and a herd of zebu. A few of his friends have had their lives transformed. But he has only found tiny sapphires, just enough to keep him going.

'Do you regret coming here?' I ask.

Batsola translates and Jean grins.

'He's got lots of questions!' he tells her. 'I can see that he's a journalist!'

But then his smile slips.

'Sometimes I regret I came here,' he says, 'but in general, there's not much difference because here or there it will always be the same. I was poor as a carpenter, and I am poor now.' He chuckles, but with the pain of genuine regret.

'What would help you here?' I ask.

He considers for a moment.

'The only thing we would need is something that could help us to see or know if there are sapphires in this particular area. Unfortunately, we don't have anything. Our materials are basic. We rely on God.'

Jean asks me politely for a gift. We never offer money in advance but there are no hard and fast rules when a dirt-poor miner has spent most of his morning chatting to wealthy foreigners. I pass Batsola some money to slip him when he is away from the other miners. He is so happy he gives her a kiss.

We drive 200 metres from the mine back into town, passing through a wooden shanty town. One young guy lazes by the road, a cheeky black and white ring-tailed lemur sitting on his shoulder.

Another man is digging a familiar hole right outside the front door of his shack. He is already two metres deep, and is passing soil up to cousins on the surface. As we film, his digging does not even slow. He is oblivious to everything but the possibility of a rich seam. Some people dig straight down from inside their homes.

Several kilos of sapphires emerge from this area each day, about half the world supply. But the vast majority of miners are poor. Nobody here is making serious money from the gems. At least none of the Malagasy.

The real value in the gems is not the price paid when they come out of the ground, but after they are exported abroad and then cut, polished and processed. Jean told me he had listened to radio programmes and knows the price he gets for small gems is just five or ten per cent of the value of a cut stone. Madagascar is trying to regulate exports, but each month between 10 and 15 million pounds' worth of gems are also smuggled off the island.

'It's always been like this,' says Batsola bitterly. 'The foreigners buy our resources and ship them out, and they make the money.'

It is a problem that afflicts most of Africa. But Madagascar need not be poor. Apart from gems, there are also deposits of titanium, ilmenite, nickel, cobalt, aluminium, graphite and oil in or around the island. Mining minerals could be a massive earner, generating wealth similar to that in Botswana. The key is to secure a good price for what comes out of the ground, and preferably process the raw materials within the country. With that in mind, a gem-cutting school has just opened in Tana, graduating experts in gemology. If the alternative to careful mining is slash and burn, mining might be the lesser of two evils.

Yet the irony is that the Malagasy have no interest in gems. They have never been part of their culture. The few that can afford to adorn themselves favour gold. I ask miners what they think foreigners use the gems for. Some have heard they are used to make weapons. Jean, like most, did not have a clue.

We go to see Thai and Sri Lankan dealers on the main drag in Ilakaka. They work and live from the protection of small wooden huts, the insides covered in gaudy lino, sitting on chairs by hatches that open on to the street. Muddy miners, conmen, shysters and chancers drop cracked and cloudy sapphires, pieces of yellow glass, blue insulators from power lines, and even the occasional clean gem, on to a plate in front of the dealers. Often the dealers do not even look to see who owns the hand. They just focus on the stone, then mutter a yes or a no.

Thais seem to cream the best gems and ship them back to jewellery factories in Thailand for cutting, polishing and mounting in rings and earrings sold globally. Sri Lankans tend to get the second-rate stones, eventually sold on shopping channels.

One of the Sri Lankans shows me plastic bags of small stones locked in a safe in his office. He tips the yellow, pink, purple and blue beads, like chips of coloured boiled sweets, on to a glass table.

'Sapphires,' he says simply. They are small, rough, uncut and underwhelming.

I finger a dull stone worth £260, an annual wage for most people here.

'How many people die to get the gems?'

'Not many,' he says, shrugging dismissively.

Outside it is dusk and the town is busy. The mayor wants to get home.

'You should not stay here overnight,' he tells us. 'It is not safe.

There are desperate people in this town. They have seen your equipment. Bandits might come and attack you or kill you in the night.'

People die in Ilakaka all the time, our drivers warn us, it is dangerous here. Batsola is unhappy about being in the town at night. There are gunshots in the darkness, a palpable edge to the town, and a casual aggression among locals. A group of burly men walk over to where we are filming and insist, menacingly, they will provide us with 'protection' for a fee. Our drivers decide they are robbers and threaten to leave us in the town. Just before the electricity is switched off for the night and the town is plunged into darkness, we pass another roadblock mounted by men with oiled AK-47s and indistinct uniforms, and break out of Ilakaka.

THE SMALL town of Ranohira is just 20 minutes away by road, but an oasis of calm. I spend a peaceful night being thrashed at pool by locals on a roadside table so close to the street a bus nearly kills me when I finally pot a ball.

As Ranohira disappears behind us the next morning, we are back among the subsistence farmers. Herds of zebu are moved slowly across the plains by cowboys, on foot and horseback, who take weeks to travel from the coast to the highland markets. Some Malagasy tribes view cattle-rustling as a rite of passage, and many of the cowboys carry old shotguns. 'It's very dangerous to be a cowboy,' says Batsola. 'They are targeted by gangs of poachers.'

Our cars pass small Tuscan villages made of the ochre earth, huge rocky hills and stone half-domes straight from the photographs of Ansel Adams. Occasionally we see battered minibuses that serve as country taxis, but there are few cars or lorries and the passage of our four-wheel drives is enough of an event to make the rural poor, who walk by the side of the road, turn and stare. Everywhere we see the effects of *tavy*.

Another example of Madagascan eccentricity. By the side of the road the living have simple, temporary houses made from bamboo branches that tremble in the wind. Next to them the dead have comparative luxury and permanence in solid tombs built to last an eternity, decorated on the outside with paintings featuring the interred and their deeds. There is an army officer, a helicopter, a painting of a herd of zebu. And on top of one giant tomb, the skulls of zebu. When a farmer dies his entire herd of cattle is often slaughtered for a mass village feast and an orgy of meat consumption. Not great for the next of kin, who must survive without their livestock.

Then we start to climb. We have reached the Hautes Plateaux, the Highlands, the home of the Merina people, who arrived from Indonesia and formed Madagascar's first royal dynasty. Farmers here use Asian techniques to terrace the land to grow more rice, squeezing paddy areas from even the steepest slopes. Buildings become more sophisticated, changing from shacks to two-storey mud houses, as we draw closer to the middle of the country, and finally reach the town of Fianarantsoa.

We arrive late in the evening and find the few guest houses and hotels full. There are rooms at a private house on top of a hill reached by steps our cars cannot climb. Local teenagers offer to help lug our bags and cases up the slope, but my Peli case holds the tapes we have shot on this leg of the trip. I curse its weight but hug it to my chest.

We are all tired and hungry and Batsola has made us salivate with her memories of scones with strawberries and cream taken in Brighton tearooms. We race for dinner at a small restaurant in town, one of the most popular tourist restaurants in the country. The two small rooms are full of French visitors who look at us, dirty from days on the road, with unreserved disdain.

There are only a few thousand French expats in Madagascar, but many have made fortunes by bribing officials to win contracts. 'Somebody who is a no one in France can be a god in a poor country like this,' whispers Batsola as we are seated at the back of the restaurant.

Familiar sounds wake me at 4 a.m. the next morning. Cockerels again. I'm losing count of the score, but I have a feeling it's 4–0 in their favour. Then the haunting sound of a muezzin's call to prayer drifts across this hill town, followed at a more acceptable hour by a peal of church bells. What a mixture. I head out to investigate.

FIANARANTSOA IS a bustling hill town with a delightful old quarter of cobbled streets and ramshackle houses with leaky roofs. Part fairy-tale, part old France, the sum total is uniquely Madagascan.

We only have one day in Fianarantsoa, and we use it to sightsee, rest, re-charge our batteries, check emails and make contact with the outside world. We are all exhausted. Anya and I call home on a crackly phone line to finalize our wedding preparations. The venue, service, booze, food and rings all still need to be tied up. Doing this on the road in Madagascar is not ideal.

At 5 a.m. the next morning my phone alarm wakes us for the start of our long journey to the east coast of Madagascar. We have already travelled by horse, car, four-wheel drive, plane, taxi, bus, ferry and boat along Capricorn. Time for a train ride.

We arrive at the station at 6 a.m., just in time to find a place in a long queue. There are three carriages on the train and two distinct groups of travellers. There are Madagascans journeying along the line deep into the highlands, who book tickets for the two second-class carriages. *Vazaha* backpackers, mostly French, buy seats in the marginally better first-class coach. We had planned to travel with the locals, but then we are told the journey takes around ten hours. We have a look in the shabby carriages and reconsider.

The train is due to leave at 7 a.m. But the locomotive is still being repaired in a shed. We wait. And wait. Batsola is told the train will not be leaving until 10.30 a.m. We head off for a second breakfast of delicious croissants in a local café. When we return, there is still no sign of the engine. Malagasy passengers have resigned looks. Foreign travellers lie on the station platform, sunning themselves and playing with child postcard-sellers, who clearly view a delayed train as a business opportunity.

Another two hours pass. There is an engine whistle from the shed. A smoking red locomotive slowly emerges, backing towards the three carriages. The passengers cheer.

The Fianarantsoa Cote Est railway line carves its way through the highlands for 101 miles to the coastal town of Manakara. Between 5,000 and 10,000 Malagasy workers died building the line, many of them buried under thousands of tons of soil and rock as tunnels collapsed. It was the sort of project only a ruthless colonial power could push through. But after the French left, the line fell into disrepair, held together by dedicated but under-funded enthusiasts.

We are allowed to stand on the front of the train as it lumbers along the line. Not in a cab. On the very front, above the cowcatcher, which is supposed to sweep stray zebu out of the path of the train, saving the driver from a collision with a horned beast. The experience is like being on the front of a giant, ageing rollercoaster, and the tracks underneath our train groan and creak unnervingly as we screech round corners.

'Whoooooooah!' I scream, leaning forward beyond the railing. Batsola does the same.

'Do you think you're Leonardo di Caprio and Kate Winslet in *Titanic*?' asks Anya cheekily. The wind rushes past, my hair stands on end and I have a half-crazed look on my face. I must look like I've been electrocuted.

From the front of the train we have an incredible view as we cross viaducts, valleys and 67 bridges. We rocket down the world's third steepest railway incline, a 3.66 per cent drop, for those interested. Given the wheezing state of our engine, it's no surprise the returning train regularly has trouble making the climb.

And there are dozens of tunnels. Short tunnels with light shining from the other end. And long tunnels that we roar through in darkness, wheels clacking like giant false teeth. I shrink into a ball, fearful we might meet a lost zebu who took a wrong turning in the night, and splat him across the front of the train.

We pull into the first hill station along our route. It is a tiny place set among banana plants. A major sporting event is underway. Hundreds of people are crowded around the tracks and the station. Then I realize we will be the sport.

Half of the crowd are waiting to board. They have a steely determination forged by a combination of tropical heat and a rare train arriving hours late. Before the train has even stopped, they fight their way through the doors. Passengers desperate to leave the train pop out between the clambering hordes like corks from a bottle.

Then as the train comes to a complete halt, a second wave of attacks begins. The rest of the crowd, comprising scores of women and barefoot children, have been waiting all day to launch an assault, targeting weary travellers with trays of bananas, cakes, sweets and bottles of water. Food comes to the open windows. One of the train guards stands on the platform trying to keep the sellers away from the *première-classe* carriage. Out of sight on the other side of the train, a platoon outflanks him and launches their strike led by the bulk of a colossal, beaming woman in a bright flowery orange dress wielding a tray of bananas. She is ferocious. The guard spots her too late and moves to intercept. He never has a chance. She sweeps him aside, climbs into the carriage and waddles through offering her wares.

We hop down to watch all this and move around the train creating yet more havoc. Without exception people are friendly, curious or bemused. The blood-letting calms. The traders have feasted on the passengers. Behind the train I am examining coffee beans drying on a rusty flat-top carriage in a siding, when the train begins to move. At first I think it is just shuffling forward, perhaps to another platform. But it keeps moving. I start to walk after it. We are in the middle of nowhere. The train picks up speed. Throwing British reserve to one side, I leg it down the tracks after the final carriage, hollering at the top of my voice, much to the amusement of the scores of locals still milling around the station. Hands reach down from the back of the train and I am pulled, giggling and not a little embarrassed, on to the back steps.

The train passes a lazy river which has the feel of the Mekong Delta. Out here villages are remote, desperately poor, and reached by well-trodden footpaths that criss-cross the red soil.

We head into the hills again and acres of slash and burn. Despite, or perhaps because of, its small population, Madagascar feels carpeted with tiny rice fields. If only rice production could be concentrated in productive areas, this could become a tropical paradise again. Perhaps one day. Meanwhile *tavy* is a blot on Madagascar, but it cannot mask

the beauty of this area. And this is still one of the world's great railway journeys.

We travel with the guard, the driver, the tourists in *première classe*
and the Malagasy. Conditions in second class could be charitably
described as squashed. We pause in a village and I wander off into a
field for a quick pee. I am gone for two minutes. When I return it is
advanced dusk. There was no preamble. We stand on the front of the
train again, underneath two viciously bright headlamps that light our
passage. In the darkness they draw every single insect in eastern
Madagascar. We are a blur of arms as we battle to keep them out of
noses and mouths. When we reach the next village we head back to
our seats in the carriage.

Walking alongside the train, I realize it is dark in the carriages.
An electrical problem means we can either have lights inside the
train or headlamps so the driver can see where we are going. There
is no contest.

It is 7 p.m. We are travelling in complete darkness and I can see
other passengers only by their silhouettes. Every ten minutes our train
is stopping to have huge bunches of bananas loaded in such a leisurely
fashion that French travellers on the train decide to help and speed
the process. Worst of all, an overpowering smell of pee permeates our
entire carriage from a single toilet two metres away that has the internal appearance of the pub toilet in *Trainspotting*. My enthusiasm for
the journey briefly wanes.

But then I look out of the window. Hundreds of fireflies flit across
a starry sky. We pull into another station for yet more bananas, which
are now being loaded into an entirely new cattle carriage acquired at
the back of the train. The platform is lit by candles and locals are
running a small shop on a wooden table, with bananas, crisps and a

few beers arranged with careful precision and pride. Kids on the platform start singing local songs, for themselves as much as the passengers. It is a haunting sound. The train guard lights flickering candles in the carriages. It is a beautiful, other-worldly scene, another unique spectacle on Capricorn.

'To us this is just a journey, but this railway means everything to those people,' says Batsola as we listen to the singing. When Didier Ratsiraka was forced from office, his armed supporters destroyed bridges and threatened to attack the railway. Villagers along the line slept outside next to the wood and steel spans that keep the FCE running. It is our railway, they told the warring politicians. Our people died to build it. You will not take it.

What politicians failed to destroy, nature easily derails. Cyclones in 2000 caused 280 landslides along the line. It was a disaster for locals who grow coffee, vanilla and bananas around their impoverished forest villages. You can't survive by eating coffee and bananas. Farmers need to be able to transport their produce to coastal markets so they can buy rice. Each year this railway shifts 3,000 tons of coffee and 6,000 tons of fruit. Low global coffee prices already meant more farmers were shifting to growing rice. Studies showed that without the railway farmers would slash and burn hundreds of thousands of acres of forest to clear land for more rice plantations. So the line had to be saved.

When charitable Americans decided to help, the railway had no bank account and was close to bankruptcy. Money was kept in a box under the director's bed. US aid and help from a Swiss railway put the trains back on track. The king of Thailand sent grass specialists to advise on the planting of vetiver grass that stabilizes steep embankments with steely roots three metres deep.

A railway line protecting a swathe of Madagascan forest. Who would have thought it?

The FCE is still not the most reliable railway, and the carriages are cramped and, at least on my trip, annoyingly dark. But the line is a thread connecting and saving a vast region of the forest, and you don't have to be a trainspotter to enjoy the spectacular journey. We cross a runway in the dark, one of only a handful of trains in the world that can claim the honour, and finally creak into Manakara just before 10 p.m. Only six hours late. As we leave the station, barefoot pousse-pousse rickshaw drivers pull and tug at our clothing, desperate for the chance to carry our 20 heavy bags. We find a couple of cabs and drive through darkened streets to a dank and mouldy guest house with damp beds that smell of sweaty armpits. I spread a bin liner across our mattress to keep Anya and me dry, and we sleep soundly.

The next day, after a breakfast of honey and bread with rat poo in the crust, we set out for the sea, the end of the second leg of our Capricorn journey. Manakara, battered by salty water, has the feel of a quiet Louisiana backwater. It is not just sleepy, it is comatose.

Batsola and I have a shandy at a canal-side restaurant and bid each other a final farewell. This has been a spectacular journey for both of us. A revelation for me; a final tour for Batsola. Anya and I will fly home to take care of some domestic business, before heading off to Australia on the next leg of this journey. But in two weeks Batsola flies to central China, to spend four years studying for a Masters, her second, in Agricultural Economics and Management.

'I know I'm going to miss my country every day,' she says, 'and I'm really grateful for this chance to travel across my island.' She sheds a tear, I get a lump in my throat, and we all have a group hug. It is all rather moving.

There are few people around as we cross a rusting bridge in Manakara, patched together with silver braces that look like sticking plasters on its red frame. I peel off, hopping into a pousse-pousse that takes me 100 metres further east towards a line of palm trees on a bank shielding a beach and the milky-blue waters of the Indian Ocean. Brian commandeers another rickshaw to join me. I reach the end of the road. Two women are selling coconuts and cakes under the palm trees. They beam at me and I wave back. I am halfway around Capricorn.

THE DRY CONTINENT

6 · WESTERN AUSTRALIA

TWO WEEKS AGO Anya and I tied the knot. You might think it was a little inconvenient to get married in the middle of a round-the-world-trip. But it was planned well before this Capricorn ramble, and what sort of person would change their wedding plans for a work journey? So we were married. I could tell you about the wedding, but you're not reading *Hello!*. You know what happens. I wore a suit. She looked incredible. We haven't had time to write thank-you cards and now we're back on the road, flying to the south side of the world to resume our Capricorn journey.

Our destination is a country twice the size of the European Union that most Brits feel they know well: Australia. It's all sunshine, *Neighbours*, an opera house, surfing, cold XXXX, didgeridoos, kangaroos and cricket, isn't it? But looking at another map on the plane heading Down Under, I'm hit by the realization that all I really know about the country is the cities sitting in a slender band of life around the south-west, sheltered behind a range of mountains called the Great Dividing Range. Stretching across the rest of the country is the Outback, a chunk of land unknown even to most Australians, urbanized and suburbanized as they are. My only real reference for the vast Outback is *Crocodile Dundee*. It's nothing personal. It's just that Australia has never been of massive interest to me. Perhaps I thought

I already knew all about it. I have another look for the Tropic of Capricorn. It hits Australia on the west coast, crosses the near-middle of the country and shoots out on the east side at the bottom of the Great Barrier Reef. Whatever I think I know about Australia, I'm about to spend weeks discovering the reality.

There are obvious differences between home and Oz. But there are also bizarre similarities. A taxi-driver from Essex takes me to Heathrow, I fly to Perth on the western edge of a country on the other side of the planet and the money still bears the Queen's head, the people drive on the left and a taxi-driver from Essex picks me up from the airport.

They say Perth is the most isolated city in the world, although when we finally arrive it seems full of office towers and the usual friendly cafés serving complicated varieties of coffee. But this is not the starting point for the latest leg of my journey. Along with Brian, who will be lugging his heavy camera again, Anya, filming on a second camera, and Louise Turner, who will be directing the Australian leg of Capricorn, I head further up the west coast to a beach next to Ningaloo Reef, one of the last major healthy coral reefs in the world, a home to turtles, manta rays and huge whale sharks travelling along warm currents south from Asia. We just have time to absorb a vision of white sand and aquamarine water, and then we are off, heading to the small town of Exmouth, just north of Capricorn and next to the blue waters of Exmouth Gulf, where I'm told hundreds of humpback whales take a break during their long journey south from tropical calving waters to the nutrient-rich feeding grounds of the Antarctic. Apparently some humpbacks feel so safe there they use it as a nursery, and even give birth in the gulf.

Driving towards the town, and a rendezvous with the whales, a tyre on our rented four-wheel drive explodes. I fumble around to find the jack and slowly change the wheel under a boiling sun, sweat running down my back. Since the moment I arrived here the heat has launched an assault. It is 40 degrees Celsuis. In Fahrenheit that's treble figures. The air seems to sizzle. This will be a tough, energy-sapping trip, and it is only just beginning.

Exmouth is a sprawl of single-storey homes, grazing kangaroos and more stifling heat. I head to the quay and a meeting on a 23-metre boat called *WhaleSong*, a former tuna long-liner, now the headquarters for a small family outfit who run the Centre for Whale Research. Curt and Micheline Jenner have been monitoring whales in this area for more than a decade and are passionately committed to protecting the huge creatures. Curt promises there are scores out in the gulf and offers to take me out to have a look.

'This is a spot where cows and calves can come to just do nothing during their migration,' says Curt. 'They can rest and get out of the swell and big winds, and build up their energy reserves. They need to put on half a ton of fat...'

'Half a ton!?' I splutter.

'Yep...of fat before they leave here and head south again for more than 2,500 nautical miles down to the Antarctic.'

'But how long before you normally spot them in the gulf?' I ask, conscious that pursuing elusive marine life poses certain visual challenges.

'It'll be 30 seconds,' says Curt confidently, 'just as soon as we move away from the quay and head out into the open water.'

Micheline, a lively, attractive woman in her forties, interjects. 'For seeing a large number of whales I'd put this gulf at number one,' she says. 'There are huge numbers here. We did a survey a few weeks ago and we saw 163 pods during nine hours of survey and most of those pods had two whales in it. We've got a density of one whale per square nautical mile and there are roughly 350 square nautical miles of gulf here that the whales use, so a whale per square mile. That's phenomenal in anyone's language.'

They are true to their word. We have only just cruised past the stone walls of the quay when I see whales surfacing to breathe. Clouds of mist are formed when the warm air shooting out of a humpback's huge lungs hits colder surface air.

'Blow at two o'clock!' shouts Micheline, spotting on the top deck.

Curt, a quieter sort with whiskers and thoughtful eyes, powers up the engine, tuned to run at whisper volume to avoid disturbing sensitive whales, and we move forward half a mile or so towards one of the blows. Then we cut the power and cruise forward at jogging speed.

But the whale has vanished. For a couple of hours we see little more than distant mist and chase shadows. Then we spot whales waving their tail flukes 20 feet out of the water, almost calling us over to take a look, and we get lucky.

I am standing at the prow of the boat, staring into the ocean, while Curt and Micheline are at the outdoor controls on the deck above, when a huge shape moves under the waves. At first it is just a darkness, then a gasp-inducing creature emerges from the deep. A leviathan. The back of an enormous marine monarch slides through the water, breaching the surface.

Other great backs surface to the side, their dark skin pocked and marked by scrapes and battles. In front of me this large pod appears to be practising synchronized swimming, one gigantic back emerging after another as if a long eel is moving through the gulf. I hang off the edge of the boat, which affords me a front-row seat as four male humpbacks follow one larger female.

'She's pregnant! She must weigh more than 40 tons!' shouts Curt excitedly over the noise of the wind, waves and whales. In just a few days she'll come to the surface, form the shape of a 'C', and give birth to a one-ton calf the size of a small family car. No wonder she's twisting and turning. But her work won't stop at birth. Every day Mum will need to produce as much as 600 litres of fatty milk the consistency of chewing gum to keep junior well nourished. Up comes a cloud of air. I spread my arms to let this life mist envelop me.

'Don't breathe their blow!' warns Micheline. 'They can have TB and all sorts of strange things inside.' I shut my trap just a moment too late.

Whales use this gulf as a sanctuary, a place to rest, a chance to layer fat reserves before the long journey south. Mothers use the waters to teach their young calves the rules of the sea. And the expectant mother in front of me feels safe enough here to give birth.

Yet the males are not gliding alongside her for altruistic pack reasons, such as protecting her calf from orcas. Just after she gives birth she'll come into oestrous and they'll try to mate with her yet again.

'There's probably an evolutionary reason for that because it means the cow has protection around her while she's giving birth,' Curt says.

'Incredible.'

'Well, these creatures have had an age to develop.'

Indeed they have. Whales are impossibly ancient, existing in their modern form for 30 million years. Just doing what they do: travelling incredible distances and migrating further than any other mammal. Whales have been recorded making 8,000-kilometre trips, an extraordinary distance.

'So how does this compare to other places you have studied or worked?' I ask Curt as we take in the scene.

'Oh, this is without a doubt the most amazing spot we've ever worked,' he says.

'In the world?' I query.

'Yes, in the world, in terms of its importance for a single population, in terms of behaviour. Here we've seen whales rolling in the mud to scratch wounds where males have been fighting. Some of the behaviour seen here has never been spotted anywhere else on the planet.'

We follow the whales, keeping a reasonable distance, as they turn towards the north-west shore of the gulf and the radio towers of the Harold E. Holt naval station, a US communications base named after the Australian PM whose term in office was abruptly ended when he vanished, presumed drowned. The sight could hardly be more incongruous. The US Naval Command chatting with crews under the waves, while this pod of giant submariners slides gracefully through the water.

The sun sinks slowly and turns the sky a golden orange. Wisps of cirrus embedded in the gold close to the horizon turn a rusty red, while thicker bands of cloud above my head hide a still deep blue sky. It is a scene for Turner to paint. I sigh in amazement. It is beautiful.

Then the pregnant cow requests my full attention. Rolling on to her back she begins slapping the surface water with her giant five-metre long pectoral fins. The sound, like a loud clapping, is playful, enticing, as it should be.

'She's probably trying to attract more males,' says Curt. 'She might be thinking those around her are weedy, and might not offer enough protection to her calf.'

The whale pauses, steadying herself in the water.

'She might even give birth in the next few hours,' he adds hopefully.

But I could not be that lucky. We watch for a few more moments until dusk turns to dark, then head back towards the port.

Inside the boat, we have time for coffee. This 70-ton HQ is a base for research. But it is also a warm home for a family of four, two zebra finches (Vegemite and Milo), and a Jack Russell called Skipper. Cutting-edge potato-growing experiments sit on a sill in the kitchen alongside children's drawings and watercolours. In the office-cum-cabin a copy of the *Happy Feet* Nintendo game sits on a cluttered table near a *Star Trek* console and seven plasma screens that control the boat.

Curt grew up on the plains of central Canada and didn't see ocean until he was 16. He's making up for it now. Exmouth Gulf is one of the most important whale sanctuaries in the world. It must certainly rank as one of the top five places for whale spotting. But that might be about to change.

Whales have long faced outright danger on the high seas. The creatures were virtually annihilated by whalers, with almost 90 per cent being killed before a moratorium was agreed in the 1960s. Japan now exploits a loophole in International Whaling Commission laws to kill up to 1,000 whales each year, targeting endangered creatures despite a global ban on whaling. But whales now face new threats even inside their Exmouth sanctuary.

'To tell you the truth,' says Curt, with a conspiratorial wiggle of his eyebrows, 'if you had contacted us six months ago I might have denied any knowledge of the whales. We didn't want the world to find out about this place and ruin it. But just in the last few months a whole raft of new proposals have been put forward for industrial development in this area, and we need to beat a drum and warn people about what they might be about to lose.'

It sounds dramatic, but I soon realize Curt is not exaggerating. In fact, his calm Canadian manner might even be understating the problem.

On the wilderness eastern edge of Exmouth Gulf there are advanced plans to build one of the world's largest salt fields, anything up to 70 kilometres long. In its simplest form, this involves building a long wall, pumping salty seawater into shallow basins on the other side, and waiting for the water to evaporate in the hot sun. Millions of tons of salt will be harvested for use in Asian industry and the manufacture of plastics.

Apart from the threat of salt leaching into the Gulf after a storm or cyclone, the salt will be shipped out in 300-metre boats with powerful engines. Sound travels roughly three times further and faster underwater than above the surface. Our boats, motors and propellers are a screaming intrusion into the world of whales.

'Imagine trying to rest with a newborn baby somewhere in a quiet spot, and dumper trucks were going by and people were banging garage doors.'

'I'd want to move,' I say.

Curt nods. 'Yes, you'd want to move and we're worried that this is what will happen with the whales. The gulf is absolutely critical for them. If they can't stay here in order to beef up the calves for the journey down to the Antarctic,' he pauses, 'well, that would be a population-threatening event.'

'Population-threatening? It's that serious?'

'Exactly,' says Curt. 'If these cows and calves can't rest they'll probably perish on their way to the Antarctic, and that'll be the end of them.'

There are plans for other development in this region. Oil and gas fields have been found off the west coast. Multinationals are lining up to secure mining- and ocean-drilling rights in areas whales pass through on their way south. Nobody really knows what the consequences will be for our marine cousins. They are sensitive creatures that dislike change and disturbance. The whales might just avoid Exmouth Gulf and this pristine sanctuary may be lost.

But development seems inevitable in Australia. It will be a recurring theme of my journey across this huge country. Demand for raw materials to house, feed, clothe, entertain and transport the population of our planet just goes on increasing. And in the vastness of this continent-sized country there are all manner of seams, mines and quarries offering the rawest of materials to fuel furnaces and feed the resource-hungry emerging economies of China and India. In Queensland in the east, further along Capricorn, the demand is for coal. Here in Western Australia it's for iron ore. The clammer for resources has created the biggest boom Australia has seen in decades, possibly the largest and most lucrative boom in the country's history.

Following Capricorn will help me to explore the story. From Exmouth our plan is to head to Newman, a mining boomtown two days inland by road. Heading further east along Capricorn will take us to the town of Alice Springs, bang in the middle of the country.

We pop round to meet Ian Steck, who will be driving me part of the way, at his home on a quiet street in Exmouth. A chunk of a man wearing shorts and a singlet in 40-degree heat, Stecky, as everyone calls him, is a classically Aussie character. We sit in the shade at the front of his house chatting about our route across the country while his grandchildren play on their bikes. Warm, witty and crude, Stecky has the slow shuffle of a man who only wears flip-flops and the

weather-worn skin of a leatherback turtle after a life in the sun working as a fisherman, a dog-catcher and the local snake wrangler.

'Woman up the road called me the other day to get one from her
garden. Big bugger. Nasty bite.'

My eyes widen. 'What do you do with them?'

'Ah, I just release them in my front yard. They don't harm anyone.'

I move my chair away from the bushes. Four dogs – acquired on
his official duties – roam around the garden. 'If I couldn't find homes
for them quickly I ended up keeping them. You can't go giving dogs
away when they've formed an attachment. It breaks their hearts.'

And his, I suspect. Stecky loves his animals, but doesn't seem
overly fond of whales. He was out fishing in his small dinghy at the
weekend and a humpback came right up to him. 'It just sat there.
Huge thing. Stared at me for about 20 minutes. Bloody thing scared
all the fish away.'

On the back of his pickup is a sticker: 'Pass the salt'. Locals in
Exmouth are split between those who worry about the whales, and
those who think the area needs more jobs and investment. Stecky is
in favour of the development. 'I don't think it will harm the whales,'
he tells me. 'And you can't halt progress.'

Up early the next morning to begin our crossing of the continent. A man in the town camping shop tries to sell us all head-nets
to repel flies.

'Will we really need them?' I query.

He asks where we're heading and snorts with laughter when I tell
him inland.

'Yeah,' he says. 'You'll be needing them all right.'

We load the Land Cruiser with water, food, supplies and a couple
of spare tyres, just in case. Stecky puts on those wraparound square

sunglasses favoured by elderly Americans with an unsavoury addiction to golf. 'Well,' he says, turning to me and offering a typically dry Aussie understatement, 'here we go.'

EACH COUNTRY on Capricorn has something new to offer. As we leave the outskirts of Exmouth and head inland, I idly compile my first shortlist for Australia. So far it has to be the size, heat and emptiness. And flies. We are being attacked by the most aggressive, persistent bush flies I have ever encountered. On more than a few occasions the damn things crawl so far up my nose I fear they might find a long forgotten route through to my ears, and fly out of the side of my head.

'They're after protein,' says Stecky. 'A few might be carrying something nasty, but really they're just a nuisance.'

I wave my hands around in impotent fury, then reach for my head-net. Stecky looks at me in disgust, then laughs.

'What's so funny?'

'Well, if you didn't open your mouth so much you wouldn't catch so many!'

'Does anything keep them away?'

Stecky produces a large can, and fumigates the car with an insect repellent brewed by the Soviet biological weapons programme. Brian and I gag on the fumes; Stecky just guffaws.

We focus back on the road. The landscape beyond Exmouth is unremittingly flat and barren. There are shrubs and moments of wispy greenery, but there is nary an inch of shade for hundreds of miles. We pass from the outskirts of Exmouth into 'the bush', and beyond that into the Australian interior, the scorched unknown, the Outback.

The central core around which Australia shapes its identity, the very harshness of life in the Outback provides a justification and counter-balance for the beauty, the pampered luxury and the sheer joy of the soft beach lifestyles around the coast of this continent. 'You feel free in Australia,' wrote D.H. Lawrence. 'The skies open above you and the areas open around you.' He was right. But Australia is too big. It is only now I am up close that I fully appreciate its enormity. We motor for hours in the heat, windows down for natural air conditioning, and reach a stretch of road widened to become an emergency landing strip for the Royal Flying Doctor Service. This feels truly remote.

I have a nagging feeling I will find this country a real challenge. Australia is too many time zones ahead of home. For these past few days I have felt zonked, drugged, and utterly devoid of energy. I am suffering severe jetlag. It is also too hot. Moving under the sun when we stop for petrol at a lonely roadhouse is like being turned on a kebab spit. Sweat is rolling down my back and the pressure from the heat is swelling my brain. Where the hell is my hat? Even Stecky is feeling the heat. He ties a small blue towel around his head as a bandana, and we crack on.

As we drive through the Outback, Stecky starts to open up. He talks with wonder about the array of venomous Australian snakes that await visitors, the rock strata, the shrubs and long sandy ridges that meander across the landscape towards the east of the country. Then we move on to his fishing, the organic broccoli he grows and how he has waited ten years to get a delivery of seeds from a particular passionflower.

'*Passiflora coccinea*. It's a bright crimson flower!' he says enthusiastically. 'I've been testing a few new plants out this year, but this is the one I've really been waiting for. It brightens the place up! The flower doesn't germinate and produce seed pods very often. It's taken that long.'

When I first met Stecky outside his house I thought there was a touch of Les Patterson, Barry Humphries' least-sophisticated comic Australian character, about him. Shame on me. Stecky is as enjoyable a travelling companion as I've had on any of these long journeys. I apologize for my initial slur. But it's not all my fault. While young folk from Down Under fill our cities, with at least 200,000 living in London alone, we are peddled a simplistic vision of Australia and Australians in films, TV and particularly advertising, which delights in making Aussies look like beer-swilling, misogynistic morons.

Much of what we think we know about Australia is a myth. Even much of what Australians think about their country is a myth. Take snakes. For visitors and locals alike, these much-maligned reptiles help define Australia as a dangerous and life-threatening country. Many Aussies relish the belief that swarms of deadly serpents are lurking out in the great interior waiting for the unwary. It fits with the national belief that the country isn't for wimps.

And yes, the definitive tome *Snakes of Western Australia* does have photographs of 76 venomous land snakes and 18 venomous sea snakes, including the (nasty) brown snake, the tiger snake, taipan and the helpfully titled death adder, which supposedly does what the name suggests. But snakes are shy, retiring creatures that often won't bite even if you tread on them. According to the Royal Flying Doctors, roughly 3,000 people are bitten each year in Oz. Between 200 to 500 lucky souls receive anti-venom and an average of just one or two die. Do you know how many Brits die annually from choking on their toothpaste? No, neither do I. But given that 12,000 Brits are taken to hospital each year after sustaining injuries while putting on socks, tights or stockings, I believe my point still stands.

Yes, I know this is a land with a ludicrous number of poisonous bugs, a caustic bush sap capable of inflicting second-degree burns, and a plant with seed-pod fur like deadly glass filaments. But you are not likely to encounter these. And hopefully neither will I. Australia is certainly hot, sunny, beautiful and welcoming. But a life-threatening country full of advertising clichés it surely is not.

I SCOUR my map as we drive. We are passing close to Mt Sheila and Mt Bruce. So much for no clichés. Aussies seem to lack a certain amount of imagination when it comes to names. The latter, far from being an insignificant tiddler, is the second-highest mountain in Western Australia. It is as if the naming committee had so much to do they just ran out of ideas. Calling another fine hill Mt Nameless shows little ingenuity, particularly when the local Yinhawangka Aboriginals had known it as Jardunmunha for thousands of years. And what about Mt Hopeless or Mt Unapproachable? Elsewhere, Mt Buggery sits next to Mt Disappointment, with both overlooking Horrible Gap and Terrible Hollow. I rest my case.

As luck would have it, our route to Newman, the mining boom-town, is taking us through Karijini National Park, the second-largest park in WA and an extraordinary world of mountains, rivers and deep red gorges. The route is close enough to justify a diversion to a new eco-lodge in the park. Wholly owned by the local Gumala Aboriginal Corporation, the lodge is seen as a shining example of cooperation between business and Aboriginals, although the staff I meet on the site are a curious mix of white Australians, Brits and even a Maltese.

Above ground in Karijini, the eye is caught by spinifex, clumps of spiky grass. Covering plains and low hills, it is a comical sight, like endless herds of fat, green hedgehogs. But the real draw here is the series of deep fissures below the surface, extraordinary chasms and gorges with steep, sheer sides lying beyond precipitous drops.

Rob Fullagar, a beefy young guide from the lodge, takes us down into Dales Gorge. On the surface the land is parched, empty of natural shade, and the temperature hovers around 40 degrees. I peer gingerly over the edge of the gorge into a scene from *The Lost World*. A hundred metres below me, nestling between great, iron-red canyon walls, trees shade a lazy stream tumbling slowly over rocks nature has cracked, with meticulous skill, along edges squarer than a mason could carve. Birdsong echoes along the cliffs.

The sun is on our necks as we climb down into the gorge. Each step seems to take us closer towards the time of creation. We drop quickly past the dawn of man, through the Cenozoic era to the Mesozoic, the time of dinosaurs, then down past the Paleozoic, back 2.5 billion years to the Paleoproterozoic era, when these rocks were laid down. It was a time before fossils, when cyanobacteria evolved and kindly pushed enough oxygen into the atmosphere to raise levels from less than 1 per cent to the current habitable level of 21 per cent.

At the bottom of the gorge there is a palpable drop in the heat. It is less like an oven and more like a pleasant sauna. We are close to the beginning of time, on a primordial seabed in a gorge carved as the waters receded.

I can see hundreds of ancient layers of iron ore in the rock, stacked like thick slices of bacon. Rob leads me through Eden, showing me lizards and huge red dragonflies, along marked tracks and past slender waterfalls towards a circular pool at the far end of the gorge.

It is quite the most beautiful natural pool I have ever seen, surrounded on three sides by high cliffs and fed by warm water leaching and pouring out of the rocks as natural showers. Led by Rob, we all slip into the cool water.

As we return, Rob pauses by huge house-sized rocks containing thick bands of a shiny material with a gun-metal hue: blue asbestos. In a previous industrial boom it was mined for sale around the world. Safe while embedded, industrial milling creates highly carcinogenic airborne fibres, and has ended thousands of lives. It riddles the gorges and rocks in this area.

Leaving Karijini, we head east, arriving at the remote Auski Roadhouse after a couple of hours. The road left leads towards an abandoned town called Wittenoom, sitting next to a site the West Australian government believes to be the most asbestos-contaminated area in the world. The road right leads to the town of Newman and a comfortable bed. We turn left. I hope it is the right choice.

Wittenoom is the site of the biggest industrial tragedy in Australian history, the country's Bhopal. Starting in the 1930s, thousands of miners spent decades hacking asbestos out of rocks in the Hammersley Range, hills of spellbinding beauty with gorges to rival those in the Karijini Park. Miners below ground laboured in shocking conditions while workers in the mill on the surface often needed arc lights to see through thick clouds of asbestos fibres and dust, even in the middle of the day. When the corporation behind the mine realized asbestos was starting to kill its workers it tried to ignore the evidence. The resulting tally of tortured deaths ranges from between 400 to several thousand, depending on which report you read. Fathers, brothers, sons and uncles all suffered endless torment as their bodies fought asbestosis and appalling cancers.

When the mine in the nearby gorge was producing thousands of tons of blue asbestos, Wittenoom was one of the biggest inland towns in Western Australia, with parks, tended lawns, a hotel, cinema, school, churches, hospital, even a race day. Then workers started dying, the extraordinary dangers of inhaling asbestos fibres became apparent, and most people fled. But piles of asbestos tailings were left abandoned around the mine. The government decided it should try to close the town and encourage remaining locals to move elsewhere. In the years since, public buildings have been torn down, utilities and services have all been cut or removed, residents have left and their houses have been destroyed. Maps advise passing drivers to close their windows. Just seven locals remain.

While the story of Wittenoom fascinates and appals me, none of us on the team has any particular desire to develop mesothelioma in 20 or 30 years' time by inhaling lungfuls of asbestos fibres. In proper BBC fashion, a lengthy risk assessment was conducted before we left London, but unlike Geiger counters for radiation, there is no handy gadget for measuring asbestos fibres in the air. We will head into the town, but we will not be taking any chances. No risky detour to the old mine for me, where evil blue asbestos sits in mounds and tailings. Disturb the dust, and you have a chance of getting a lungful. Even the town might not be safe. Officials believe tailings from the mine were used to build gardens and parks, and in place of sand to construct buildings. If the wind starts to blow we will turn tail and run.

I ask Stecky what people in Western Australia think of Wittenoom.

'They know it's hazardous, so people avoid it like the plague. Nobody stays there for very long.'

'Should we be going there?' I ask.

'As long as we don't stay long and we try not to breathe too much, we should be okay.'

We drive down a dirt road towards Wittenoom, the Hammersley Range on our left and a flat plain to our right, flashing past a small government sign warning that inhaling asbestos is not entirely conducive to long-term health. But there is no barrier, nothing physical in our path that could prevent or even discourage us from entering the town. And then, among the high grass on our left, a few single-storey blocks hove into view. Small suburban roads, cracked and pot-holed, lead off the main highway into what was once a cluster of neat homes. The homes that remain are now almost all either derelict or dilapidated. Most have vanished. There are hundreds of empty lots. We stop by one house and I wander over for a look. Three kangaroos leap out of the front garden and bounce off into the bush. Nature is fighting back, gradually retaking the town, one house at a time.

On the edge of town, a tad closer to Wittenoom Gorge and the mine, I meet Meg and Frank Timewell, two of the remaining seven residents. Frank is 72. His upper arms are thicker than my thighs and he has a grip-crushing handshake. Meg is 61, with bright eyes and a wholesome laugh. They are a tough Outback couple with steel for spines. They need to be strong. In the last couple of decades they have watched their town die around them. Their friends have gone. The church where they were married was destroyed last year. Their homely bungalow is stuffed with billycans and jerrycans and the tools survivalists would need to survive in the aftermath of a nuclear attack.

I ask Meg what services they have lost as the government tries to encourage them to leave.

'We don't get rubbish clearance, no road maintenance, no fire service, no police.'

'What about electricity?'

Meg laughs. 'Nah, the electricity has gone so we provide our own from generators. The post was just recently taken away from us. It's frustrating having to travel nearly 300 kilometres to pick up your mail.'

'So where's your nearest shop?' I ask.

'That'll be in Tom Price, that's a 460-kilometre round trip.'

'So how easy is it for you to survive out here?'

'It's easier than you might think,' says Meg.

'Even without the government providing your services?'

'Well, it's not very nice, but this is how we've lived all our lives. We've always lived bush, never lived in a city, never ever. We don't want to live in a town. It was hard initially, but after a couple of months you get used to it.'

'We've lost a lot,' says Frank, 'but the thing is, we've not lost our pride.'

'And you've not lost each other,' I say. 'But I still can't under-stand why you won't just leave the town.'

'This area is in our hearts,' says Meg. 'It's really hard to describe, but if I've got to go to Perth I don't like it at all and can't wait to get back. Once we cross back over the Tropic of Capricorn, suddenly we're home.'

'It's going to take more than the government to get me out of here,' says Frank.

'We're not going. The government will have to chain me up to get me out,' says Meg with utter defiance.

'We're not bloody going,' growls Frank slowly. 'Simple as that.'

But surely, I suggest, the town is contaminated and the government just wants you to leave for your own good. They burst out laughing.

Meg has heard the state wants to build a railway through Wittenoom Gorge to extract more iron ore from an undeveloped iron ore deposit in the Hammersley Range, which can be seen through her kitchen window, glowing in the sunlight. Whether this is true or not, in a country where property prices rival those of Tokyo, government offers of roughly £20,000 to buy their home are clearly derisory. If the state was really worried about the health threat to Meg, Frank and the remaining die-hards, and was really trying to get them out, it will need to add another zero to their settlement offer.

After a cup of tea, Frank and Meg take Brian and I on a quick tour of the town in her battered vintage Land Cruiser, pointing out empty lots once home to the local hotel, shops, post office and the pub Meg ran. After a cider or two, Frank could occasionally be found playing the harmonica or singing 'Danny Boy' from the top of one of the tables. His eyes sparkle at memories of the 'drink the pub dry' party they had before the building was pulled down. 'Now *that* was a weekend,' he says, nodding wistfully.

Frank's eyes stray from the road and Meg leans over to tug on the driving wheel of her car as we stray close to the kerb. 'Be careful with my baby,' she says, playfully slapping him on the leg. They are a devoted couple, utterly in love.

Back home, we sit outside on the porch and Frank takes out his teeth and starts to play a mouth organ. It is a haunting sound, but he cannot manage more than a few bars.

'It's my lungs,' he says. 'They're not so good anymore.'

I say nothing, but a shadow falls over our conversation. He passes me a stubby, a bottle of beer, and we put our feet up and watch a cloud ambling across the Hammersley hills. 'Look,' he says, 'how could we leave here when we have such an incredible view.' His eyes have a faraway look and he shakes his head in wonder. 'You should see how the mountains change colour through the year.'

I spend the afternoon with Meg and Frank and when it's time to go I feel sad to leave.

'You're such a lovely couple and so brimming with life. It upsets me to see you here in this town that has died around you. You'll be okay though, won't you?'

'Ah, we're fine, don't you worry about us,' says Frank. They share a look and giggle. 'We've got each other. We've got all that we need.'

They look at each other lovingly, and Meg strokes Frank's arm.

'I think Meg fancies Frank,' I say to both of them.

'Meg will always fancy Frank,' says Meg. And they give each other a quick squeeze.

We bid them farewell and head out of town towards the old mine. I presumed the government would have blocked access, but we pass no warning signs or barriers. The old tarmac has not been repaired and the surface is cracked and broken. Stretches of road are missing, and Stecky powers our four-wheel drive across rocks and pebbles. Suddenly I realize we are grinding rock against rock, and decide this is as far as I want to go.

We stop by the road and I look up the gorge towards the mine and then down at my feet. There are bands of asbestos shining in boulders all around us. In this form it is relatively benign. But when milled, or ground, perhaps even by tyres churning rock against rock, it can become airborne. Or so I've been told. What do I know? I'm not a geologist. The risk might be low, but the sun is setting and I feel I have seen enough.

As afternoon turns to dusk, we drive slowly back towards the Auski roadhouse. Kangaroos have a nasty habit of diving in front of cars, perhaps because they panic when they see the lights, or because they try to reach kids or family on the other side of the road when the noisy steel beasts come hurtling along. Scores of roo corpses line the roads. They are an upsetting sight. It is amazing kangaroos are not endangered.

N IGHT FINDS us an hour or so from Wittenoom, in simple rooms at Auski, a vital staging post for burly truck drivers in a country where distances are measured in light years. We watch regional television of such mind-numbing parochial awfulness that I pray for *EastEnders*, and eat fish and chips in the diner. Below the waist my clothes have taken on a muddy, dusty hue. Above, I have the appearance of a small child, my T-shirts marked by the sort of unidentifiable food stains that result from eating on bumpy roads.

While Anya and I wash our smalls in a sink, we are startled by a ferocious-looking eight-eyed spider beastie sitting quietly on the wall. Fight or flee? I take a snap on my digital camera and Stecky and staff identify a huntsman spider.

'It'll keep flies and mozzies out of your room,' Stecky tells me. 'Just let it be. It's fairly harmless.'

I don't like that word *fairly*. Anya and I wring out our clothes, keeping our four eyes on Huntsman while he watches us with eight.

Waves of nausea and gut stirrings wake me during the night. I creep to the toilet once, twice, then three times. It might be something I ate, but it might also be the sheer challenge of crossing Australia. I am coming to terms with the flies, but the stifling heat is crippling, and we have a long way to go. Even at 6 a.m. fingers of hot sun are creeping through the thick curtains in our room. By late morning the temperature climbs to 40 degress Celsius. We could not have chosen a worse time of year to be making this journey.

When my stomach finally calms enough for me to stray more than ten metres from a toilet, I wander over to the roadhouse to find a ride. Parked up in long straight lines on the huge lot outside are a dozen of the biggest trucks I have ever seen, giant engines towing three or even four trailers. These are the legendary road trains of the Outback. They make a standard articulated lorry look like a Reliant Robin.

Over breakfast I meet up with Graham Wilcox, driving a three-tanker truck back further south to his own roadhouse right on the Tropic of Capricorn. We have arranged that he will give me a lift, and we head out towards his gleaming white rig. It is a one-minute walk, but the sun is merciless. 'You're lucky the weather is so mild,' says Graham with a smile. 'It's not even up into the proper forties yet.'

From a distance Graham's rig stretches across the parking lot outside the Auski. Up close from the front the trailers seem to disappear into the distance. There is a heat haze around the last trailer. Graham asks me to take my shoes off as I climb into the front cab. Another stereotype bites the dust. No dirty truck, the inside is a vision of luxury that would put a Rolls Royce to shame, with walnut facia, brass trimmings and burgundy padded-leather the colour of the earth outside. 'Easier to keep clean,' jokes Graham. Mod cons include satellite phone, a fridge, DVD player, small cooker, and air conditioning throughout. The cab behind the front seats is larger than some city studio apartments, with two fold-down beds and crisp sheets. No toilet, unfortunately, so my troubled guts will need to behave. The train is 49.6 metres long, weighs 143 tons and is carried on 70 tyres, each costing around £350. Total cost: £500,000. Behind us today is 120,000 litres of fuel. We're at the front in the Prime Mover, which sounds and looks like something out of *Transformers*. Tugging all this along under the hood is a 550-horsepower Caterpillar motor. The whole thing is a beast.

We start rumbling along at a sedate speed. There is a power to the vehicle and a weight to the fuel behind that even expensive shock absorbers cannot disguise. This truck never lets you forget it is a train. And stopping is not just a matter of applying brakes.

'You have to be careful with the brakes because sometimes the friction can start a fire around the wheels,' says Graham, in a matter-of-fact, don't-worry-about-it sort of a way. 'Then you have to decide whether to blow it out with your speed, or stop and try to get an extinguisher on it.'

I try to digest this explosive Catch 22. The road train has a stopping distance of about one kilometre, by which time the fire could be spreading under the fuel. If Graham accelerates to let air put out the blaze it will take him even longer to stop if the fire does not die.

Graham warms to his theme. 'Yeah, then there's bush fires. As I was driving back from the coast yesterday there was a bit of a burn by the side of the road.' Graham, it transpires, had been forced to drive 120,000 litres of fuel through a blaze raging on both sides of the road. Didn't he see the flames in the distance, I ask.

'You have to make a judgement about stopping. Usually it's best to keep going. If you stop the train the fire could reach and surround you. And then you're really buggered.'

We power our way down the road towards Newman and the Tropic of Capricorn Roadhouse, or the Cappy, as Graham calls it. We are heading ever deeper into the centre of Australia.

We cross into the East Pilbara Shire, the largest council area in the world.

'Everything is huge out here,' says Graham, 'the size of the trucks, the length of the trains, the scale of the Outback.' He pauses. 'And the size of the salaries people are earning,' he adds with a wink. The resource boom is pushing salaries through the roof in this region. Truckers earn AUS$100–150,000 (£50–75,000) a year. A fantastic salary in a country where earnings are traditionally lower than in the UK or US. No wonder teachers and nurses are handing in their notice to join the boom working as truckers or miners.

Graham is doing better than most out of the boom, driving his truck, running the roadhouse with his wife, and investing in the shares of mining firms finding new deposits in the Outback. His business empire includes two road trains, two other fuel trucks and two roadhouses. Graham already has 24 staff and will soon need more. Hoteliers have asked if they can build scores of new rooms at his roadhouse to provide more accommodation for workers joining this modern gold rush. 'I think this boom has real legs,' he says. 'We're shipping to China at the moment. Next will be India. This is going to last.'

Graham tells me when the Gulf War started they did not hear about it in the roadhouse for four days. He thinks he is isolated. But I have a feeling he is right at the centre of world events. Like few in Europe or the US, people out here in this remote corner of Oz really have a sense of the new world order, a global economy driven by China, and perhaps one day India.

We drive to Newman, but Graham cannot pause on the incline as we pass the town. Stopping on a hill in this train is not an option. Another four Prime Movers would be needed to get us rolling again. We head 18 kilometres south of the town to his roadhouse for a fry-up.

I make it to Newman later in the day. The wind is blowing in from the Great Sandy Desert and it is damnably hot, passing 40 degrees.

Around the edges of the town, temporary housing is being brought in on the back of huge lorries to provide homes for workers drawn to this remote mining outpost. Camps of 'dongas', cabins the size of shipping containers, are springing up. House prices have rocketed. Even pubs have been converted into housing. *Australian pubs.* Sacrilege.

The reason lies under the ground: rich, bountiful supplies of iron ore that feed the furnaces in China and the great emerging economies. Estimates put the total reserves of ore in the Hammersley Range at more than 30 billion tons. A decade ago there were five mines around the region. Now there are nearly 20, with more projected to open.

Dawn the next morning finds us around the back of a BP petrol station in Newman waiting with a group of miners for a bus to the nearby Mt Whaleback iron ore mine. Time for the shift change. Next to me is Justin Edwards, a 26-year-old former recruitment consultant from Melbourne, built like a prop forward, who moved out here with his girlfriend to drive a 240-ton mine-dumper truck the size of a large house and secure a hefty rise in salary. Justin is chipper and lively at this ludicrous hour, but he is used to it, working weeks of alternate day and night shifts at the 24-hour mine in exchange for longer periods of rest. 'And better pay,' he tells me with a happy smile.

We shuffle on to the bus, packed with burly miners, and head into Whaleback. The production set-up here is very similar to the diamond mine I visited in Botswana just a few months ago. Vast quantities of dirt and rock are taken out of a giant hole in the ground, driven out of the pit and chucked through crushers. Except in Botswana the miners were after millions of pounds worth of sparkling stones, and here they are after millions of tons of iron ore.

Everything is on a colossal scale. The Whaleback pit, 6 kilometres long and 2 kilometres wide, is the largest of its type in the world. I stand on the rim and watch an explosion clear a new shelf of 300,000 tons of ore, a tiddler compared to the largest blasts at Whaleback, often around 1.3 million tons, enough to cause the planet to ripple in shock. But the force of this blast still pushes huge clouds of dust into the air. As it rises, the sun catches the different colours. It has a terrible beauty.

Soon Justin will be among the drivers gathering to shift the ore out of the pit. Sections offer ore rich enough to weld straight out of the ground, ore so dense a chunk hardly bigger than a football weighs more than me. BHP, the company behind Whaleback, earns around £2.5 million every day from this mine and has built a railway line to shift the ore to the coast and waiting ships. Their trains are the longest and heaviest in the world. I watch one being loaded. It is 1.2 kilometres long, with 200 carriages, each one holding 120 tons, pulled by five locomotives. There is a palpable sense of urgency in Newman, as if they are feeding a benevolent hungry giant who might rise at any moment and wander off. Which, of course, they are. If China finds another cheaper source of ore the boom will end.

Until then the men riding this boom work hard. After getting sweaty in the dust they gather with their mates, play poker, or down beers in Newman's few bars and taverns, still wearing their blue and orange overalls and heavy boots. These are not what you would call classy joints. One is run by a slab of a chap called Pidge, his name helpfully tattooed on the back of his head, perhaps for easy identification during a busy Happy Hour.

That night I join Justin and a dozen or so other workers outside their dongas on a Newman camping site for a barbecue. There is much ribald banter, as you might expect. These are blokes living in an excessively blokey atmosphere, and working in an almost exclusively blokey world. But their first thoughts, after admitting they are all here for the money, are not about beer or footie, but about the difficulties and damage working out in the mine is doing to their wives and relationships.

'It's hardest on our partners,' one hulking miner says gravely. 'But we pull together.'

Far from wives and lives, I expected *Lord of the Flies* behaviour from these guys. But barbecued grub and slabs of stubbies seem to encourage introspection and reflection. It becomes a back-slapping therapy session.

I am witnessing that most Australian of concepts: mateship. An uncomfortable social code for many new arrivals, burdened as they are with the frigid culture of colder lands, mateship involves manly men being overtly friendly in a way that elsewhere invites suspicion. The heat of Australia and the ongoing privations of the Outback have always fostered mateship. In this sort of climate and environment there is no choice. If you don't pull together you don't survive. So we all clink bottles, discuss their relationships, slap each other on the back, and then head off to our respective beds for an early night. They have another 5 a.m. start in the morning, heading back out to the mine to make their fortunes, while I will be heading east again. Next stop: the Northern Territory.

7 · NORTHERN TERRITORY

Alice Springs is our first stop in the vast Northern Territory. The town has a romantic image, eulogized by Nevil Shute in *A Town Like Alice*. Despite being the second-largest town in the Territory it is really a provincial place, a draw for Outback tourists and Australian eccentrics who take a fancy to life in the middle of nowhere.

Although small and isolated in the centre of Australia, close to the Tropic of Capricorn, Alice is rapidly becoming the world centre of the lucrative Aboriginal art market. In the 1970s a white teacher gave brushes and paints to elders at the settlement of Papunya, 240 kilometres north-west of Alice, and suggested they paint their 'Dreamtime' stories. Their extraordinary dot creations, vivid, rich and redolent with history and meaning, were the beginnings of an entire industry. Sotheby's Aboriginal art auctions generate more than £3 million a year, with about half the works heading overseas, while one work by the late Emily Kame Kngwarreye recently sold for the record sum of £450,000. Now some unscrupulous dealers bribe indigenous artists with grog (alcohol), drugs, even Viagra, to get them painting.

I wander around art galleries along the sunny main shopping street in Alice, almost all staffed and owned by whites, full of Aboriginal art selling for scores, hundreds and often thousands of pounds. Browsing for hours, I am hypnotized by paintings with exotic, unfamiliar swirls and shapes, all with clear purpose but hidden meanings. In the highly reputable Papunya Tula gallery, one of the few owned by Aboriginals, vibrant, colourful works sell for between £200 and £20,000. They are stunning, irresistible. Anya and I raid our savings to buy a canvas at the bottom of the price range.

Down an alley off the main street we stop to rest with our Capricorn souvenir at Bar Doppio Café, a wholesome hangout that plays Tracy Chapman on the stereo and serves the freshest juices and food in town. A scattering of women wear long flowing dresses with new-age jewellery. It is hippy heaven. I can overhear folks at the table next to us discussing how a friend had gone off the rails: '...but then he had an amazing drink overflowing with Tibetan herbs,' says a happy soul wearing a patchwork dwarf hat. She produces a bottle of pills from a rainbow-coloured string bag. This is surely the only café in town with a leaflet for the visit of His Eminence the Seventh Dzogchen Rinpoche in the toilets.

An elderly, barefoot Aboriginal woman shuffles in, hustling for change. She is broken, decrepit, with matted hair, a battered, puffy face and the thousand-yard stare of a person who has suffered endlessly. And she is old. My heart drops when I see the aged begging. It is the sign of a collapsing society. But even in here it is seen as normal. She passes unnoticed, waved politely from tables. She leaves with a few coins. Nothing is resolved, but the problem is transferred.

Alice is one of the main towns in a region home to some of the oldest Aboriginal communities in the country. Just off the main street, groups of Aboriginals sit quietly on a grassy knoll selling cheap paintings of debatable quality. Others simmer in drunken huddles, their voices occasionally rising as rows or fights explode with sudden force. Most white Australians seem to keep their distance, skirting them with a wide berth.

I know Australia's first people have been fighting a long, losing battle with the bottle for decades. But to find out more about Aboriginal life in the Northern Territory I visit the offices of an indigenous radio network, which broadcasts from Alice, and meet up with Floyd Doyle, a warm, friendly, mixed-race local Aboriginal journalist. A tall, burly bloke, with sparkling eyes and idle growth around the beginnings of a Mohican haircut, Floyd tells me almost all of the addled souls I have seen in the centre live in dilapidated houses in town camps on the outskirts of Alice. Originally established during a time when Australia practised policies similar to apartheid, the camps were stuffed with souls forbidden from living in the white centre unless they worked for a licensed employer. It was a despicable and effective way of keeping the town almost exclusively white.

It seems most of the 19 town camps are now in a desperate state. Over-crowding, alcoholism and unemployment have fostered extraordinary rates of violence and pushed the murder rate in Alice to ten times the national average. Alice Springs now holds the unenviable title of stabbing capital of the world.

The problems in the Alice town camps are replicated in other remote Aboriginal settlements across the Northern Territory. Since the 1970s huge tracts of Outback land have been returned to Aboriginals, who now own almost half of the land in the Northern Territory, and can use a permit system to exclude outsiders. Aboriginals have effectively been left to run their own communities, but this attempt at self-determination has often been a tragic failure. While some communities banned alcohol, kept children well nourished and raised school attendance figures, in others school attendance collapsed, violence became endemic, and kids became malnourished as parents spent their money on grog. Critics say the government watched from afar and twiddled thumbs as many communities stagnated or rotted due to inadequate funding, leadership, education and opportunities.

But now the snowballing effects of worsening conditions in Aboriginal communities, a new report on child abuse in Aboriginal settlements, and a general Aboriginal life crisis, have finally forced the government to take action. After years ignoring the country's first people, it has decided to take control of their lives.

I have arrived in the Northern Territory at a crucial moment in Aboriginal history. Amid much fanfare, the Prime Minister has created a powerful government taskforce, composed of the army, police, health and social services and headed by a major general, that is launching an unprecedented programme of 'intervention' in Aboriginal areas. The government plans to take back control of 70 communities, banning alcohol, introducing compulsory health checks and quarantining welfare payments, so perhaps 50 per cent of welfare money will be given in the form of food vouchers. The taskforce started work a few months ago, and has already started intervening in remote communities. Critics call it an invasion. Others think it is a one-shot chance to save Australia's Aboriginals.

LEARNING MORE is difficult, because outsiders must obtain permission or permits to visit most Aboriginal communities in the Northern Territory. But we have been granted access to the 200-strong settlement at Titjikala, south from Alice, and Floyd agrees to accompany us, translate, and generally act as an intermediary with people who often view outsiders with justified suspicion.

Leaving Alice early in the morning we drive for hours on unmade roads along the sandy fringes of the Simpson Desert, spotting wild camels and the occasional kangaroo hopping around dunes amid the stark, dry land. We power our way through sucking sand, and eventually arrive in a small settlement marked by abandoned cars, litter and run-down houses. We have timed our visit to coincide with the arrival of representatives from the new government taskforce, who are dropping by for a progress report. They land at a dusty airstrip in the bush and drive into the community. The group, full of mainly white medical, social, police and military professionals, meet a handful of Aboriginal leaders, but most locals have left the community for a sports festival hundreds of kilometres away, and the few who remain appear disinterested.

The taskforce leader, Major General Dave Chalmers, is wearing combat fatigues, which have unfortunate connotations of invasions. But he is a genuine, no-nonsense sort, who knows Australia's first people have been left behind. He talks with a degree of emotion, at least for an army officer, about an Aboriginal man who when told his grog was being stopped, asked with incredulity what he was supposed to drink. 'As if there was nothing else,' says the general, shaking his head in disbelief. I ask what's upset him the most since the taskforce started work and he mentions an abuse case in which a young lad was being sexually abused by a 15-year-old, who in turn had been abused when he was a child. 'The youngest lad will probably go on to be an abuser,' says the general. 'Three generations ruined.' When he says he wants to help, I think he means it.

But are the Australian government and people really willing to invest in their Aboriginal communities? The problem has been too easy to ignore for too long.

To my eyes this community is in a sorry state. I ask Floyd, who grew-up in the northern city of Darwin, for his opinion. He nods slowly, shrugs, then purses his lips. 'It's not too bad actually. This is pretty much what [Aboriginal] communities are like.' He senses my disappointment.

'Y'know mate, I think you might be applying your European mindset,' he says charitably. 'These people definitely need help, better health care, better education. But just because they don't live like the whites doesn't mean there's not happiness here. Out here it's all about family. You go to an old people's home in this country and there are no Aboriginals, because they're all at home, in their own beds, with their own families, being cared for, not farmed out to the state. It's a beautiful thing. It makes me feel proud that when I get to that age, I'll be looked after.'

Aboriginals still have enormous respect for the elderly and the concept of family in a way Europeans, so desperate for their own space, so obsessed with the cult of youth and so often dismissive of repositories of knowledge and life experience, will never fully understand. So how has the whole idea of intervention been received, I ask Floyd.

'A lot of people are happy some action is being taken,' he says. 'Police, yes they want; health, yes they want; education, yes they want because numeracy and literacy is very low. But two things Aboriginal people don't want to hand over is land because it's a bargaining chip with the government, and the right to have permits that keep people out of the community.'

'Aboriginal people fought hard to get those rights,' I say.

'Yep, particularly for land. And we know that under a lot of these communities there are lots of minerals: gold, oil, gas and uranium. And you can see China and India are after our resources at the moment. People here suspect the government wants to sell parts of the Northern Territory off to China for coal, and they're really scared about that.'

We pause outside one overcrowded home to watch a young man preparing an outdoor pit fire to slow-cook a metre-long goanna monitor lizard he has just caught out in the bush. 'That's good meat,' says Floyd. 'Tastes a bit like chicken.' The sense of community is everything. Meat from the goanna will be shared among his family and the extended clan in neighbouring houses. When the neighbours go hunting they'll share their catch. 'We look after each other,' confirms the hunter, a shy young man called Michael.

'Family is everything for us,' says Floyd as we hop back into his car. 'It's even more important for this desert mob. If my brother's telly stops working he'll come round and ask to watch or borrow mine. But if the same happens here they can just go round to their brother's house and take his television. No messing. Yeah, kinship rule's strong out here, mate.'

THE SIGHT that greets us over the horizon is familiar and comforting. We are approaching perhaps the single most recognizable natural feature of our planet, an icon used to celebrate, promote and market Australia in every territory of the world. With the view comes a sense of achievement, of attainment, of finally arriving at one of the greatest sights on Earth. It is a thrilling and evocative view. Uluru, better known to me by the European name of Ayers Rock, is arguably the largest sandstone monolith in the world, left exposed to the empty blue sky after all around it has weathered and eroded away.

From a distance Uluru is a frame-filler. As we drive closer it becomes strange and exotic. Giant walls of orangey-red rock soar

348 metres (1,142 feet) into the sky. It is 9.7 kilometres (six miles) around the base. The scale is almost unsettling. Drive around this oval rock and it pops into sight from unexpected angles, filling the rear-view mirror, reflecting off a wall of glass on the side of a viewing coach.

Of course the reality of this mass tourist site is a little different to the air-brushed postcard version. This is no longer a particularly remote place. Around 500,000 people visit each year. At the sunset viewing point they flock to watch the rock gently changing colour. Car parks are full of adventurous Americans, Europeans and Japanese who travel out here to the middle of the country to park in a line and stand in a line and click their cameras in unison. They take a few snaps of The Rock at sunrise and sunset, then trot back to a sterile resort complex to sit in air-conditioned restaurants.

We have travelled to the rock with Vince Forrester, a talented artist and Aboriginal elder, from Alice Springs, a five-hour drive away. Vince is middle-aged, mixed-race, with a long ponytail worn under a battered Akubra hat. He smokes like a trooper and has the pallor of a man who has enjoyed life. He reminds me of Keith Richards.

Before dawn the next day, Vince wakes us in our hotel for a sunrise trip to Uluru. We drive out towards the rock, passing signs that still refer to it by its European name.

'*Ayers?*' says Vince dismissively, with the dramatic intonation of a Pentecostal preacher. 'What's *Ayers* got to do with it? I've got Ayers on me bum, mmm-hmmm.'

We find an area of low hillside overlooking Uluru marked with metal stakes from which flutter incongruous pink ribbons. The stakes ring an area planned as a new £10 million sunrise viewing area for visitors. Local Aboriginals from a community called Mutitjulu, just a kilometre or two away, where Vince has strong connections, are disappointed they are not involved with the construction. They say their proposal to have a coffee stand in the area has been rejected. 'Two old guys got £200 for checking no sacred sites would be disturbed. That's all we'll get out of it,' says Vince bitterly.

We sit on the ground as our yellow sun rises from the bush behind us, flooding Uluru with light and scorching it with early morning heat. It is an earthy, spiritual sight. You would need a heart of stone to not feel connected to the ancients who have sat and wondered at this sight for thousands of years. Vince picks up some fine red sandy soil and lets it run through his thick fingers.

'We are not *from* this land, we *belong* to this land,' he says slowly, his voice rising and falling with the lilt of Martin Luther King. The hair on the back of my neck stands tall.

As the sun climbs we drive around the base. While the view from the car parks is instantly recognizable, trotted out thousands of times on book covers, postcards and tourist brochures, the rock up close is alien and surprising. The sides are vertical and smooth, with gravelly innards exposed where rockfalls have shorn giant boulders from the face. It looks like nothing I have ever seen anywhere. I feel like an ant looking at a giant sleeping elephant. My guidebook says this an insel-berg, the protruding head of a vast mountain of arkosic sandstone that extends miles below the surface, but my heart says it is something huge that has gently crashed to rest on the surface of our planet. See Uluru from its base and it feels like an interplanetary offering. Something that may one day wake and rumble to life.

We stop by a steep slope where visitors can clamber to the top of the rock, clinging to a simple guide rope for dear life. Dozens have died over the years falling from the rock. Trying to catch a flying hat seems to be a popular cause of accidents. Apparently one man tripped while racing down the rock when he mistakenly thought his tour bus was leaving, and fell to his death.

The local Pitjantjatjara and Yankunytjatjara Aboriginal people have signs imploring visitors not to climb their sacred rock, particularly if they are going to kill themselves, but middle-aged folk with thunderous thighs are heading upwards. They look as though they puff going upstairs. I cannot understand why anyone other than a semi-professional would risk the climb. For tumbling flesh, the surface of the rock is like a giant cheese grater.

'When they roll down they need to be *scraped* up, mmm-hmm,' says Vince. His gruesome emphasis makes me shudder.

With Brian, Anya and Louise, we take a walk around the base and Vince shows me shrubs and bushes on either side of the path that have been used for medicine and smoking pleasure for thousands of years. Plants and trees can treat arthritis, headaches, diarrhoea and much more. Surviving out here requires specialization and intimate knowledge of the terrain and wildlife. Aboriginals even know that a clear liquid squeezed out of the anus of a bush cockroach has antiseptic properties. *How* they discovered that, I can only imagine.

As we stroll, Vince tells me about Aboriginal Tjukurpa, 'creation law', which explains how the world was created and offers guidance on living in harmony with nature. For Aboriginals, Uluru is a holy place and the beating heart of a region where they have lived for more than 20,000 years. For Vince, every rocky crag of Uluru has a story, every boulder a tale. A giant gash in the base of the rock is weathered smooth with a back wall that curves like a huge crashing wave. Another gash is a women's sacred site, Mala Puta, the pouch of the female hare-wallaby. Rocks are ancestors turned to stone, and over there is the Blue-Tongued Lizard Man. We walk to Kantju Gorge, an ancient site where rainwater flows down a vertical rock face rising around our heads to form three sides of a square several hundred metres above. The scale and the age is thrilling and frightening.

Just as I am contemplating eternity at Kantju Gorge, several coachloads of tourists arrive. Vince is standing at the edge of the path, looking upwards with his hat tipped back.

A loud couple with two youngsters and a baby stop to ask him whether they would be safe climbing the rock with their tiny son early in the morning. The child is just a few months old. I think they are mad, but Vince responds politely. He mentions the heat, the two-hour climb up, the two-hour climb down, and the easy death that awaits the unwary. They take him seriously.

'Excuse me,' an Italian tourist then asks Vince with hesitant respect, 'but are you Aboriginal?'

'Yep,' says Vince with natural pride.

'Can I take your photograph?' Vince stands straight. Snap, snap.

Visitors here are desperate for interaction with Aboriginals. The tourists often have more respect for Australia's first people than white Australians do. Yet just a handful of workers from the indigenous community appear to be employed at the hotel resort near Uluru. The hotels are missing a trick.

We start walking back to the car and find ourselves behind another tourist couple. Suddenly Vince leaps a foot in the air, shoves me backwards and shouts. '*SNAKE!*'

On the path in front of us, a thick, deadly, camouflaged king brown is rearing its head. Vince's warning stopped the couple in front treading on the snapper, the third largest venomous snake in the world. As it slips away into the undergrowth it seems to turn its head to check if we are following. 'That's a vicious one,' says Vince, holding me back. 'I betcha that one would chase us if we moved towards it.' Suddenly I wonder if my scepticism about the dangers posed by Outback snakes was a tad misplaced. I check the ground with more respect.

VINCE HAS taken us around the base of Uluru and shown me this most other-worldly of rocks. The next day he suggests we meet him in Mutitjulu, the local Aboriginal community, home to the traditional owners of this land.

A meandering road runs around the base of the rock. On the opposite side of Uluru from the hotel complex, a side road leads away from the monolith. We pass three signs next to the road prohibiting entry to liquor and the unauthorized, and just a short distance down this side road we find a sight no tourist sees.

From a distance Mutitjulu is a small community of broad streets and ramshackle houses hidden from the ring road around Uluru by tall shrubs and bushes. But draw closer, and obvious features leap out. Quantities of rubbish are spread around liberally and an apparently limitless number of mangy dogs roam the streets. I drive our car down the main street, agog at the conditions. We have turned from the Developed World to the Devastated World.

In 1985 the people of Mutitjulu were given title deeds to 1,325 square kilometres around Uluru on the condition it was all leased back to the government for the benefit of the nation. It was an enlightened attempt to give Aboriginals symbolic control of this spiritual rock along with an annual rental income for inclusion of their land and their rock in the Uluru-Kata Tjuta National Park. So this should be a model

Aboriginal community, profiting from its ownership of Uluru and its sheer proximity to the rock.

But here in Mutitjulu things have gone badly wrong. The government claims the community has suffered from alcoholism, domestic violence, petrol-sniffing and child abuse. Rental money for Uluru became just another form of 'sit-down' money, the miserly welfare cheques thrown at Aboriginals – usually free of any reciprocal requirement to find work – that encourage those in remote communities, empty of employment, to do little but drink and fester. So houses in Mutitjulu are falling apart, gates hang open, there is rubbish and broken glass everywhere, along with rotting mattresses, car parts, bottles, cans, packets, bags, tins, bits of this, bits of that, much of it swept into piles like sand-drifts of crap. I am on the set of a post-apocalyptic movie. Living well away from the Uluru tour buses and the coaches, these are Australia's shadow people.

In search of Vince, I drive down a road sparkling with broken glass to the main community offices, painted the yellow, black and red of the Aboriginal flag. The offices, which look like a collection of wooden huts, are busy with elderly men asking about welfare payments and locals discussing what the government taskforce is planning. Everyone seems to have a complaint against officialdom. Norman, a small, friendly, wizened old man who spent 20 years teaching National Park staff how to manage the environment around Uluru, complains he was dismissed without a pension. Several community elders, who have extravagant ideas about hot-air balloon flights for visitors and laser light shows, are angry the management of the National Park are not allowing them to start a tourist business. It is hard to know the truth of their claims.

I cannot find Vince, so outside I take in the scene back on the main street. To one side of the offices is a clinic. Across the road a couple of trees and dilapidated shelters provide shade for groups of men and women escaping the 40-degree heat and scorching sunshine. At first they appear unfriendly, even sullen, and the mask slips slowly. There are yet more dogs. One couple in the community are said to have at least 70. Then I hear a scuffling at my feet. A small, scab-ridden puppy is gamely eating the contents of a used, rotting nappy.

It now seems hard to believe, but Aboriginals and tourists used to live next to each other around Uluru. The old Ayers Rock camp-ground, where baby Azaria Chamberlain was snatched by a dingo in 1980, resulting in an infamous court case, was just behind where the Mutitjulu community offices now stand.

Dorothea Randall, a busy, harassed, mixed-race Aboriginal woman who is running the local council, walks me over from her office to a group of derelict houses at the edge of the community. She blames their condition on inadequate government funding. These are properties just a few hundred metres from the base of Uluru. The rock dominates the view. These houses are sitting on one of the most valuable pieces of land on the planet, offering year-long views of this most lucrative of tourist sites. If they were rented to visitors these homes would be guaranteed year-round occupants. But no tourists come here, let alone stay here, and these houses are decrepit, vandal-ized and empty save for rubbish, flies, excrement and torn pages of magazine porn. One remaining door inside the first house bears the childish scrawl: 'Fuck this room'.

Vince appears and we take a longer walk around the community. I like Vince. He's a proud and generous man, and a doting husband and father. A good, spiritual soul. But at first he doesn't want to

Above: Western Australia – the extraordinary circular pool in Dales Gorge, inside Karijini National Park. The whole scene is straight out of a shampoo commercial. A dip in the refreshing waters is the perfect reward after a sweaty walk.

Right: Western Australia – a tight squeeze through rocks in a gorge in Karijini National Park.

Above: Western Australia – Frank Timewell, one of the remaining seven residents in the town of Wittenoom, which sits next to a site the West Australian government believes to be the most asbestos-contaminated area in the world.

Above: Northern Territory – Barbara Tjikatu, a senior elder from the Mutitjulu community next to Uluru, also known as Ayers Rock. Barbara says: 'If we go out and hunt kangaroo, we share it among us. But the government's not sharing money from Uluru. We're being discarded like the rubbish.'

Below: The icon of Australia's Northern Territory: Uluru, known to Europeans as Ayers Rock, is probably the largest sandstone monolith in the world. Giant walls of orangey-red rock soar 348 metres into the sky. Dozens of tourists have died while climbing it.

Left: Northern Territory – Uluru is an inselberg, the protruding head of a vast mountain of arkosic sandstone extending kilometres below the surface. From the base it feels like an interplanetary offering, something that may one day wake and rumble to life.

Left: Queensland – during Australia's worst drought students are still studying at the Australian Agricultural College in Longreach, an outpost of learning in the Outback.

Right: Queensland – Simon with Peter Batt, who farms cattle and sheep on 183,000 acres in the remote Outback. Peter's land has not had proper rain for seven years. The effects of the drought are causing misery across the Outback. Reservoirs are drying-up, revealing old towns cleared decades ago to make way for water. Milk and wine production, wheat, rapeseed, barley and cotton-lint harvests are collapsing. Farmers are selling their land for peanuts. About half of the stations around Peter are empty. People are giving up.

Left: Queensland – the extraordinary beauty of the Great Barrier Reef, the world's largest coral reef chain, stretching more than 2,000 metres along the Queensland coast, and part of a marine park occupying an area larger than Italy.

Above: Argentina – out on a hunt for wild honey with Roque Miranda from a Wichí community (right) and Petiso José, a lad from the village (left). Simon is wearing a natty bag over his head as protection against thousands of furious bees.

Right: One of the great engineering wonders of the modern world, the Itaipu hydroelectric dam in Brazil.

Below: The Iguaçu waterfalls in Brazil. The falls are taller and four times the width of Niagara.

Above: Chile – Rosa Ramos, the vice-president of the Atacama People's Council, at the extraordinary Tatio Geysers, the highest geothermal field in the world. Between 6 and 8 a.m. every morning on this flat patch of land, clouds of steamy water are pumped high into the cold mountain air by scores of geysers, ranging from bubbling tiddlers to giant infernal whoppers that roar like mini volcanoes.

Above: Argentina – John Palmer, an English anthropologist, and Roque Miranda, leader of a community of Wichí indigenous people at Hoktek T'oi, stand amid devastation. Loggers have been using two bulldozers to drag heavy chains through the forest. The Wichí have lived in the forests of northern Argentina for thousands of years, but now their community is under threat of extinction.

Chile: Tuyajcu, a beautiful mountain lake 4,000 metres above sea-level in the high Andes, the great spine of South America that also marks the border between Chile and Argentina.

Above: John Palmer, who has lived in northern Argentina for decades, studying the Wichí people and marrying into a community, with his wife Tojweya and boys Benedict and Terence – both an impossibly cute confection of Wichí and English blood.

Above: A graphic display in a museum in an old torture centre in Asunción, the Paraguayan capital. This was the same cell where Dr Joel Filártiga was extensively tortured. The former Stroessner regime employed torturers that conducted interrogations while victims were dumped in vats of excrement, and ordered opponents to be cut up with chainsaws to the accompaniment of the Paraguayan harp.

Above: Paraguay – a hunter with Margarita Mbywangi, the cacique, or chief, of a community of indigenous Aché in Kuetuvy village in the Mbaracayú forest. When Margarita was five-years-old her village was attacked by Paraguayans and razed to the ground. She was found hiding nearby and kidnapped, sold into slavery. Eventually she returned to her community to give them wisdom learnt from contact with the outside world and is now likely to be elected as a senator.

Below: Simon with children from the Aché community in the Mbaracayú forest. There can be few groups on the planet forced to adapt and change so quickly.

accept that Mutitjulu is in a terrible state. He complains that outsiders always focus on the rubbish and the dogs. I gently suggest this is hardly surprising, given that both are present in abnormally high quantities. And the litter crisis is even worse away from the main street. Burnt-out and abandoned cars sit on bricks.

'Of course it breaks my heart to see the place in this condition,' Vince finally concedes, touching his chest with a pained expression.

We walk past an Aboriginal woman sitting in the dust and dirt outside her house. Three filthy half-naked children are playing with bits of rubbish. She seems not to notice us, or them. A general listlessness pervades the atmosphere. I am overwhelmed and confused by the suffering here. Mutitjulu reminds me of badly run refugee camps, or the resettlement camps for the San on the edge of the Kalahari. But in some ways Mutitjulu is worse. Such conditions and suffering should not exist in one of the richest countries on Earth. It is a desperate situation.

Spontaneous conversations are not easy. This community, numbering around 250, is on a par with that of North Korea for insularity. I try to talk with two youngsters, aged perhaps eight and ten, who are playing ball and bouncing on abandoned mattresses at the back of the community. They are friendly, without an ounce of surliness. But their English is limited, an educational failure instantly condemning them to life on the margins in English-speaking Oz.

'It's terrible,' says Vince. 'I can read and write better than some youngsters here. Can you believe that? Surely each generation should improve on the last, shouldn't they? Here it's the other way around. Conditions are actually deteriorating.'

Local explanations for the problems and litter are confused or contradictory. The obvious historical target is the government. But the state has not fully abandoned this community, as shown by the clinic, a primary school, and a new police station staffed by five fine officers who really care about the community. Vince tells me that before the taskforce arrived and began taking control a few months ago the place was spotless. Yet much of this rubbish has the worn colouring of garbage left out under the sun for years. People here seem to have an aversion to sensible rubbish disposal bordering on the pathological. Everyone dumps litter on the ground. Surely this community has not spiralled into this dreadful state in a few months, or even a few years, but over decades?

In search of answers, I sit down under a tree on a bare patch of land in front of Uluru with Barbara Tjikatu and Judy Trigger, two senior elders from the community. Their clothes are tatty at the edges, they have worn faces and tired expressions. These women are the backbone of their community. In recent decades they have contended with unimaginable social challenges.

Through an interpreter, they tell me there has never been a serious issue with child abuse in this community, that it has all been blown out of proportion, and that they are sick of outsiders criticizing the way they live. Petrol-sniffing was cured by the community, they claim, even before the government introduction of non-sniffable fuel. 'We work as a family and we have strong culture here,' says Barbara.

At first I think they are blind to reality, but they do not deny there are problems. I ask them what they think has gone wrong in Mutitjulu, and they blame most of the issues on a lack of government funding.

'[The] difference with us is that what we have, we share,' says Barbara. 'If we go out and hunt kangaroo, we share it among us. But the government's not sharing money from Uluru. We're being discarded like the rubbish.' Then she finishes her cold soft drink and throws the can to one side. There is no irony in her action. It is just another bit of trash to add to the pile.

The issues here run deep. They cannot be solved with a quick apology, a group hug or a charity telethon. Aboriginals now live nearly two decades less than white Australians. Aboriginal infant mortality rates are double those of white Aussies. Aboriginals are roughly ten times more likely to be in jail and seven times as likely to be murdered. Indigenous domestic assault rates are eight to ten times those of white areas. Some remote communities have endured spiralling abuse, with children molested and raped. Reports suggest around 30 per cent of 13-year-old indigenous girls in the Northern Territory have sexually transmitted diseases, while the gonorrhoea rate among some indigenous children in Western Australia is said to be 186 times the rate among mainstream kids.

Make no mistake. This is a shame that stains Australia.

Why do Aboriginals suffer such appalling privations, such a disparity in living, such stunted, empty, violent lives? What is to blame? Who is to blame? How has this jolly, friendly, enlightened, lucky country managed to so fundamentally fail its first people?

AUSTRALIAN Aboriginals have the oldest continuous culture in the world. These are a people who probably arrived in Oz during the last ice age and have successfully passed the very essence of their civilization across the ages, so Aboriginals today in many parts of the country can still understand and forensically interpret the complex meaning of ancient rock and cave paintings thousands of years old. Extraordinary, eh?

Yet their very longevity and history makes their current tragedy all the greater, cursed as they are by the irony that most new arrivals in their land, since the time of transportation, have been people desperate to forget the past and start anew.

There is an amnesic disorder among immigrants who arrive in a new country after the battles have been fought and the blood of massacred locals has seeped into the earth; a disorder that can slowly poison a new nation. Whether it is European arrivals in the New World, or expats across every corner of the planet, the later arrivals too often ignore what happened before. They think they have clean hands. And so it is easy for modern Australians to deny their personal culpability for the ongoing suffering of the first people of this country.

Conquering lands has always been a messy business, but by the time Brits arrived off the coast of Oz 200 years ago there were certain lawyerly technicalities surrounding territorial occupation. The government in London side-stepped the legal issues by deciding that although Aboriginals were clearly resident in Australia they were Aboriginal, so they didn't count. So Britain could claim the land.

In the decades that followed, European settlers treated indigenous people as one group and first tried exterminating the locals and then, in the 1950s and 1960s, assimilation. Missionaries and the government encouraged and forced them to settle together in communities. But there is not one Aboriginal community in Australia. There are hundreds. They are not one collective but a commonwealth of nations with more than 700 language groups. At Wadeye, the largest indigenous community in the Northern Territory, the population of around 2,700 people is still divided into three ceremonial groups, seven tribes and 24 clans. And forcing them to live together inside communities has created intense social problems in a culture where ancient traditions mean it is still forbidden for sons and mother-in-laws to interact.

There are more deep wounds. Over the decades, vast farms appeared on traditional Aboriginal hunting grounds. Game vanished, slaughtered by farmers who did not like prey taking lambs or calves. Herded together on settlements, Aboriginals stripped the surrounding land until there was nothing wild left to eat. Food became a commodity bought with cash from whitefella shops, not hunted on long quests. Hunter-gatherers were stripped of their role. Over decades, Aboriginal men were emasculated. Then unlimited quantities of alcohol became available. Even when Aboriginals banned alcohol from their land, illicit 'grog-runners' used four-wheel drives with balloon tyres to smuggle beer across the Outback into remote communities, charging four or even ten times the normal price for a liquid that blots out the present and pushes the drinker into a spiral of suffering.

And the state? Until the 1960s Aboriginals in some parts of Australia did not even have parental rights over their children. The state effectively owned them. Until 1967 Aboriginals weren't even counted in the census. Australia has treated its indigenous people appallingly.

I go to see Bob Randall, one of the most senior Aboriginals in Mutitjulu. He's a storyteller, songwriter, and former Indigenous Person of the Year. He's also Dorothea Randall's father. As a child Bob was one of the 'stolen generation', taken from his parents and raised by the state. He has a wise face, like an Aboriginal wizard. We sit on plastic chairs outside his well-kept home and he patiently tries to explain what has gone wrong in Mutitjulu. According to Bob, and others I spoke with, the community was thriving 15, even 10 years ago. Locals worked in the schools and health clinic. But then there were government cutbacks. Funding in Mutitjulu and elsewhere was slowly eroded. People lost their jobs and became dependent on welfare cheques. They became idle and lazy. Ganja, petrol-sniffing and grog took minds. A rot set in.

But Aboriginals are not, of course, free of blame. Some of the underlying problems are their own cultural shame. Endemic spousal abuse by Aboriginals has been noted since the first arrival of Europeans, and insulation and isolation from mainstream society has not always helped. In some remote areas Aboriginal men have used an entry permit system to exclude outsiders and bully their communities, particularly women and young girls. Some elders have even used tribal law and tradition to justify rape. The Australian judiciary has made the situation worse. One Aboriginal elder recently claimed the 14-year-old he used for anal sex had been promised to him as his wife, and he was teaching the girl to obey him. He was sentenced to just one month in jail.

All the problems in Aboriginal communities have been compounded by a lack of sophisticated Aboriginal leadership, a lack of thoughtful Australian politicians, and a succession of governments throwing welfare cheques at communities as quick financial sops for deep-rooted problems. Yet the astonishing thing about Australia's indigenous crisis is that the numbers involved are comparatively small. There are a total of 460,000 Aboriginals. They make up just over two per cent of the 20 million population, compared to the six per cent who come from Asia or the Middle East. The government in Canberra now has a surplus running into billions of pounds. Why doesn't it, why *hasn't* it, used the money to lift indigenous communities out of penury? Instead the entire mess has been left to stew. For decades.

The modern legacy of all this history is dystopian communities and an institutionalized racism that sees much of the country treat Aboriginals with contempt. For all its sunny, 'lucky country' image, Australia has a confused relationship with its first people.

This is still a country where I hear a radio DJ using overtly racist language on the radio without censure or sacking, where normal folk write letters to the media calling for Aboriginals, 'feral creatures', to be shot. As I wander across the country, perfectly friendly, outwardly decent Aussies of all ages and classes openly make the sort of snide or racist comments about their national minority that have long been deemed unacceptable elsewhere. They denigrate what they should elevate. Other governments have adopted a policy of declaring their indigenous peoples 'national treasures'. It might go some way to restoring a sense of dignity to this tortured people.

Until then Aboriginals will remain the shadow people, living in communities on the outskirts of Australian country towns, wandering through shopping centres or sitting in listless groups under trees on sunny knolls. Australian whites offer cheery greetings to all and sundry. Even Poms. But when whites and blacks pass each other in the street, outside stores and on pavements, they invariably pass without even a glance. I am not the first outsider to notice they exist in separate dimensions.

Travelling across Australia, I have seen just two of Australia's first people working in jobs that involve interaction with the public, one as a steward on an internal airline and another in a restaurant at Uluru. And yet this is a surprisingly multicultural country. More than a third of people in Sydney were born in another country. Outside Aboriginal areas you will see more black African faces than indigenous ones. At a lonely roadhouse on my journey, 300 kilometres from anywhere, the staff were Africans and Chinese, all of them developing broad Aussie accents.

This apparent failure of Aboriginals to hold down normal jobs and integrate into mainstream Australian culture irks and perplexes many whites. Even strict Muslims have sought to adapt to Australian beach life by creating 'burqini's', natty two-piece outfits featuring a loose top, head covering and leggings that conform to Islamic dress codes for lifeguards like Mecca Laa Laa, who is rapidly becoming an Aussie icon. But the integraters are the new arrivals. Should Aboriginals dilute their souls to fit in with the whites?

The strength of my feelings on this whole issue surprises me. We Europeans like to think our colonial crimes are in the past, that our hands are clean. But in Australia the Aboriginals are still suffering under the rule of the whitefella, and I dislike the taint of association. It makes me angry with Australians for failing their Aboriginals. And yet I can see that Aboriginals must also take more responsibility for their own condition. On our second day in Mutitjulu, Norman, the elderly man I first met in the community council offices, takes Brian to see an old spear in a squalid house where he lives with his blind, disabled wife. The couple have been devastated by the murder of their daughter six months ago in Alice Springs. After her death, as tradition dictates, Norman and his wife left their house because the spirit of their daughter was still present. Norman also had to rid himself of his daughter's possessions. He asked park rangers to help remove her car, but he claims they would not help him. So he put a match to the car where it was parked. He *burnt* the car. In his front yard. Destroyed it.

White Australia cannot understand such waste and destruction. And nor do I. It is one thing to cleanse the possessions of a nomadic hunter-gatherer, quite another to torch steel and clothes in a settled community. Many societies, including European, have or had such traditions. Remember in Madagascar, how people would slaughter herds of zebu belonging to the dead? At least there everyone had a feast. But even in Madagascar, in remote parts of a country lacking much contact with the outside world, people now realize such profligate waste is self-destructive. Norman's Aboriginal traditions have stubbornly rejected such twenty-first-century updates.

Death seems to drive one of the thickest wedges between the indigenous community and the white mainstream. White Australians cannot understand why Norman burns the car, nor why they should employ an Aboriginal worker who will insist on leaving his job, sometimes for weeks on end, to attend the funeral of a distant 'cousin' in a remote part of the country. How can two such diametrically opposed cultures ever find common ground?

As we meet again on my final evening in Mutitjulu, Vince explains to me what white Australia still fails to understand. His wisdom can, perhaps, be distilled into a single sentence. Aboriginals are a proud and ancient people whose very refusal to integrate, to live like the rest of mainstream Australians, to keep their yards clean and tidy and take regular nine-to-five jobs, is both the self-harming behaviour of a traumatized people, and a final act of defiance and rebellion against the white state that has taken their land and destroyed their sense of purpose.

AFTER SPENDING several days around Mutitjulu and Uluru, it is time to drive the 280 miles north-east back to Alice Springs, from where we will be heading east to Queensland and the coast. We strike out at dawn one morning, and by 9 a.m. the temperature is up to

33 degrees Celsius and the road takes us through the broad, open, Capricorn savannah. At the very start of this journey in Africa I found this landscape excessively hot and barren. Now I am starting to love it, appreciating the warmth and relishing moments of green. As we drive I feel tension slipping away and I start to unwind. It is, quite honestly, an enormous relief to put the complex problems of Mutitjulu behind us.

But I cannot relax for long. Arriving back in Alice we discover an indigenous group has agreed to take us out in the Aboriginal camps that surround the town. So on our last evening in the Northern Territory, Brian and I go out on a Night Patrol around Alice with a local Aboriginal organisation, looking for drunks and trying to prevent violence among the indigenous community. We travel in a twin-cab Land Cruiser with a cage on the back with two benches and handcuffs on an overhead rail, visiting half a dozen of the 19 indigenous town camps that surround Alice, a legacy of Australia's apartheid past, a history the lucky country now tries to airbrush from memory. Apart from the police, few white folk visit here. For most people in Alice these camps are just sources of rumours and stratospheric crime figures.

The roughly 2,000 permanent Aboriginal residents in Alice have 1,000 relatives visiting from the Outback each year. But there are only 191 houses in all the camps, so each building holds a huge family. In a few areas strong families have created happy homes in well-kept houses, but several of the town camps, particularly those in wasteland outside the town limits, are as bad as Mutitjulu, full of rubbish, broken hopes and rotting houses. In some there are a dozen people in a room. Roslyn Forrester, the 35-year-old Aboriginal leader of the patrol team, a considered, thoughtful woman who lives in the Larapinta camp, admits overcrowding has long been a problem.

'For us our aunt is also our mother, our cousin our brother,' she says as we drive slowly through the camps. It is all about the clan. 'If someone from the family comes in from out bush they have to be allowed to stay.'

And nobody can ask them to leave, even if, as is often the case, tribal law has forced them to leave remote communities after a rape, drunken violence or abusive behaviour. A number of men in Alice town camps will be stabbed or speared for their crimes if they return to their Outback homes. It is a recipe for social disaster.

As the hours tick by and evening becomes night, we shift from patrolling to a taxi service, running intoxicated grandparents back to their camps from the centre of town. So much for the new dry laws. We pick up one woman who turns out to be the sister of the grand-mother of one of the patrol. Then we are stopped by the auntie of another patrolman.

'I'm going to drink!' she stands by the car shouting at us, already drunk. 'Ain't no boss tell me no. I'm gonna drink!' She is old, frag-ile and ravaged by booze. The two women go into the cage on the back of the patrol car and we cruise the streets looking for more passengers. A large shoeless woman in her early sixties with a shock of dishevelled bright hair, wild eyes and a bandage on her leg steps from a dark alley into the headlights. She flags down the patrol car and asks to be taken home. When she sees my white face in the front seat she squares up aggressively. 'I didn't kill my husband!' she shouts, entirely unprompted. 'It was an accident!' Apparently she stabbed her man a few years before and is now out on parole. She shouldn't be in the centre of town, let alone drinking.

We drive all our passengers back to the Aboriginal camps, now dark and empty of street lamps. Some are quiet and sleepy. In others moonlight illuminates groups of animated men. Our tyres crunch over broken glass and we drop the stabber at a home where about 20 people are gathered outside under the stars, half-asleep on beds around a small television. They live amid an almost biblical scene of destruction, as if a whirlwind has passed through, emptying the contents of the entire house. The stabber is shouting. She wants us to find her blanket. We refuse, she starts mouthing threats and abuse, and we scarper.

There are only a couple of thousand Aboriginals in Alice, but in 2006 the Night Patrol helped 5,474 people after 9,396 'encounters'. Night after night on these patrols, the same people have the same problems. They are burdened by alcoholism, ill health and psycho-logical problems. Mainstream society has let them drift too far from the shore.

As the night progresses, some passengers seem to be waiting for their booze cruise home. The four patrollers know the name of almost every Aboriginal in Alice. Caring as the crew are, I can't help thinking they risk reinforcing unsustainable welfare. These elderly folk realize they can get pissed in town and the patrol will then magic them home. The Night Patrol risks becoming a sticking plaster, help-ing with the symptoms of the underlying problems, but unable to offer a cure.

Yet when leadership emerges and funding is provided, the indige-nous community can do so much for itself. For more than a decade almost half the permanent Aboriginal population of Alice Springs have opted to receive welfare payments in the form of food vouchers to ensure money is not spent on grog. The vouchers can only be spent on food at one supermarket, 50 per cent owned by the local Aboriginal council.

As I stand chatting with Roslyn at the entrance to a camp, waiting for one of our drunk passengers to disembark, I aim a kick at an old can of lager by the side of the road. 'I think some in the government just hope we'll go to sleep one day as Aboriginals and wake up white,' Roslyn mutters, almost to herself. She snorts at the thought. Then she turns to me and adds, in a conciliatory tone: 'But I know somehow we're all going to have to learn to live together.'

Aboriginals refuse to live like white Australians, but they have not found an alternative path in the modern world. As individuals, humans can be endlessly adaptable, but as groups we can be slow to change. And even then groups don't change when they are told they should, but when they tell themselves they must. If lives are to be transformed, change must come from within Aboriginal communities.

While the current suffering of Aboriginals rivals few other groups around the world, they are not the only indigenous group suffering the death of their culture. On this journey I have already seen what has happened to the San in southern Africa, pushed from their traditional homes and hunting grounds and now languishing in hopeless resettlement camps. In both Botswana and in Australia many politicians just want the San and the Aboriginals to submit, and join mainstream society. It seems the death of the indigenous way of life, and their individual cultures, is the price of unity, of the emergence of a single global civilization and domination by Western international values. And it is a terrible price to pay.

8 · QUEENSLAND

WE TRAVEL east from Alice to Longreach, a Capricorn town at the heart of a huge cattle and sheep-farming region in western Queensland, flying a circuitous route via Melbourne on the south coast and Brisbane on the east. As a small propeller plane takes us the final leg across Queensland towards Longreach, the landscape below starts to change. Green slowly gives way to parched brown. Much of Australia is in the grip of an appalling drought.

Longreach is an archetypal Outback country town. It has a saddlery on the main street, along with an Outback outfitters, a live-stock agency and a hotel with an old-style Western front. A four-wheel drive pickup pulls up and a cowboy gets out. Well, he's wearing the gear, and his stock dog is tied up in the back. It looks like a town from the 50s. But along with pretty buildings in the centre of Longreach, including a beautiful railway station, a cosy post office that makes you want to send a letter, and a huge Masonic lodge, Longreach has a few other sights deserving of the trip.

A little way out of town a Qantas 747 is parked at the tiny country airport, a touch of incongruity that makes me think of those small American towns that distinguish themselves by displaying the world's largest rubber-band ball, or the largest collection of matchbooks. Apparently tourists who have flown all the way from Brisbane on a tiny propeller plane are then keen to wander around the spacious interior of a jumbo. At least there is a connection. Qantas (Queensland and Northern Territory Aerial Services) had its original headquarters out here in this small town.

But the real draw in Longreach is the Australian Stockman's Hall of Fame, a paean to the good old days of Outback life, when men were pioneers and sheep were scared. The museum has been a huge success, drawing coastal city-dwellers out here to rural Queensland thanks to Australia's continuing love affair with the Outback. City-folk still throw wistful glances at the world immortalized in 'Clancy of the Overflow', Banjo Patterson's wonderful poem about a shearer and cattle drover:

And he sees the vision splendid of the sunlit plain extended,
And at night the wondrous glory of the everlasting stars.

I wander around the museum for a perfectly pleasant couple of hours, awed by the fortitude of men and women who survived and thrived in this landscape before the arrival of the twin eureka inventions of air-conditioning and the four-wheel drive. Little did the first settlers know they were sitting atop the Great Artesian Basin. Our driest continent has the world's largest store of underground water, occupying a staggering 20 per cent of the land mass of Australia. Nature seems to love such irony.

But water under the surface is often no use to those above it. Much of the basin is still too deep to be pumped economically, and without water the first white settlers struggled, relying on seasonal rains and wells. Drought, according to one display in the museum, has always been a part of Outback life. Between 1895 and 1903 some 50 per cent of livestock perished due to drought. The current Big Dry, as locals are calling it, is much, much worse. In some areas around Longreach it has not rained for more than six years. This is probably the most serious Australian drought in more than 1,000 years. Around 70 per cent of the country is affected by the drought, including all of the major cities. Many scientists think the drought is caused by climate change, and that Australia is the first advanced, first-world nation to really experience environmental changes that one day may affect us all.

But what do the locals think? After overnighting at a motel, Anya, Brian, Louise and I pop round to the Australian Agricultural College in Longreach, an outpost of learning in the Outback, to meet Peter Scott, a gentle teacher with an intense love of the great outdoors. He wears the college uniform of Blundstone boots, blue jeans, a shirt and an Akubra broad-rimmed hat. When Peter was at school he'd work with his Uncle Laurie, driving cattle from the area around Brisbane to places like Longreach. 'I'd grab my swag [a cross between a sleeping bag and a tent] and off we'd go,' he says fondly. 'It was an amazing life.'

The life of a stockman has a powerful allure. Despite the drought, youngsters still come from across the country to learn the skills. At seven in the morning down in the cattle stalls I find three lads and four lasses, jackaroos and jillaroos in the Aussie parlance, already working hard, learning how to divide up meaty cattle and feed them into well-used holding pens for tattooing and branding.

Cows are pushed and shoved through a narrow barred corridor until they can be forced, one at a time, into a crate-like cage. I do not find it a pleasant sight. First the head is held tight, as if the animal is in the stocks, then a pole is cranked and the side of a cage closes, trapping the cow. Brands have been heating in a gas furnace and the students learn how to apply a mark. The sizzle of flesh makes each cow buck and scream. For such docile creatures cows can put up a surprising amount of fight when confronted with the pain of a red-hot poker. A smell of burning hair floats through the shed. After they are branded several cows are de-horned. A huge cigar-cutter is produced and the trapped cows have their horns chopped unsettlingly close to the skull. The animals writhe in pain and fear as blood spurts red on to the dust. I blanch. One of the students sees my face. 'Bit messy, eh?' she says.

When they've finished branding a dozen or so, we chat about the drought. One blonde 18-year-old student, her Akubra perched at a jaunty angle, tells me the Big Dry is hitting her parents, who run a farm, or station, particularly hard.

Yet the general feeling among the youngsters here is positive, even optimistic. Even if they are witnessing the first strikes of climate change, and the temperature is going up a few degrees, the jackaroos and jillaroos seem to think Aussies will adjust accordingly. 'The Australian farmer has always been adaptable,' confirms Peter Scott as we move rams into a shed for feeding. But I can see he is not completely convinced. 'A lot of people around here think this drought is part of nature's natural cycle, and new rains are round the corner. But yes, I personally think something *has* changed.'

I ask Peter what will happen to the farming industry if climate change bites. 'It's tough to farm in the Outback at the best of times,' he says. 'If global warming really does hit then we'll have to change the way we farm. We won't be able to farm these.' He waves his arm over a group of thirsty merino rams. 'Cattle will also become prohibitively expensive. Farming out here will become unsustainable.'

As we leave the college, Anya spots a sign for the Australian Meteorological Department. On the edge of the Longreach airfield, in a small building at the base of what looks like a stubby lighthouse, or something slightly more phallic, researcher Robin Paton is preparing to launch a weather balloon carrying a shiny aluminium capsule. Radar in the lighthouse will follow the capsule as it zips across the country.

'And that,' Robin, a grandmotherly soul with a kindly face, tells me, 'is how I measure wind speeds above us.' Her office is cool, calm and computerized, full of screens and sensing equipment. I stand well away as Robin takes wind readings and checks the weather patterns out here in central Queensland. Then I ask: does she think the drought is down to climate change?

'I'm at the coalface here, generating information for the head office to collate and study,' she pauses. 'But yes, I think it's global warming, and I think it's been happening for a while. I was here in the early nineties and even then elderly town residents were saying the weather was changing. They used to tell me how they had frost in winter in the old days and hosepipes would freeze. Well that *never* happens now.' She looks over her glasses at me to emphasize the point.

Robin tugs me towards a noticeboard displaying a laminated A4 sheet headed 'Climatological Extremes for Longreach Aero[drome] Using Data from 1949 to 2005'. The first set of figures it records lists the highest temperature for each month of the year, with data back to 1966. Not one record was set in the 60s or 70s, Most are from the 90s or this current decade. In fact, 2005 was the hottest year on record, with 2006 following close behind. Along Capricorn and the Equator, from African villages to South American cities, everywhere I have been travelling in the last few years, older folk say the weather is changing. Globally, nine of the ten warmest years have happened since 1989.

There is a popping sound from the computer. 'Excuse me,' Robin says, turning away, 'that means the weather balloon has just blown up.' She spots my look of concern. 'Don't worry, it's perfectly normal. It expands as it rises higher. Eventually that's what it does…'

she makes an exploding motion with her hands. She breaks off from chatting to deal with the balloon and file a live weather report for the local radio station, and I head off.

To get a sense of what life is like without rain, I want to visit a cattle farm. Robin had told us about an area to the south of Longreach hit hard by the drought. A few calls to a local journalist and a farmer support group helped to put us in touch with Donna and Peter Batt, who run a remote cattle station called Eldwick. Apparently their land is parched. Donna gives directions over a crackling line, and we plot a route on our map to a dot called Eldwick.

The next morning we drive for two and a half hours towards the settlement of Stonehenge along a narrow, single-lane tarmac road through an unremittingly barren, washed-out landscape. When a four-wheel drive approaches from the other direction, roughly every half hour, both vehicles leave the safety of tarmac and half-drive on the dirt.

'Where have you come from?' asks Brian politely.

He half turns his back, and puts his hand to his head, as if searching for the answer. He wrestles internally. 'I'm not really sure,' he says finally.

So we leave him to his journey, and continue with ours.

Stonehenge is deathly quiet. The settlement of a few houses, some parked cars and lorries and one solitary pub appears deserted. There is not a soul to be seen. It's almost creepy, like one of those movies where a predatory beastie has stalked and supped on the locals. Imagination works overtime in the Outback. We consider stopping but find the silence of the place unnerving, so we turn right by the pub, head over a cattle grid, and speed on towards Eldwick.

Another half hour on the road, and more than a couple of wrong turns, and we are finally on the right track. This landscape is as bare as any I have ever seen. It's as if the top rug of nature has been pulled away, leaving a dusty Martian surface. To increase the size of their grass pastures, farmers have used huge steel chains dragged between tractors to clear the land of trees and shrubs. So after years with no rain there is simply nothing left.

We stop by the unmade rutted track to feel the dry soil. A few lines of poetry by Dorothea Mackellar rumble around my head. 'I love a sunburnt country, a land of sweeping plains,' she wrote in 1904. But these plains aren't sunburnt. They're scorched. Farms have been reduced to dust bowls. The dreams of pioneers have evaporated and suicide rates have soared. Australian farmers, devastated by the drought, are killing themselves every few days. Then a willy-willy, a small, swirling tornado of dust, appears off to the left. It gathers pace, heads in my direction, and circles around our car, lightly covering us in dirt. What a bizarre experience. It seemed to aim for us. No wonder Aboriginals think a willy-willy is the soul of the dead.

We press on, coming to another lonely fence running up to the road, with another cattle grid ready to take the weight of the hire car. A sign poking out from the endless dust announces our arrival at Eldwick, an 80,000-acre station with cattle, sheep and the home of Donna and Peter. For the farm buildings take a left, for the homestead take the right. Another few miles, and across the empty plains a green oasis hoves into view.

Donna and Peter are in their mid-40s, somehow younger than I expected. They're worldly, lovely, fun, embarrassingly hospitable, and keen to explain the attraction of Outback life. But first I have a snoop around. Their attractive single-storey house has large, airy wooden rooms, with an almost colonial feel, backed by a huge – at least to my squashed urban eyes – range kitchen.

This is the proper Outback. The Never Never. A land of rugged shearers and drovers. Peter and Donna's nearest neighbour is 20 kilometres away. They own this station and a couple of other 'patches' of land totalling more than 180,000 acres. One of their neighbours farms 1.2 million acres. That's three times the size of London and nearly 30 times the size of Glasgow. Town is more than two and a half hours away and Donna hasn't been for six weeks. Groceries and fresh food are delivered twice a week, and left in their mail box ten kilometres down the road. But despite their apparent isolation, they are completely in touch with the outside world. A stack of recent *Economist* magazines have been well thumbed and a satellite provides them with a fast broadband connection. Just two days ago, Peter bought a truck at a live auction on the Internet.

'The net has changed our world,' says Peter. 'When we first came out here we didn't even have a phone. That was tough. Particularly with four young children.'

Outside, their house is surrounded by a modest garden, a moat of green grass and plants. But beyond their fence is the reality of the Big Dry. Mile after mile of dry, hot, arid soil. I stand on the verandah with Peter, looking out over the endless plain.

'It might be hard for you to believe,' says Peter, 'but when the rains come, all that out there is green. Beautiful green grass waving in the breeze. Like a sea. And then it dries out and goes a lovely yellow.' He goes to find some photographs to prove his point. One shows a luscious rainbow over a prairie. But the photos are at least a decade old.

We watch grey clouds skitting above our head.

'That looks like rain, doesn't it?' I ask Peter.

'Nah,' he says slowly, his eyes scanning the sky. 'Those clouds are just teasing us.'

Peter is out here every day. Often several times a day. Checking the clouds and hoping, praying for rain. 'It's been seven years now since we had good rain. I'm still hopeful. We're both optimistic. The rain has to come some time, doesn't it?'

They need a few good storms and a consistent drenching for life to take hold and the plain to become green. With water comes grass for their sheep and cattle. Feed for their business. I ask Peter whether he thinks the drought might be a sign of climate change.

'I really don't know,' he says with a sigh. 'I'm not convinced. I don't feel I've seen hard evidence. I think this could just be the natural course of life. There's been terrible droughts out here in the past. This is a hot, dry country. This is what happens, isn't it?' Peter needs reassurance that one day the Dry will end.

He pauses. I ask if he thinks about what might happen if the scientists are right.

'If it *is* climate change, all this will have to go. There's no way you can farm cattle and sheep out here without rain. It's simply not possible.'

And then the grey clouds begin to yield. A few drops. It seems unthinkable, but rain begins to fall. 'Can you believe that?!' I say excitedly. 'How long is it since you had a flurry like this?'

Peter laughs. It is the bitter laugh of a man whose endlessly malfunctioning car starts to run perfectly as soon as a mechanic is looking under the bonnet. Would you believe it, he seems to say. We've had no proper rain for seven years and then as soon as you turn up we get a shower. Unbelievable.

But the splattering, the best for eight months, is short and hardly dampens my T-shirt. It will take more than that to bring an end to the drought. The effects of the Big Dry are causing misery across the Outback. Reservoirs are drying up, revealing old towns cleared decades ago to make way for water. Milk and wine production, wheat, rapeseed, barley and cotton-lint harvests are collapsing. Farmers are selling their land for peanuts. About half of the stations around Donna and Peter are empty. People are giving up.

Australian wildlife is also taking a hammering. Camels are invading remote farms in their search for water and being killed by trains as they lick morning dew off the tracks. Kangaroos, which are thought to have halved in number, are hopping into towns to eat the municipal grass.

Nobody should doubt this is the future that, in some way, awaits us all. America and China are already dealing with their own droughts. The Horn of Africa is suffering a terrible period of dry weather, at the very least exacerbated by global warming.

Peter takes me and Brian out in his Land Cruiser to feed the cattle. With no grass for them to nibble, he needs to provide a supplement. Tara, his ageing stock dog, still excited and lively well into her twilight years, is perky on the back of the pickup. We load cottonseed meal on to the back of the car and drive off across the dust. Peter's land runs to the horizon in three directions and to the base of a range of low hills in the other. It is an extraordinary expanse of land.

'You need this much to have cattle, because the land here is bare at the best of times,' he says. But this is not the best of times. This is the worst of times. The dryness of this land is startling, unnerving. There is no moisture in the soil, no life growing above the ground. Before the drought nothing really troubled farmers out here. Eagles would take lambs, and Peter and Donna had problems with dingos a few years back. The dogs attacked their sheep, sometimes just chewing on their backsides and leaving the poor animals to suffer a horrible death. Sometimes the dingos just ate a single kidney from a sheep.

They would settle for those problems now. Rain levels on their land are equal to those of a desert. We drive for 15 minutes across the empty land, passing through a few fences that divide the land and separate cattle from sheep, until we spot a herd of 30 cows waiting expectantly for their grub. They dart backwards as we pull up, nervous and tense. Their full bodies surprise me. I was expecting skin and bones. Peter has sold cattle and rented space on the few neighbouring stations that have any dry grass to keep them fed. All at enormous cost. We dump the cottonseed into large plastic vats, and watch them graze.

Back at the house, Donna has been preparing dinner. She has invited neighbours over for a feed and a chat. One family drive 103 kilometres to get here. They are jolly, positive and optimistic. Jim, a tough old station owner, wags his finger as he tells me he's been doing some calculations. 'Them upstairs now owe me 40 inches of rain, and I'm relying on them, I'm *expecting* them to deliver.'

All of the remaining farmers sound like gamblers to me. They've bet their lives on arid pieces of land in the centre of Queensland, and now, after years of doing well, they just can't face the possibility they might not get enough rain in the future. They know all about China building two coal-fired power stations each week, and the vast forests that are being chopped on every continent. They just don't believe nature's payback is happening in Queensland.

'Why would it happen to us, out here, of all places?' queries Jim, taking a swig of rum.

'Well, why not?' I say.

He shrugs. Then he queries the rate of change.

'I just don't think things could change that quickly,' he tells me. 'I can see how cutting down all the trees will have an effect, but I don't think we'll see the consequences in my lifetime. These young 'uns will have to deal with it.' He points at his well-built sons on the other side of the table. And everyone laughs and sinks beers and Donna's delicious lasagna. Because the alternative is too awful for them to contemplate: if this *is* climate change, and no more rain is on the way, it will wipe out their farms and their lives.

WE CHAT until late and then rise early the next morning. I am on a farm, but no cockerels disturb my sleep, thanks to Kelly the killer stock dog. After attacking the chicks, she has been banished to the back of the farm buildings, where she sits forlornly.

Out here, farm work must start before the sun rises high and the temperature rockets. Peter has a plan to get me working as an apprentice jackaroo. Behind the house he has a corrugated iron shed the size of a small aircraft hangar packed with well-used cars, machinery, engines, bits of engines, and a few trail motorbikes. He fires up a junior one for me and I climb aboard. It is 5.30 a.m. I comprise one part hangover and several parts exhaustion. I haven't owned a motorbike for 15 years and I can't even remember how to change gear. After the briefest of recaps – one sentence, in fact – Peter is gunning his own bike, and we are racing out across his land. The mind sobers and clears at incredible speed when confronted with potential danger. Within 100 metres of the house my head feels as if it has just taken a dip in an icy Norwegian fjord. I am completely focused on self-preservation. Speed alone seems to keep me upright as I skitter and wobble along a gravel track and the back of the bike bucks and slides.

Dawn sun blazes the sky a deep, flaming red as we shoot across Peter's land, riding along an empty track through bare land for a good 15 minutes before turning right along an endless fence. Another ten minutes and we reach the most incongruous of sights. At a crossroads in the middle of bleak nowhere, a rusty steam engine holds a signpost to another 80,000-acre station Peter and Donna have bought from owners who have sold up so they could move to Tasmania. A sign pointing at the stomach of the steam engine, which once lived off coal and fire, indicates where mail and supplies can be left for the station owners. We ride on, past the empty station house, across three cattle grids and a couple of huge paddocks, until we finally spot a flock of 150 sheep. We pause for Peter to give instructions.

Peter wants to muster the flock and move them from one dead, dry field to the final grassy paddock on his land. This is the last remaining area of vegetation that sprung up after a brief flurry of rain eight months earlier.

The sheep are graciously compliant. I ride behind them and they move as a flock along the side of a fence. Peter gives me a thumbs-up from the other bike. With a turn of the throttle I am pushing along beside them, bouncing across the uneven ground. I outflank and outpace them to reach the gate to their final pasture and they pause, held against the side fence by Peter on his bike behind and me at the front. I swing the gate, hop back on the bike, gun the engine and swing the bike around to the side of them. It is enormous fun. With a gentle push and a holler, a couple of sheep at the front of the flock make a break for it through the open gate and the rest follow, pouring through like a wave and banking perfectly to the right towards dry grass. A beautiful sight.

The grass is parched and yellow, but it will provide the sheep with nourishment for a few months. And then?

'Well, if we haven't had rain by then, I'll have to get rid of them, sell them on,' says Peter. 'It's not ideal, but what can we do?' He shrugs his shoulders and chuckles.

It's impossible not to admire his resilience. Donna and Peter are two of the most pragmatic people I've met. I would be tearing my hair out. They are struggling out here and if the rains don't come the bank will come knocking. Yet they are still laughing and joking.

But consider the wider situation. Australia is already the most climatically difficult of the continents humans can call home. And the UN Intergovernmental Panel on Climate Change (IPCC) has warned that the annual flow into Australia's Murray-Darling river basin, an area the size of Spain and France combined, that provides 85 per cent of the water used for irrigation, will fall by up to 25 per cent in the next few decades. The future does not look good for Australian farmers.

The experience of Peter and Donna suggests the future isn't looking great for many of us. By 2050 there will be around nine billion of us on the planet. Feeding all of us will require a doubling of global food production. How can this be achieved when water scarcity is increasing, when 1.8 billion people will be living in countries suffering from severe water scarcity by 2025? The latest UN reports state clearly that by 2020 harvests could be halved in some countries.

There is an appalling irony to this Australian drought. In recent years Australians have been the world's worst emitters of greenhouse gas per head of population, thanks to their obsession with burning coal to generate electricity. The country emits almost as much greenhouse gas as Italy and France, which have three times the population. Yet few here seem to make the connection between Australia's role as both perpetrator and victim. Australia and the US were the only two industrialized nations that refused to ratify the 1997 Kyoto protocol (until new Prime Minister Kevin Rudd signed the document in December 2007).

This country has helped to cause climate change even as Donna and Peter suffer the consequences. As the Outback endures drought, the whole country still rides the resource boom, harvesting every mineral it can find at enormous expense to the environment.

At the start of this journey I wondered what evidence of climate change I would encounter along Capricorn. Looking for lessons in the Australian experience is not rewarding. If Aussies are anything to go by then our species will ignore the reality of climate change and our role in creating it even as we run ourselves over a cliff like lemmings. What fools we are. At least Australian politicians should be honest with the people. Tell them the Outback may well become virtually uninhabitable and impossible to farm, but at least the country can make money from human need and greed, flogging iron ore, coal and anything else that can be mined to the rest of the planet.

If I were an Outback farmer ravaged by drought I would sell my cattle and sheep and start prospecting for minerals on my country-sized land. However hot it gets, the climate lesson from Australia is that we'll all just turn our air conditioning up a notch and ignore reality even as the planet begins to boil.

DRIVING BACK towards Longreach takes nearly four hours due to a pause for an ice-cold beverage in the pub at Stonehenge. The lack of customers and the warmth of the staff suggest it is a charitable venture established to provide comfort on the dusty highways. After reaching Longreach I had planned to turn right and start driving east towards the coast during the late afternoon. But I'm exhausted. It is amazing how much one Englishman can smell after a few days in the Outback. I reek. We head to a motel and I shave and shower in delicious cool water.

The next day the Capricorn Highway takes us east. We drive for two hours through pretty 50s country towns, tidy towns (winner, 2000 and 2003) and past public exhibitions of garishly coloured farm machinery, and then see a sign telling us Rockhampton is still 578 kilometres ahead. Harumph.

We approach the Great Dividing Range and the landscape is gradually transformed by greenery and solid trees. Another 90 minutes and we are driving past fields of green crops, through Jericho, Alpha and into Emerald, a bustling town with a row of car washers (no shortage of water here) and a 25-metre-high recreation of one of Van Gogh's sunflower paintings. On a giant easel. No, really. Then on, through Blackwater, the coal capital of Queensland, emerging next to a railway line along which runs heavy trains pulling 40, 50, 60, even more than 100 wagons loaded with coal. They roll along slowly, probably because they need to avoid the next train in front of them. I count seven going towards the coast and seven heading back west completely empty. This area has 34 operational coal mines extracting more than 100 million tons of coal each year. It is Australia's single most important export commodity. Further evidence that Australia is making a fortune from the resource boom even as farmers just a few hours to the west of here are suffering an endless drought brought on by carbon emissions. Nobody is connecting the dots.

We overnight at a motel in the town of Rockhampton, just 40 kilometres from the coast, in a motel with bare rooms and a curious smell. Rockhampton on a Saturday night reminds me of Newcastle on New Year's Eve. Gangs of pissed-up girls roam the streets bellowing and belching, pursued by gangs of boys hoping to snare a stray. The next day, at a marina in Gladstone, just to the south of Capricorn, I finally reach the coast, run towards the sea, and get stuck in thick, gloopy mud. It is an unspectacular end to my crossing of mainland Australia, but my feet will touch one final bit of Oz before I follow Capricorn to South America. At Gladstone Airport we hop on to a chopper for a short flight out across the sea towards Heron Island, a tiny dot in the ocean and the last patch of Australia on Capricorn before Chile.

The chopper turns as we rise from the airport and head out east towards the tropical azure sea. This area of the coast seems packed with heavy industry. Just back from the sea, a huge power station provides the juice for an even larger aluminium smelter, one of the biggest in the world, while through my glass footwell I can see the water's edge and a coal-loading facility churning away. More than a dozen merchant ships are lined up neatly off the coast, patiently waiting to receive their load.

'Captain Cook passed this way a few years back, naming the headland to the left Cape Capricorn,' says Peter the pilot. We rise another 500 feet above Australia's east coast, providing a panoramic view as we race along the southern border of the tropics.

In front of me, along Capricorn, I can see shapes and circles forming on the horizon into distinct islands and cays. In the dim distance is one of the natural delights of the Tropics. The Great Barrier Reef is the world's largest coral reef chain, stretching more than 2,000 kilometres along the Queensland coast, part of a marine park occupying an area larger than Italy.

Below me I can see small patches of land growing out of the sea, all covered with lush greenery and surrounded by white sand. The sea is changing colour. Azure, aquamarine, even jade. The chopper ride is short, fast but intense. A real visual thrill. Heron Island shimmers into sight. It is pure, unadulterated tropical beauty. A tiny dot of an island made of coral perched right on the reef. But I am not coming here just because it is beautiful, although admittedly that helps. Heron Island is home to one of the worlds pre-eminent marine research centres, the biggest in Australia in terms of research and teaching output, and one of four global centres conducting a huge World Bank project on the effects of climate change in coral reefs. What a place to work. Close your eyes and imagine a tropical paradise. Here it is.

We drop closer to the island, preparing to land. In the seat to my right, Peter is requesting landing permission and checking wind speeds. I can see the heli-pad on the edge of the island next to a boat jetty. A dark shape juts out of the water, the rusty wreck of a once-powerful nineteenth-century gunboat cruiser. I can see other structures poking out between trees and palms on the island, a resort, the research centre and a few buildings for rangers protecting the national park. We drop out of the sky, settle snug on the ground next to a sign welcoming us to Capricornia Cay and I leap out and trot away from the spinning blades just like they do in the movies. It has all been very exhilarating.

We arrive on Sunday and have a late afternoon to explore before visiting the research centre in the morning. We check into the hotel, a fairly responsible attempt to put a resort for more than 200 guests on a remote tropical island. Buildings are kept below the treeline, drinking water is desalinated, liquid waste recycled for island plants and solid waste taken back to the mainland. I am full of gleeful expectation as Anya and I carry bags to our room. Will I trek full circle around the island? Snorkel on the reef? Stroll around admiring the 70,000 black noddy terns nesting, fishing and breeding around this coral cay? No, instead, I am ashamed to say, I fall asleep. Like an old buffer who has had too much excitement, I lie down for 40 winks and find myself struck by narcolepsy.

'Whooooooooooooah, whooooooooooah.'

Spooky sounds, the mournful cry of the muttonbird, one million of which nest in the Capricorn Bunker Group of islands, eventually wake me for dinner, but I am so late the waitress tells me with a cheery smile that the ovens have been switched off. Perhaps I would like a steak and kidney pie while watching the evening film, *Finding Nemo*? Not my most impressive day of Capricorn exploration.

I AM ON an island, well away from farms and their dreaded cockerels. But during the night the muttonbirds keep me awake with their haunting sounds. They are a choir of ghostly voices. Curiously, they don't make much mention of the birds in adverts for the island and many visitors find them a pest. I find them soothing. But I wish they'd let me sleep.

In the morning I rise, bleary-eyed, and finally set out to explore. Muttonbirds are nesting in the ground outside my room and all across the cay. They are adorably hopeless creatures, queuing up on inland runways to take off for a day's fishing, and then crash-landing on their return. There are birds everywhere, like nowhere I have ever been. I duck three times as noddies fly along pathways at head height towards their ragtag leafy nests, held together by sticky guano. Visitors are occasionally whacked by two-kilo birds. You have to keep your wits about you.

Down by the beach there are rays moving slowly along the shore. Shy reef sharks patrol in the shade. Wildlife on this island is up close and personal. Like wildlife in the Galapagos, birds and marine life here do not seem to mind close contact with humans. Heron Island is an area of just 42 acres. It has the heat, look and feel of the Maldives, but with more wildlife. And cheaper prices.

I walk around the island to the University of Queensland research centre, a collection of low-rise industrial buildings, to meet Dr Selina

Ward, lecturer, researcher and president of the Australian Coral Reef Society. Selina, as she insists on being called, is in her mid-40s, tanned, fresh, even bubbly, with the infectious love of her subject that marks out a fine teacher. She is the sort of academic who makes you want to study.

We gather snorkels, masks and flippers, nattering away as we walk the 100 metres to the beach and a rigid boat that will take us out to the Great Barrier Reef. I ask what Selina loves about her work. She tells me the reef is one of the most biologically diverse environments on the planet. Only rainforests rival coral reefs for their sheer wealth of species.

An immense natural structure that can be seen from space, the Great Barrier Reef is the largest and most diverse reef system in the world. A broken jigsaw of 2,900 individual coral reefs spreading for 2,300 kilometres along the east coast of Queensland, it includes 300 coral cays and 600 islands. The largest marine park in the world protects the reef, over an area of 344,400 square kilometres, from Cape York in the north to Bundaberg in the south, just below Capricorn.

We head out on the boat over aquamarine water and snorkel above a rainbow world of craggy coral, fissures and a swarm of exotic marine beauties, with serene angelfish, black and white humbugs and bright iridescent parrot fish all just metres from the beach. The reef is home to 1,500 species of fish, 360 species of coral and 17 species of sea snake. And around 8,000 species of unloved molluscs. There are thousands of different animal and plant species on Heron Reef alone.

The ability of most coral to build this reef is down, in no small part, to its close symbiotic relationship with zooxanthellae, microscopic single-celled organisms living in the tissue of the coral polyp. The zooxanthellae and the coral work together, with the coral providing the zooxanthellae with a home, nitrogen and phosphorus, and the zooxanthellae using sunlight to make oxygen and sugar from water and carbon dioxide, which the coral uses for food and respiration. The zooxanthellae in turn uses carbon dioxide, pumped out by the coral as a waste product, during photosynthesis. If only we could all live together in such perfect harmony. Feeding each other and eating our neighbours' waste.

Just as in the complex ecosystems I saw in southern Africa, everything fits together, with plants, corals, scavengers, coral predators and filter feeders all relying on each other for survival. Reefs cover just 0.3 per cent of the oceans, but support at least 25 per cent of all fish species. They are also shock absorbers, protecting millions around the world who live by the sea from the ravages of the oceans. But they are fragile, subject to the whims of our changing climate.

After an hour of enduring the marine life on the reef, we climb out of the water into the boat and I discover the backs of my legs have changed colour. Apart from a finger mark at the back of my left leg, where I remembered to apply a lonely streak of sun-cream, they have turned bright red. I quite liked it when they were a pasty white.

'Don't worry,' I tell Selina, who is giving me a sympathetic, that's-going-to-hurt look. 'It's traditional in my culture.'

The hot sun dries us within minutes and Selina takes me for a reef walk. She must have done this a thousand times, but she still has the excitement and curiosity of an undergraduate. Looking down plastic tubes like reverse periscopes takes us from the dry world above the waves into a watery world of extraordinary and exotic creatures.

A sea hare has delicate light green skin with chocolaty-brown swirls on its back. It looks like a huge snail that has lost its shell, the sort of creature that your brain tells you shouldn't really exist. It has the softest velvety skin of any creature I have ever touched.

Vacuuming their way along the bed are sea cucumbers, which

breathe through their anus and spew out a stream of sticky goo if threatened. If that doesn't work they can eviscerate themselves, chucking out their digestive systems as an offering to a pursuer. Still being chased? The cucumber can then eject its bright red respiratory system. As if it hasn't suffered enough bodily trauma, some varieties also let their kids develop in their colon, and then split their sides to release them.

As we move further from the shoreline, we pass patches of healthy brown coral. Then Selina shows me a patch of coral just below the water that has faded to an off-white eggshell colour. This bleaching of the coral occurs when the vital zooxanthellae separates from the coral. It is a huge threat to this pristine environment, and it is happening more frequently.

Before 1980 this sort of bleaching was limited to tiny amounts of coral. Then during the 1980s coral bleaching began affecting larger areas of reef. In a mass bleaching in 1998 more than 50 per cent of the Great Barrier Reef was affected and more than 15 per cent of the world's coral died. During early 2002 vast areas of coral again changed colour from healthy brown to deathly white. Sometimes coral will slowly recover. Often it dies.

Selina and other coral experts are sure the problem is caused by climate change. Coral can only exist in a certain temperature band. A comfort band, if you like. Too hot or too cold, and coral bleaches and usually dies. Australia has been enduring record-breaking heat in recent years, but climate change is also allowing cold weather from the Antarctic to flow further north to New South Wales and Queensland, causing water temperatures to plummet. Bleaching is now happening with greater frequency and greater intensity than ever before. It is a catastrophe for the reef and a disaster for the oceans. But it is also an indication to the rest of us, as if proof were still needed, that our planet is being transformed. The reef is like a canary in a coalmine. The bleaching is climate change happening right now.

To illustrate the fragility of this ecosystem, Selina snaps a short piece of coral. Back in her lab she attaches a pipe to an oxygen tank and uses the pressure to blast air and water at the coral, stripping the outer core of life from its surface. Within seconds the living coral tissue is gone, leaving the dead skeleton behind. Coral life clings to just the surface of coral. It is fantastically fragile, vulnerable to even subtle changes in temperature.

We walk through the research centre, along a wooden boardwalk and past dorms and accommodation huts, to a raised platform over-looking a building site. Concentration of carbon dioxide in the atmosphere is now 25 per cent higher than it is has been for more than a million years, and until a few months ago there were huge water tanks here measuring the effects of carbon dioxide on coral. The tank experiments could have helped us to understand how life around the planet will be affected by increasing carbon dioxide in our global environment. Unfortunately the building site in the back-ground is the aftermath of a fire at the research centre a few months back that saw much of the centre, water tanks and experiments burnt to the ground. They are rebuilding, but it is taking time to get all their experiments started again. I can only hope they move quickly. We need accurate information about our changing world.

Before the Industrial Revolution there were 280 carbon dioxide particles per million (ppm) in our environment. The station had one tank containing 380 ppm, which is the current level, and another containing 560 ppm, which is at the very bottom end of projected future ppm for the year 2100, as predicted by the IPCC Special Report on Emissions Scenarios, which estimates a range from 541 right up to 970 ppm.

As carbon increases in the atmosphere, so it increases the acidity of the oceans. Acidity levels in surface water, where most marine life thrives, are now known to have risen by 30 per cent. This is probably the most significant change in the chemistry of our seas for 20 million years. That's worth repeating. For 20 *million* years. Put simply, rising atmospheric carbon levels raise ocean acidity levels, which in turn makes it harder for creatures such as plankton, on which almost all other marine life ultimately depends, to survive.

'We hadn't finished our experiments, but it was clear life didn't like the increased carbon dioxide,' says Selina drolly, with a smile that indicates massive understatement. Playing God with ecosystems has unforeseen consequences, as I have already seen in the national parks and game reserves in southern Africa. But for humans to alter the ecosystem of the oceans will have incalculable consequences for all life on earth.

Selina and I take another walk along the beach on the north side of the island and she shows me more incredible marine life just centimetres from the shore. There are cowtail rays resting in the water, 10, 20, 30 of them, all lined up facing the vanishing sun. A loggerhead turtle swims past, poking its head out of the water. Soon it will be time for hundreds of loggerhead and green turtles to start nesting on the island, travelling enormous distances from nearby feeding grounds in south-east Queensland or as far away as Indonesia and New Caledonia.

They are not the only long-distance travellers who make it to Heron Island. Apart from the 30,000 human visitors who come from around the world each year, pods of whales pass Heron Island travelling between feeding grounds in the Antarctic and the warmer waters of eastern Oz. Intercontinental bird visitors also make regular appearances, with seven species of migratory wading birds travelling from as far, in the case of the delicate Pacific golden plover, as eastern Siberia and western Alaska, and northern Europe and north-east Siberia for the long-beaked Whimbrel. Despite its diminuitive size, Heron Island packs in the sights.

'In your heart,' I ask Selina, 'do you think this reef is going to survive?' She looks at me and considers the question for just a moment, then puts her head on one side.

'I want to believe that humans can change and cut their emissions.' She pauses again. 'But I'm not sure we'll be able to move fast enough.' The UN IPCC report of 2007 predicts catastrophic damage to the Great Barrier Reef. So are we going to lose it?

'Well,' says Selina carefully, 'I'm pessimistic about the future.'

Across the water dark clouds are gathering over the Great Barrier Reef. Selina glances at her watch.

'Sorry,' she says. 'I have to dash. I've got a class to teach in ten minutes.'

We say warm farewells and she jogs off down the beach, leaving me to settle down on the white coral sand and watch the rays in the water.

And then it hits me. I started this leg of my journey thinking the Capricorn areas of Australia are so remote they would be among the most isolated of the entire line. But in fact Australia is economically linked to the outside world, thanks to China's demand for resources, it is joined – virtually – thanks to the new wonders of the Internet, and as the industrialized nation most sensitive to climate change, Australia and Australians are clearly in the same environmental boat as the rest of us. As climate change worsens, more of us will suffer the way some Aussies are already. Australians often feel cut off from the world. But in actual fact they are completely connected.

I finish my journey across Australia by the sea right next to Capricorn. It is dusk and lightning strikes fork through the sky. I raise my head to the heavens and light rain washes over my face.

MOUNTAINS TO METROPOLIS

9 · CHILE

I AM SITTING on a railway sleeper at an old Western-style railway station called Prat on the edge of a barren desert a few kilometres inland from the coast of Chile. A ferocious, dusty wind is blowing, and a corrosive smell floats in the air from hundreds of tons of sulphuric acid (*acido sulfurico*) leeching from 40 freight cars just 20 metres away. The cars are waiting for three diesel engines and a driver to take them across the Tropic of Capricorn and towards vast copper mines in the Chilean wastelands.

Around the station the land is barren and empty, with fine dust the colour of Horlicks and not a blade of grass breaking the monotony. It is a greyer version of the Batt's farm in Queensland. But there the drought is new; here it has been this way for centuries. I am on the edge of the Atacama Desert, the most sterile patch of land on the planet, which stretches for 1,000 kilometres from the south of Peru into the north of Chile. Swathes of the desert are said to have had no rain for hundreds of years.

This is the beginning of the final leg of my Capricorn adventure, a journey through a slice of Chile, the northern tip of Argentina, then Paraguay and Brazil, where – barring disasters – the entire escapade will end on the Atlantic coast just before Christmas. Sitting next to me under the creaking Prat sign is Constanza Mujica, a sharp, focused

30-year-old university lecturer from Chile who will guide me across her country. She has already performed a classic piece of 'fixing', arranging with the FCAB railway line for us to travel along their freight line as we head inland into the Atacama Desert and east across this narrow country, a bizarrely thin strip of a land averaging 180 kilometres wide, but running 4,000 kilometres from north to south. The distance from Norway to Nigeria, as my guidebook helpfully points out.

But back to the start of this trip. I reached Prat station after a long flight to Santiago, the Chilean capital, and another flight north to the coastal town of Antofagasta. Brian has reoccupied his position behind the camera, and travelling with us on this leg are director Dominic Ozanne and assistant producer Fiona Cleary, who speaks fluent Spanish. We started the journey where Capricorn hits the Chilean coast, on a small promontory looking out across the Pacific. Incredible to think I had just been thousands of miles across the ocean in Australia.

First stop after the coast was a Capricorn monument in sight of the sea. Constanza had arranged for me to meet Jorge Ianiszewski, a writer on astronomy who provided the measurements for an enormous arched structure that marks the line and also acts as a solar observatory. Jorge, an excitable sort, leapt around the monument as he explained how the sun would throw a shadow below the arch during the time of the solstice, when the sun would appear to be directly overhead.

'The solstice is coming!' he said. 'On 22 December! Just over four weeks from now, and the solstice will be upon us. You must stay here until then. We will be having a big party.'

'Well, that would be lovely,' I replied, 'but unfortunately we still have a long way to go.'

I had already decided to cross South America and arrive on the east coast of Brazil just in time for the solstice. It should be a splendid end to our journey around Capricorn. Just so long as we can cross the Atacama Desert, the Andes Mountains, which mark the eastern edge of the Atacama, and whatever other obstacles South America decides to throw our way.

Visiting Jorge's monument, the most impressive on Capricorn, was a chance to blind a fellow Tropic enthusiast with a few nerdy facts. In my quest for Capricorn information, Mick Ashworth and Kenny Gibson from the peerless tome *The Times Comprehensive Atlas of the World* had patiently explained to me that over an eon the Tropic of Capricorn crawls around in a band between roughly 22.5 and 24.5 degrees. According to Mick and Kenny's calculations, in the year 2000 the line was at 23° 26' 21.448". By 19 November 2007 it had moved to 23° 26' 17.76". Because it moves by tiny amounts, the precise length also varies. On 19 November 2007, Capricorn was 36,748,889.697 metres long: 36,749 kilometres. Jorge agreed: it is quite a distance.

'But doesn't the fact the line moves make static Capricorn monuments a little redundant?' Constanza asked diplomatically as we left Jorge and his monument.

I laughed. 'Yes. Probably over long periods. But it only really moves an insignificant distance each year.'

Jorge's monument lies just beyond the outskirts of Antofagasta, a coastal town founded by a Brit on slopes between low hills and the sea. The town appeared to be a permanent building site, with endless traffic jams to match. Cars and trucks thundered through the streets, fresh from mines in the region.

'This town looks like a mining town,' I said to Constanza.

'This *country* is a copper and mining country,' she countered, smiling broadly. 'You know, nearly 40 per cent of all our exports re copper. Everyone in Chile knows copper is vital to all of us.'

Yet again, new China is having an enormous impact on Capricorn. Prices for copper have soared in recent years, thanks to demand from the superpower. Chilean mines are working at full capacity and money is pouring into the national coffers from the state-owned mining company.

Which is why I find myself just outside Antofagasta, sitting on a railway sleeper at Prat Station, waiting for a copper freight train to take me into the Atacama. The FCAB line shunts huge quantities of supplies towards great copper mines close to Capricorn in the Atacama, and then takes the raw materials back out towards the coast. After visiting diamond, gem and iron ore mines on each previous leg of my Capricorn journey, I'm all mined-out. So no visit to the copper mines for me. But who could refuse a ride along Capricorn on a huge mining train? As we wait for the train to be readied, Constanza and I glance at a local paper. The front page has an arrow pointing up the page to show the direction of copper prices.

'We've all become *obsessed* with the price of copper,' says Constanza with more than a trace of regret. 'All they seem to talk about on the news is copper prices and business. And since we signed a trade agreement with China last year, every Chilean businessman or farmer dreams of selling just one apple, or one *any*thing, to every Chinese guy.'

I smile. I've heard this before on Capricorn. The prospect of one billion new Chinese customers seems to be getting everyone excited.

Constanza sighs. 'We Chileans are changing. People used to say we are the British of South America, because we like order, and we like things to be neat and tidy. And we have a long democratic tradition...'

'...despite the ups and downs of the occasional military dictatorship,' I interrupt.

'Yes, but apart from that we're a very stable country, with low corruption. But now we've become obsessed with business. If we're not careful we'll become like the Argentineans.'

'What's wrong with the Argentineans?' I query, slightly bemused.

'Surely you know everyone in South America hates the Argentineans?'

I shake my head meekly, having missed the subtle nuances of interstate relationships on the continent. Everyone hates the Argentineans?

'Well, they're so proud and haughty, and they walk around thinking they are the best in the world. And now many Chileans are walking around like that. And that's not how it used to be. Perhaps we've become a little bit more arrogant and selfish. Perhaps that's the price we must pay for economic success.'

Just as that thought settles, the station controller announces it is time to leave. An endless procession has been assembled, comprising dozens of full tanker cars of sulphuric acid, empty flat cars and railway trucks. The whole convoy is 800 metres long. As we inch our way out of the station, Constanza and I are travelling at the front of three locomotives, a powerful monster crewed by a driver with a square jaw and muscular frame that have earnt him the nickname Mr Incredible. The train rumbles along slowly through a parched landscape, dragging its weighty load, and Mr Incredible tells us about the perks of crawling through the desert.

'There is so much beauty out here,' he says. 'The most extraordinary sunrises and sunsets are in the desert. You see the land changing colour as the sun emerges or falls. Sometimes the beauty is such I hear music in my ears and feel I am watching the very dawn of creation.'

'Chileans are poets,' I say to Constanza with a smile.

'Yes,' she laughs. 'Well, we do have two Nobel prize-winners for literature!'

The tracks take us alongside the Pan American Highway and we chug along next to articulated lorries carrying fuel, metal and lead, tootling horns at each other and waving out of windows, over low hills and round bends until we see a green flash by the roadside. Four ordinary, lush trees, absurdly inappropriate in this desiccated land, mark the presence of a roadside café just a few hundred metres from Capricorn. The line itself is marked by boulders at the roadside. Mr Incredible has passed this way countless times but today we shake hands and celebrate the crossing.

Just past the line, we hop off the train at a remote, prearranged spot where Constanza has positioned two drivers and two hired four-wheel drives. We greet, shake hands, load bags and head east, turning off the busy Pan American Highway and taking quieter roads, greasy strips of black tarmac, through the dusty edge of the Atacama Desert in the direction of the town of San Pedro de Atacama, where we plan to spend the next few nights.

Without hundreds of tons of sulphuric acid behind us, we barrel along at speed, only occasionally getting stuck behind huge trucks carrying spare parts, enormous new tyres and then finally colossal buckets for dumper trucks that work the desert mines. I have found huge mines along Capricorn on each leg of this journey, but Capricorn is not uniquely blessed with underground mineral treasures. Nature laid down the riches hundreds of millions of years ago, and over time the great land masses shifted and moved, spreading treasure around the world. But because so much of Capricorn is empty land, it is infinitely easier to mine and extract along the line than in the sweltering jungles of the central tropics, or the busy over-populated areas of the temperate zone, much of which was quarried for riches many centuries ago.

We overtake more trucks on the road, then we reach a summit at 1,000 metres. A mountain in Britain, but just a hill on the edge of the Andes. At the top I imagine I can feel the first effects of our elevation in my throbbing head. I have been badly affected by altitude sickness in the past and I am nervous about our route east over the Andes. Altitude sickness can affect anyone, young, old, fit, slovenly. Our journey across the Andes is asking for trouble, as we take our fragile human bodies nearly 5,000 metres above sea level, more than half the way up Everest. Some can adapt to such an alien environment by rising slowly from low to high altitude. But not all. If susceptible, headaches and nausea usually come first, followed by vomiting. Above 4,000 metres there is the very real danger of a pulmonary oedema, normally spotted when a victim starts coughing up white fluid from the lungs, and then possibly even death. I am susceptible to altitude sickness, and the likelihood of someone in our group suffering serious symptoms is about 1 in 5. So we must be careful. The only reliable treatment is to descend, but in Antofagasta I also bought supplies of a drug that can help with acclimatisation. Side effects are tingling in the fingers, a warping of the taste buds, and a constant need to pee. No wonder locals call them piss pills.

I reach for my pack of tablets, down the first, then spend a few moments indulging in altitude hypochondria, before we are over the hill and my fears are replaced by wonder as the vastness of the Atacama really opens before us for the first time. We stop to soak up the view. The Atacama sits on an ocean of land between the Pacific and the peaks of the Andes, the great spine of South America that also marks the border between Chile and Argentina. It is not a desert of golden sands, but a barren land of rock and gravel, a landscape that soaks solar rays and glows pink, orange and red as the sun rises and sets in the heavens above.

Air in the Atacama is nearly always dry and cool, its moisture having been lost as the wind passes over the great land mass of South America. It is dry here, impossibly dry, with some areas receiving just 2 per cent of the moisture in the Sahara or California's Death Valley. So dry and alien Constanza tells me NASA uses the Atacama as a double for the Moon and Mars when engineers are testing equipment and machines.

Rumbling into the town of San Pedro at seven in the evening, the low sun is casting long shadows down dusty streets lined with small adobe buildings. Our cars nose down back streets as we hunt for a hostel with spare rooms. Down a narrow alley, a small Atacameño woman takes us to simple rooms made of mud and cheap pine.

We wake early the next morning, our slumber brought to an abrupt halt by a lonely old dog that barks with the determination of a zealous cockerel, and we head out to explore the town. We are in the desert but here there is greenery and life. Trees, bushes, birds, insects. And tourists. Thousands trek out here every year from all four corners to experience life in the Atacama.

San Pedro is a true oasis, a small zone of life in the shadow of the Licancabur volcano created by the nourishing waters of the Vilama and San Pedro rivers, both of which flow down from the Andes Mountains. I find it extraordinary that people can survive and even thrive out here. But the most astonishing aspect of life in San Pedro is explained in the town museum.

The Spanish came over the mountains to the Atacama in 1540, hunting for gold, just a few decades after the Incas and using their fabled Inca Trail. More than 1,000 local Atacameños had fortified a nearby hill, but when a few dozen Spaniards appeared on horseback the Atacameños thought they were facing centaurs (half man, half horse) and immediately surrendered. The Spanish decapitated the Atacameño leaders and terrorised the rest.

But before the Europeans arrived, the Atacameños had been living in the desert for more than 11,000 years. I think of what Vince said to me as we sat next to Uluru. The indigenous Atacameños are not from this land. They *are* this land.

So Constanza arranges for me to meet Rosa Ramos, a local guide and vice-president of the Atacama People's Council. Diminutive, attractive, with a proud Inca nose and dark skin pulled tightly over sharp cheekbones, Rosa is a voluble, fiery campaigner. Across the continent the indigenous people of South America are discovering a new voice and a new power. In Bolivia one of their own has taken the presidency. Here in the Atacama the indigenous community is protesting against mining companies exploiting rare sources of water. Rosa wants to show me what might be lost.

THE NEXT day we leave San Pedro together in four-wheel drives, taking long, straight roads that eventually cross the Tropic of Capricorn amid vast emptiness. We pause under rich blue skies to savour the scene.

Just next to the road is the Inca Trail. A narrow footpath, it runs in a straight line before taking secret twists over arid mountains to my left. To the right is an empty, open, salty pan of dry nothingness.

'It's so dry,' I wonder aloud. 'It amazes me people can live out here.'

Rosa smiles knowingly; perhaps I am not the first to offer this astonishing insight. 'It is hard here, but San Pedro is an oasis in the desert. When I wake up I really appreciate the greenery – every morning – because this is what lies beyond. It's so dry that when it does finally rain your senses are overwhelmed with the new smells.'

Water, explains Rosa, is everything out here. 'Usually it rains once a year, perhaps January or February. Rain comes over from Bolivia, and maybe we have about 100 millimetres a year. It's not much. But flowers start to grow and *Pachamama*, Mother Earth, tells you she's happy.

'We have a ceremony called *talatur* where we thank *Pachamama* for giving us water,' she continues. 'And the men spend time digging out channels to make the river run faster and the women cook for all the men and give them drinks and water. After it ends the people from the community all give thanks to Mother Earth, and the leader of the community burns coca leaves in celebration, always facing the volcanoes, because at the top of the volcanoes is the doorway to the world of our gods.'

Off to our left an active volcano is gently snoozing, its smoke rising lazily into the clear blue sky. It seems to fit perfectly in this desolate landscape. We are now 2,504 metres above sea level, and the effects of altitude are becoming clearer. I am definitely not imagining the throbbing in my head. Dominic seems unaffected, but Brian and Fiona are also feeling the altitude. We swallow our piss pills, and Rosa offers all of us some coca leaves. Used for thousands of years to stave off hunger on long treks, they also help the human body to adapt to high altitude. She hands me a pinch of dry leaves to put into my cheek pouch, where the leaves soften, moisten and leach the taste of bitter tea. Then we are back on the road, and our cars begin to climb. Within half an hour we are at 3,500 metres and my GPS, which also measures elevation, ticks onward: 3,514, 3,516. A tiny fraction of humanity lives at this height around the world, but out here we pass through a small village full of smiling locals busy building new homes and refurbishing old buildings. They are used to the altitude. We rise to 3,887 metres, nearly three times the height of Ben Nevis, the tallest mountain in the British Isles, and cross another plain covered in dry yellow grass, similar to the spinifex of Australia. This is the *altiplano*, the high flatlands.

Another hour of driving, rising slowly on rough, cratered, unmade roads, and we reach 4,000 metres. We crest a hill, round a bend, and suddenly, from the bottom of a wide bowl nestling between enormous grey mountains, there is a glimpse of turquoise. We have reached Tuyajcu, a beautiful mountain lake. It is the colour of the tropical seas, bordered by a mixture of white salt and sulphur that give the appearance of the coral sands of Heron Island. It is stunning. I almost cry at this extraordinary beauty, the sheer other-worldliness of this place. And on the far shore I think I can see birds. We take a track that circles the lake and park for a quick picnic, then creep slowly across the marshy land towards the edge of the lake, puffing and wheezing from the lack of oxygen. Are my eyes deceiving me? I am more than four kilometres above sea level in the high Andes, and in front of me there is a tropical lake and scores of bright pink flamingos.

Flamingos! Here they are a deeper shade of pink than their cousins in Africa or the Caribbean. Waddling on thin, spindly legs through the briny pool, they munch silently on tiny shrimp.

'We believe that the water here comes from the gods that live in the volcanoes,' Rosa tells me. 'The gods give us water in the middle of our desert. My people have been around here for thousands and thousands of years and we use this place in the way it's meant to be used. We come here to bring our sheep and goat and llamas for pasture. And we come here to meditate.'

Rosa and I stop at the water's edge, and she points at a small metal barrier that has been placed across a stream running from the lake. This is why we are here.

'This high lake is vital to the indigenous people of this area,' she says. 'But one of the mining companies in the area have applied to drain water from the lake to use in their mines and also tap into more water that lies under the ground. We're desperately worried the mining companies will destroy the lake and upset the delicate biodiversity of this area. They've already taken water from other lakes in the area and bled them dry.'

Rosa accepts that mining is also vital to the Chilean economy. But she tells me that the companies don't need to take this water.

'They can bring it from the coast,' she tells me as we watch a flamingo wheel around the lake, then swoop in to land. It is an exquisite sight. 'Of course it might cost a bit more,' she adds, 'but that's a price we should pay for protecting this lake and this area.'

We sit on the edge of the lake, watching the flamingos. This area is not even a protected national park. So a mining company can walk in here and try to take the water from the lake. I have to agree with Rosa: it is epically stupid.

On the way back from the lake, we take a right turn and climb a grey, powdery hill towards a village called Talabre. After telling me what the mining giants are doing to lakes in the area, Rosa wants to show me how the people of the Atacama respect and use water. Talabre is a tiny indigenous community, home to around 200 people, with narrow, unmade streets and small one-storey houses made of volcanic stone.

On the edge of the village, a trickle of a stream flows down a narrow canal perhaps 30 centimetres wide and lined by perfectly cut stones. This water, a rare sight in the desert, has been captured from wider streams cascading off the Andes to the east.

'Every drop of water is precious out here,' says Rosa. 'Look how carefully they use it to grow vegetables and fruits.'

She points at a tended allotment, irrigated by the narrow channels, where Andean potatoes, quince and plums are growing. A large two-foot-thick black pipe also brings Andean water from a wider stream for a small hydro-electric station in a building hardly bigger than a shed. The force of the water powers a whirring turbine, providing power for the village, and the spent water races out of the base of the shed.

Luis Soza, a thick-set local man, wanders over to check what we are doing. I ask him whether any water from the plant is wasted. He almost looks offended.

'Absolutely not,' he says in Spanish. 'It flows down to a small reservoir and is used to water crops.'

The village has only had 24-hour electricity for four months. I ask Luis whether life has changed. He has a serious, almost severe appearance, but suddenly a smile crosses his face.

'It's been a huge change. It's transformed our lives. Now we have lights in the darkness, fridges that keep food from rotting in the summer, power for our tools, drills, welding machines and televisions.'

He takes us back into the village to meet his wife Antonia. A brand-new, water-efficient washing machine is sitting in the cosy front room, ready to be moved into the kitchen. I ask whether her life has changed since the arrival of electricity and she can hardly contain her excitement.

'Oh yes,' she bubbles. 'Really everything changed. Life is so much better now. It used to take me hours to do the family washing, now it will be so fast.' She pats the new washing machine like a pet.

Their two children, Catherine, 5, and Leonardo, 11, sit on a comfy sofa giggling as their lanky white visitor bashes his head on the electric light fitting. I crouch down.

'So now you have a television what are your favourite programmes?' I ask them both.

'*The Simpsons*!' squeals little Catherine immediately. She's a big fan of Maggie, Homer and Marge's youngest child. Leonardo prefers an art show for children on the Disney Channel.

Even out here, in a tiny village 3,500 metres high on the edge of the Andes and the Atacama Desert, there's no escaping globalization. Around similar villages, in similar lands, I have heard Westerners bemoaning the arrival of electricity in quaint rural villages and the changes it brings to traditional lives. Of course change can be difficult and ruinous, but surely it is outrageous to prevent others from obtaining what the rest of us already enjoy? Running water and washing machines liberate women from much of the drudgery of housework. Lights enable kids to do their homework after dark. Fridges protect food and medicines. I look at the back of Antonia's new washing machine and spot a familiar label: 'Made in China'. In the next decade, no doubt, the superpower will sell the West sturdy cars, computers and TV sets. For now it churns out cheap fridges and washing machines, products we Europeans often take for granted, to the evident delight of Antonia, Luis and families in millions of homes across developing countries.

BACK IN San Pedro, Constanza wakes all of us offensively early the next morning and we collect Rosa from her adobe house and drive through the night for three hours, climbing above 4,000 metres again, before dawn breaks and illuminates steaming chimneys on a mountain plain. We have reached the Tatio Geysers, the highest geothermal field in the world.

Between 6 and 8 a.m. every morning on this flat patch of land, clouds of steamy water are pumped high into the cold mountain air by scores of geysers, ranging from bubbling tiddlers to giant infernal whoppers that roar like mini volcanoes. That collision of hot and cold creates endless clouds of mist. Constanza has not been here before, and we both feel a sense of awe as we walk across the field with Rosa, through billowing steam and past pools of water that glint in the early morning light.

We are not alone out on the field. Hundreds of tourists have made the journey, setting out as early as 4 a.m. from their hotels in San Pedro. But it is still a magnificent spectacle.

Yet all this water and heat has mining companies rubbing their hands with covetous glee. This thermal energy could be harnessed for the mines. The geysers are threatened. And again, the geysers are not in a national park or on protected land.

We spend the rest of the morning around Tatio, then hours of driving on bumpy roads takes us just a few miles to the west of San Pedro, to the Valle de la Luna, the Valley of the Moon. It is a sight that lives up to its name, with sand dunes and soft hills eroded into a lunar landscape by centuries of wind, and curved hillsides that look like giant claws have gouged at the land. Rosa barbecues some sinewy llama meat for us to eat and we settle on the side of a dune, facing east, admiring the view.

'When you live in a city you don't have time to appreciate what's around you,' says Rosa. 'Living in the desert, every feature of the land is exposed. Out here, you feel very near to your gods. This is like a paradise for me.' She pauses, then turns to me. 'Don't you agree?'

I look out and the setting sun is turning distant mountains a glorious reddy-pink. The land is barren, stark and extraordinary. It is like nowhere else on earth.

'Yes, Rosa,' I say. 'It is beautiful. Truly beautiful.'

As darkness collects around us, brilliant stars pop to life in the heavens. These skies are the clearest and least polluted anywhere on earth. An appropriate setting, elsewhere in the Atacama, for the location of billion-pound telescopes that peer deep into space. Scientists and engineers are building one called the Atacama Large Millimeter Array (ALMA) out here, a collection of 64 giant dishes due for completion around 2011 that will become our biggest eye on the sky, with a resolution ten times sharper than the Hubble Space Telescope. ALMA will probe the very birth of our universe. It may help us to understand the mysterious 'dark matter' and 'dark energy' that comprises 90 per cent of our universe. It may even be capable of answering one of the biggest questions of all – one extraordinary in scope and scale: whether our universe is actually just one of millions of universes.

My mind, already focused on munching barbecued llama, cannot deal with such fantastical notions. Lying on my back in the Atacama and gazing up at the stars, all I know for sure is that this area of the desert, which might soon help to unlock the secrets of our very existence, is worthy of more human respect. I can only hope the Chilean government, and the Chilean people, wake to the threat and protect the lakes and the geysers in this area. To have it degraded at all, let alone to lose it, would be an utter tragedy.

The next day it is time for us to cross the Andes. We bid farewell to Rosa and leave San Pedro, have our bags checked at a Chilean customs point, confusingly located on the edge of the town, and aim our cars east towards the border with Argentina. There are few other vehicles around as we climb, up and up, on steep roads. As the GPS ticks past 4,000 metres again, I really start to feel the altitude: breathing is difficult, my heart is racing, my fingers shake. The road takes us through a dusty, reddish Martian landscape. We saw the moon last night, now Mars today. After driving for an hour, clouds appear in the distance.

'The mountains stop the clouds and rain from crossing into Chile. They are *that* high. So they get the rain on the Argentinean side and all we get is the dry wind,' says Constanza.

'It doesn't seem fair,' I say.

'Well, they have grass for their cows, and we have our copper mines. It's not all bad.'

The border between the two countries is drawn in the middle of nowhere, high in the mountains. As we approach Argentina, I bid farewell to Constanza, who will travel back to the coast of Chile with the cars and drivers.

Gloria Beretervide, our Argentinean guide, is parked by the road on the Chilean side of the border. I feel like a lucky baton being passed from one fixer to the next. We are horrendously late, but Gloria greets us warmly, gives us the gentlest of ticking-offs for making her wait out in the high-altitude cold for three hours, and we cross into the very northern tip of Argentina.

10 · ARGENTINA

FROM THE beginning, Argentina is different. We drive into the far north of the country, where the remotest of border posts mark a line between the largely sterile Chilean Andes and the more fertile Argentinean foothills. A biting wind tears past a couple of dusty immigration huts where our passports are checked and stamped by officials suspicious about our reasons for crossing. A tatty poster outside a grubby toilet shed warns of the dangers of dengue fever, spread by the pesky mosquito. There has been a huge outbreak of the disease across the region. Then we are off across high-altitude plains, driving past shy vicuñas – a goat-sized cross between Bambi and a llama – that scurry around, nibbling at greenery.

Mile by mile, the landscape becomes ever greener as we slowly descend from the high mountains. First there are more tiny bushes. Then valleys of trees.

I am still intrigued by what South Americans think of each other.

'The rest of the continent doesn't seem to like Argentineans very much,' I suggest to Gloria, an elegant journalist in her forties from Buenos Aires.

'Yes, they hate us. Because we think we're the whiteys of Latin America.'

'I heard one joke a couple of times in Chile: How does an Argentinean commit suicide? He jumps off his own ego.'

Gloria laughs. 'And it's so true!'

We motor for hours, arriving after dark in the valley town of Tilcara, close to Capricorn but still at more than 2,000 metres, and check into a hotel with a roof that leaks buckets of rainwater during the night through light fittings and skylights.

In the morning we eat a breakfast of soggy toast, damp with the rainwater leaking through the roof, and Gloria explains our plans. Following Capricorn through northern Argentina will take us through an area with the most important concentrations of indigenous communities in the country, so as we head east we want to discover more about the Wichí people, traditional hunter-gatherers who live across the region. But first Gloria wants to introduce me to one of Argentina's most precious exports. She will be taking us to visit a vicuña ranch near Tilcara, just to the north of Capricorn, where vicuñas are kept and sheared for their fibre. Just a tiny amount is harvested from them each year, but it is the finest and softest fibre in the world, softer and more luxurious even than baby cashmere, and much more expensive. Apparently the state gift offered by Argentina to dignitaries and foreign leaders is often some form of vicuña fabric. The Pope has a vicuña poncho.

As we drive out of Tilcara, we pass small, pretty houses and pause in a charming town square where an elderly man from the local indigenous Wichí community is selling handicrafts next to an antique truck. I am amazed it still runs. It is a museum piece, a lorry driven by traders in the 1930s, now held together by the careful application of gaffer tape. Outside Tilcara, in the same narrow valley, we stop at a Tropic of Capricorn monument. All around us men are working fields of crops by hand and by tractor. The land is sunny, green and fertile. With craggy red and grey hills on each side, it is something of an idyll.

Ten minutes further north and we arrive at the ranch owned by Hugo and Maria Robles, a delightful middle-aged couple who own 44 vicuñas. Hugo is a dark man with a broad hat and the air of an academic. Not surprising, given that he is also a local university professor. His wife, the descendant of Danish settlers, has distinctly Scandinavian looks. A huge barbecue is sizzling away over a fire on an enormous round grille, and as we eat lunch with farm workers we chat about the extraordinary vicuña.

Hugo explains that Incas revered the creature and sacrificed it to their gods. When the Spanish arrived they called vicuña fibre New World Silk, and hunted the animal to near extinction. Until just a few decades ago the vicuña was endangered. Then the Argentinean government introduced strict controls on the trade in the fibre and encouraged indigenous communities to breed the animals. The programme helped to save the vicuña – there are now thought to be more than 200,000 on farms or roaming wild across this region – but it has been less successful at helping indigenous Argentineans. In truth, it is mostly middle-class farmers who make money from the vicuña trade.

Maria disappears into a back room of the house and emerges with a fist-sized quantity of fibre shorn recently from the little creatures. It is astonishingly light and soft. I try on a tank top made from vicuña fibres. It has a pattern and style untouched by the trends of post-war fashion, but it is silkily soft. If bought in the shops, the price would be astronomical. Coats made from vicuña fibres can sell for £30,000.

Time to meet the source. We have arrived at the farm on a day when several of the vicuñas are due to be injected with a dose of calcium and vaccinated against disease, so Hugo takes us to a small paddock where a herd of vicuña eye us nervously. One needing calcium struggles violently as it is wrestled to the ground. It looks delicate and fragile. I gaze into its almond eyes, stroke its head and mutter soothing words as a farm worker carefully injects a shot of purple liquid into the animal.

'You really need to see them roaming free,' says Hugo. 'We have more in another larger field waiting to be vaccinated. They're quite a sight.'

So Gloria, Brian and I join Hugo in a battered old farm four-wheel drive and we head up a steep track just behind the Robles' whitewashed farmhouse to a huge, shrubby, hilly field where 14 vicuñas are busy munching the grass. After a recent shearing, they look as though they have had a bad trip to the hairdressers. Startled by our car, they rocket off, arcing around the top of the field at about 50 kmph.

'They're a bit fast, aren't they?' I say to Hugo. 'How on earth are we going to trap them?'

'Yes,' he rubs his chin. 'It can take a while. One time we wanted to vaccinate just one of them and it took us three days to capture him. We were all running around the hill exhausted.'

The vicuñas are so nippy the only way of grabbing them is for a group of workers to fan out along the hillside and then encourage or force them to run down between two long fences that funnel the creatures towards a pen. Today, of course, this human chain includes Gloria and me. Lacking qualifications and experience, I run towards the vicuñas, flapping my arms like a giant flightless bird, until I realise everyone else is standing still and looking at me strangely. So instead I make cooing catcalls like the rest of the workers, and together, after protracted exertion and endless hillside sprinting, we finally manage to get a couple of vicuñas to run down the funnel.

In the pen they are shy and scared, and they dart around at high speed looking for an escape. I am supposed to be guarding the main gate to the pen, but one of the vicuñas treads on my toes and leaps past me to freedom. The final one appears cornered.

'Come on,' I say, trying to be reasonable. 'You need to have your vaccination. It's for your own good.'

He is not listening. And he has spotted a hole in our human fence. The farm worker to my left is distracted. The vicuña dives for the gap, a cry goes up from the farm hands and we scramble for the little beastie. But it stumbles through a water trough on the ground, drenching us with water, and zips off up the hill.

The farmhand looks at me in disgust. I spread my arms and shrug my shoulders.

'You left the gap,' I point out. 'No use blaming me.'

I ask you, what was I supposed to do? Wrestle 20 kilos of high-grade poncho into the mud?

I turn to Hugo, who watches the rear-end of his vicuña heading back up the hill with a resigned air. It is clearly a sight he has seen many times.

'No wonder their fibre is so expensive,' I tell him. 'Nobody can catch them.'

IF WE ARE to reach the Brazilian coast for the solstice our schedule must be ferocious, so we leave Tilcara at dawn the next morning and head out of the valley towards the town of Tartagal, further east along Capricorn. It is the final stage of our descent from the Andes, and we drive along roads that take us down through the Yungas, the cloud forest of the Andean foothills, where thick, fluffy clouds envelop and surround the car, to the tropical, dry forest of the lowland Chaco plain.

Overnight there was heavy rain and the road is flooded with mud, rocks and boulders. Pedro, our driver, skilfully navigates long stretches that have been washed away, driving over loose ground or diverting through muddy fields. In the front passenger seat, I watch Pedro's driving for a while and realise he is expertly professional. No need for nerves. I fall into a deep sleep and only wake as we rumble into Tartagal four hours later.

The Capricorn area of Argentina around Tartagal is home to thousands of Wichí families, so Gloria suggests I meet John Palmer, an English anthropologist who has lived out here for decades, studying the Wichí people and marrying into the community. After years in the forest, he now lives in the town, in a small house on a quiet street next to a dirt road, and comes to his front gate as we pull up outside. He is expecting us.

John is 54, with the distinct, honeyed tones of John Mills. He is thin with white hair and pale, tight skin, and smokes a small brown pipe from the corner of his mouth. He came out here as a student while at Oxford, became entranced with the Wichí people, and wrote a book on their culture. We sit on wooden benches under shade outside his small house drinking tea and I ask why he finds them fascinating.

'They are a very gentle, very peaceful people, eschewing all forms of violence,' he says softly. 'They have very little, but that is the key to their harmony. Possessions and wealth encourage tensions and problems.'

But now the forest on which they depend for their life and purpose is rapidly vanishing around them due to logging and deforestation for farming. John wants the wider world to know the very existence of the Wichí is under threat, but I can sense he is not entirely happy about introducing outsiders into the Wichí community.

As we chat, John's wife Tojweya emerges from the house with their two bashful young boys, Benedict, two years old, and Terence, just one, both an impossibly cute confection of Wichí and English blood. Tojweya is many years younger than John, with deep eyes and a warm, beautiful smile. She has long black hair, parted in the middle and pulled tight over her caramel skin.

'How did you two meet?' I ask John.

'Ah. Well, in Wichí culture it is the women who choose the men they want to marry,' says John, pushing a wad of tobacco into his pipe. 'I knew Tojweya's sister Victoria when I was living and working in the forest with the community, and one day, after I moved into the town, Tojweya turned up on my doorstep and said, "I have come to see you." And that was how our relationship started.' He looks at her lovingly, and they share a shy smile.

'But can men court the women they want to marry?'

'No, not at all. To the extent that if a Wichí man pursues a Wichí woman, people say he is being feminine.'

The Wichí sound fascinating. John agrees to take us out of the town to Hoktek T'oi, a Wichí community in the forest around Tartagal. The Palmer clan will be coming with us. John picks up Benedict and tickles his stomach.

'Let's get into the car, Benny, we're going to see Uncle Roque.'

We gather supplies and head out of town towards the community, turning from the tarmac of town to a broken patchwork of road leading out into forest. The Wichí at Hoktek T'oi are a small community living on their own land in the forest, what biologists would call transitional forest between the Yungas cloud forest and the tropical, dry forest of the Chaco plain. The road is currently being 'improved' and upgraded, which means it will eventually become a sleek tarmac thoroughfare for trucks and lorries.

'The Wichí think the road will mean they can get into town more easily,' explains John. 'But what they don't realise is that there will be a wave of traffic heading in the other direction.'

A more stable road makes it easier for ranchers and loggers to exploit the forest and take the trees the Wichí depend on for their very survival.

'These roads sound the death knell for forests and people of the forests,' says John.

It is a story repeated, with minor variations, around the world. Research has shown that 85 per cent of deforestation in the Amazon, for example, occurs within 30 miles of a road. First to explore the deep forests are the prospectors, hunting for oil, gas or minerals. After clearing small drilling areas, they carve tracks through the trees for their researchers and geologists. Loggers follow the prospectors, widening the initial tracks and levelling huge areas of forest. Next come the ranchers, who tarmac the roads and use them to truck out their cattle or crops. Finally come the settlers, often the rural poor who are persuaded to try their luck in a new area of forest. And so the great forests of the world are attacked and annihilated.

Every day we are losing 20,000 hectares of forest, an area more than twice the size of Paris. And that appalling figure is low because it includes the planting of plantation forests, sterile environments empty of natural wildlife. When plantation forests are excluded, the rate of forest loss is around 40,000 hectares every single day.

As we drive towards the Wichí settlement, we pass through huge areas of deforested land now used for crops.

'What's being lost here is a unique bit of ecotone forest, a combination of two different types of ecosystem, the Yungas and the tropical, dry, lowland Chaco forest,' says John. 'The ecotone forest combines trees species of both of those ecosystems. It's the only forested area of its kind on the Tropic of Capricorn.'

Eventually we turn right off the wide track, down a short driveway, and into the small community of Hoktek T'oi.

'We're here,' John coos to Benedict, who is sitting on his lap. 'Now where is Uncle Roque?'

The community, a home for around 60 people, is compact and a little mucky. But it has an immediate homely feel. Extended families gather outside small mud huts topped by corrugated iron and surrounded by rough fences made from spiky branches. We pass one set of homemade goalposts and cross an overgrown football pitch tended by a herd of hungry goats. John tells our driver, Pedro, to aim for a community building, a barn-like structure with open sides guarded against insects by torn wire mesh, where the team and I will be sleeping on a concrete floor, and where Roque Miranda, the president of the community, has been patiently waiting for our arrival.

Uncle Roque is a reserved 48-year-old. He greets John warmly and us politely, and we sit down to explain the purpose of our visit. Then I ask Roque for the latest news on the deforestation affecting their community.

'The machines have been attacking the forest just near the village,' he tells me through John, one of the few outsiders who can speak the rich language of the Wichí. Bulldozers have been working just a few hundred metres from the village. There is no time to waste. With Roque and John leading the way, we head out into the forest to check what is happening.

We take a narrow path out of the village and walk for just 50 metres between overgrown bushes, until we find a smart new fence in front of a vast empty field.

'This forest was cut down a few years ago,' says Roque. 'It was our forest. We have lived here for generations. But ranchers just started to chop it down. The bulldozers tried to come through our village. They tried to destroy our village.'

I swing my head to look at John, who is translating. I cannot quite believe what I am hearing.

'Does he really mean they tried to use the bulldozers to destroy the village?' I query.

He nods.

'Unbelievable, isn't it?' But yes, that's how they are treated.'

We walk on beside the fence, along a narrow track next to bushes that would not appear out of place on an English country ramble. We cross another track, newly widened, with fresh gouge marks where bulldozers have ripped and scraped at the terracotta soil, and walk down a side track surrounded by thick forest. Then a scene of complete devastation appears to our left.

A long, wide swathe of forest has been torn from the ground. Trees, young and slender, old and thick, have been ripped and uprooted, all in the same direction, between two wide trails marked by caterpillar tracks. The leaves on the trees are still green. The trees have just been felled, only days earlier. Once this forest was a home to pumas, tapirs and jaguars. Now it is the frontline in the battle to protect the lungs of our planet. The place where the war is being lost.

'They use two bulldozers here,' John tells me. 'They drive down each track with a heavy chain between them. The chain rips and tears at the trees, uprooting and pulling them out of the ground.'

The Wichí heard the noise of the bulldozers just a few nights ago. Men from the village ran out to where the chains were being used, and pleaded with the drivers to stop their work.

'They told us they could not stop,' says Roque. 'They said, "This is our job." But we pleaded with them, and eventually they agreed to pause. They sent someone to talk with us and he tried to bribe us by offering us wood from the trees they have felled.' He snorts in disgust.

As I stand among the devastation listening to Roque, I am reminded of the famous photo from the time of the Tiananmen Square demonstrations. A young man, carrying plastic shopping bags, briefly blocked a column of tanks by walking in front of them and refusing to move. These villagers, with their gentle sincerity and simple pleas, face similarly impossible odds against bulldozer drivers. There are perhaps 50,000 Wichí across this region and the destruction of their forests has caused starvation among some communities. Loggers have smashed homes, blocked roads into villages and even destroyed water pumps, forcing some communities to drink contaminated water from ditches and ponds. This land is legally Wichí land. By rights, they should be protected here. But this is a remote and corrupt region of Argentina, and national or international laws on indigenous land ownership are rarely enforced.

Then, snaking along the ground just to the side of the track, I find the main weapon in the war being waged against the Wichí. A solid steel chain, 100 metres long, of extraordinary thickness and weight, curls around a patch of remaining forest where it has been left until bulldozers return and the looting of the forest can start again. It is blackened with the sap of the countless trees it has felled. I can only manage to lift the first two links. It is a chain for an anchor on an ocean-going liner. A chain for securing a battleship to a wharf. Here it is being used to cause immense destruction by a Panzer division of forest killers.

'Who makes these chains?' asks Roque in bewilderment. 'Who makes the machines? Who are the people doing this to our forest?'

We walk along beside a twisted, mangled mess of trees. Roque stops, visibly upset. He pauses and says just a few words. John listens, then lowers his head. 'He says, "This is death."'

Our cars and drivers have come to find us, and we set out to find the bulldozers responsible for this devastation. We continue driving along the same track, and find more areas of deforestation. Every 80 or so metres there are bulldozer-width trails driven through the forest at right angles to our track. I wonder what they are doing. And then I realise they are planning to chain the forest between the trails. Everything is marked for obliteration.

Another ten minutes of driving, and we see the results. This is an area where the trees have been chained out of the ground, then pushed by bulldozers into huge stacks of wood roughly 50 metres apart and half a kilometre long. In a final obscene act in the deforestation tragedy, these wood stacks will all be burned.

I can see the look of pain on Roque's face. He cannot fully comprehend what is happening here. We drive around the edge of the stacks, barrel down a narrow track, and find the metal agents of this destruction parked by the side of the road. Two yellow Caterpillar bulldozers with bright shovels at the front, four metres wide and two metres high, are waiting to start work. The cabs where drivers sit are protected, almost armoured, with reinforced roofs and thick mesh to stop falling branches from injuring the operator. At the back of each creature is the coupling that takes the deadly chain. Soon they will be felling again.

THAT NIGHT I sit with Roque, John, and half the village on rickety benches under a lean-to shack around a small fire. After seeing the destruction of the forest they are depressed and disheartened, and I wonder whether they will find solace in a few beers. But John tells me the Wichí generally dislike alcohol. They only drink around the time of New Year, when they get completely drunk, spend a few days sobering up, and then abstain for another 12 months. This is how many indigenous communities in South America used alcohol for thousands of years before the arrival of Europeans. But when traders started taking bottles of hard liquor to remote communities deep in the jungle, many succumbed. Countless indigenous communities in South America have appalling problems with alcoholism. Not the Wichí. Instead of alcohol I drink cups of tea with them, brewed in a blackened kettle on the fire, and light from the flames flickers off the faces of a dozen children who sit in a semi-circle opposite the solemn elders.

I ask Roque whether he is hopeful about the future for his community. He stops to consider, and then tells me sadly, 'When I was young I was excited about what life had to offer. But now the years have passed and it has become clear nobody seems to want us to survive. We don't know what's going to happen. All we know is that it's destroying the world that we live in.'

He pauses, and John and I wait for him to continue. The village is listening closely. Roque's words reflect the pain of the entire community.

'What are the children going to live off?' he asks rhetorically. 'What are the children's children going to live off? We're being systematically driven out of existence. I do not know if we have a future.'

'Roque,' I ask, 'the outside world is doing this to your forest. Is there anything else you want to tell us?'

'Yes,' he replies. 'There is something else I want to say. And it is that I want people who live a long way away to know the problems we are facing here. Because the people who live close to us are the people who are causing the problems. The government has pretended to make us part of the country by giving us identity documents and saying we are Argentine. But this is just a lie. It's completely untrue. They're not making us part of their system. They're just causing us to lose our way. They're stealing our land. They're reducing us to utmost poverty. The only hope we have is of people like you who live far away. Please take our message.'

I am squashed on to the end of a bench. I rest my forehead on my hands, partly to hide the tears in my eyes. There is bewilderment and a palpable fear of the future in this community. And the experiences of other indigenous people I have met on my journey suggest they are right to be scared. How long can they survive?

With the forests vanishing around them, this community struggles to support itself. John has distributed quantities of rice and flour we brought for them, as they requested, but they do not have enough spare food to provide for us. So after talking with Roque, John and the community late into the night, until the fire is just smouldering embers, Dominic and I walk back through the darkness to the community hut, where the rest of the team are already asleep. I pop some solid fuel tablets on a tiny fold-out cooker under my mini stove and boil some water to re-hydrate a pack of chicken curry. And then to sleep.

At about four in the morning, the faintest of sounds stirs me from my sleep. Cocks are crowing. But this time I just turn over. I am wearing thick ear plugs. Cockerels 4, Reeve 1. It's taken a while, but I'm learning. Then roughly an hour later, my bedding starts to move and a muffled sound wakes my brain. Hooves? I fumble for my torch and spot the door of the hall ajar. I shine the light at my feet. Frozen in the beam, a goat is tugging at my sleeping bag. Ah well, you can't prepare for everything.

GIGGLING CHILDREN wake me in the morning. Through bleary eyes, I see tiny faces pressed up against the huge mesh panels at the side of the hall above my head. They are peering intently at the team and I as our strange pale forms stir in the hall. Pedro, our driver, passes us cups of hot *mate*, a drink like concentrated green tea that helps to wake the brain.

One of the watching children giggles at us and shouts something over her shoulder. John, who has come to wake us, listens, then laughs uproariously.

'What did she say?' I ask.

'She said, "Look! Monkeys! Come and watch! They are so funny!"'

When my mind finally engages gear, we go to find Roque. He wants to take all of us out into the forest again. This time in search of wild honey.

With Roque leading and Petiso José, a young lad from the village, onboard, we drive out of the community in our four-wheel drives, because the forests nearest the village have already been levelled.

'Is it getting harder to find wild honey?' I ask Roque.

'Yes. Much harder,' he says. 'We have to go further and further away from the village.'

Fifteen minutes from the village, we turn right, going from one unmade track to a narrower trail. At least here there is thick forest on either side. After a few more minutes, we stop and abandon the cars. Roque is carrying an axe, machete and a string bag with a tight weave which he will wear over his head as protection if we find any wild bees.

We walk down a thin forest trail, along which play scattered shafts of bright sunlight, looking for honey. It doesn't take long. Roque spots bees returning to a nest in the centre of an old, rotting tree. He points at a small hole in the trunk. There are dozens of bees gathered around the entrance.

Roque and Petiso clear an area of ground just a few feet from the tree and gather some twigs for a fire. Smoke from the blaze should calm the bees and make them dozy. But it rained last night and the twigs will not light. Lucky they have me here. I pull out a can of insect repellent and with the help of a lighter turn it into a flame-thrower. Soon there is a small blaze and smoke wafts over the nest. Roque starts preparing for his attack. He tucks his trousers into his socks, rolls down the sleeves of his shirt and pulls on a thick pullover. Then he puts the thick string bag over his head and picks up his axe.

'Careful,' says John. 'The bees are not going to like this. You might like to get your fleece on, that will help to protect you from being stung.' I still have it tied around my waist.

I zip it up tightly, tucking the bottom of my trousers into my socks as Roque hefts the axe over his head. He swings it down against the trunk, just below the nest. There is an instant reaction. From inside the trunk the calm buzz of thousands of bees becomes an angry roar. Squadrons emerge from the trunk to confront the attackers. Roque is surrounded, but his headgear and thick clothing protect him from attack. His axe keeps swinging. Furious, the bees switch their attention, buzzing around my head. Then I feel a sharp pain in my left arm and two more stabs in my right arm, and I start to panic. I wave my hands around my head, trying to fight off a small swarm. But of course this just makes them even more angry.

'Try to be still,' says John calmly. He is standing to one side, but as the bees buzz around he is motionless

'I'll keep still when they stop attacking me!' I shout, flailing my arms impotently. I brush several bees off my face, quickly pull a mesh bag over my head, and try to breathe slowly.

Roque is still axing the tree.

'The nest is too big and the tree is too rotten,' says John. 'They'll have to bring the tree down.'

Part of the trunk is already resting on a thinner, younger tree. Roque swings his axe at the trunk once, twice, then shouts a warning.

'He's saying it's going to go,' says John. 'Be careful, Simon, the trunk might spring back.'

Then, with an almighty tearing noise and a deafening crash, the tree collapses to the ground. It is a bit of a shock.

'Bloody hell!' I exclaim.

Roque starts axing the side of the trunk as if cutting out a tumour. A dozen strokes and the trunk tears open. He uses the axe head to prise the trunk apart. Inside is a mass of honeycomb. It is golden, glistening and glorious. Perhaps the bees can sense they are about to lose their treasure. I try to stay calm as their buzzing increases. Roque reaches for his machete, starts cutting slabs of honeycomb out of the trunk, and drops them into his bucket. Then he cuts a smaller slice and passes it to me. It is fresh, wild honey, and I stuff it greedily into my mouth and suck on the nectar. It is light, sweet, gentle on the tongue and packed with flavour. It tastes like no honey I have ever eaten. Roque watches my face closely.

'It is delicious,' I tell him.

He nods, smiles proudly, then points at the side of the honeycomb and lists the flowering trees and shrubs the bees have feasted upon for their pollen. He is completely in touch with his environment.

We stand by the felled trunk, bees buzzing around. 'We're being denied our own food, and offered Western food, but it's not as healthy as the food we can get from the forest, and you have to pay for food in shops. And where do we get money from?' says Roque.

'The key thing is that indigenous cultures are non-monetary-based cultures. All transactions involving money are completely alien to them,' says John. 'They live off nature in the purest sense of the word. And that doesn't mean living like an animal. It means understanding your environment. A millennia of experience to master the art. And they really are masters of the art of living off the forest.'

As John talks, Roque cuts a chunk of brown honeycomb, darker than the rest, pastes the honey syrup on top, and eats it like toast.

'What's that?' I ask, pointing at the brown base.

'Bee larvae.' And with that he passes me the half-eaten chunk. I can see white larvae where his teeth have bitten. I wish I'd kept my mouth shut. But I take a bite through the squishy larvae and chew thoughtfully. Disguised by the honey, the larvae taste of nothing, but the sensation and knowledge of what I am eating are enough to put me off. Don't swallow the wax, John tells me, just a moment too late.

Roque then motions for Brian and Dominic, who has a rasping, dry cough, to come over to the trunk, and passes them chunks of wild honey, a natural antiseptic.

He points at Dominic's neck. 'It will help your throat,' he says.

The bee strikes are becoming more desperate, so Roque gathers his bucket and we head away from the nest. On the path, I pause and lift the head-net from my face, thinking I am safe. A kamikaze bee launches a frontal attack. I see it heading straight for my eye and swat unthinkingly with both hands. But the bee scores a direct hit on the end of my nose.

'Aaaargh!' I yelp.

'We must go now,' says Roque. 'Another, bigger swarm will be coming.'

Finally, when we are a safe distance from the nest, we stop by the path on the edge of the forest for another golden feast. Eating and sharing the honey, Roque is as happy as I have seen him. Out here in the forest he looks like a completely different man.

'Last night you asked when Roque and the Wichí last knew happiness,' said John. 'Well, it's at times like this. Hunting; gathering; when they are living as they have lived for generations.'

'How long do you think the Wichí have been doing this?' I ask him.

'We're in a forest so it's hard to find evidence from rocks or stones. But I think they've almost certainly been here for 2,000 years, and there are some indications they have been here for 11,000 years.'

'Without our trees we will never be able to do this,' says Roque as he gorges on honey. He passes me another delicious slab to suck and relish. I slurp noisily, but with a lump in my throat. Because the tragedy is that by the time you read these words the bulldozers may have finished their work and Roque, this Wichí community and their forest world, may all have vanished.

THE FOLLOWING day, Gloria takes Brian and I north to the border with Bolivia, just a 40-minute fast drive from Tartagal. We are on a shopping trip, looking for presents for our families, and we negotiate stroppy guards, cross a busy border and arrive in the bustling market town of Yacuiba. Bolivia is a country experiencing a revolution. The indigenous people have taken power behind the banner of President Evo Morales, a trailblazing indigenous politician who is inspiring people across the continent. Our trip is largely unsuccessful, although Brian does manage to buy a lasso for one of his sons, and within three hours we are back in Argentina.

But I am struck by the fact that almost all the faces on the streets of Yacuiba are indigenous. Shopkeepers, traders, shoppers, taxi drivers, hustlers, policemen. There are faces from the Toba, Chorote, Chulupi, old hunter-gatherer tribes; from the Avi Guarani tribes from the Amazonian area; and even people from Wichí communities who found themselves on the Bolivian side of the fence when borders were drawn.

'Their original culture has been completely smashed,' says Gloria.

Their lives and their tribes have been swept up by the whirlwind that is the all-powerful global cult of money. Magnetised, usually against their will, they become part of it. Slaves to the same system that drives my culture, your culture, and our world.

Is this what will happen to Roque's Wichí community? I wish I could say they will keep their own sanctuary in the forest and live happy, peaceful lives. But it will not be so. Gentle people tend to be walked over in our modern, grasping world, and a force is breaking upon their village with the power of a tsunami. If the experience of other indigenous people is anything to go by, first it will take their land, then it will suck them into towns and poverty.

It is with that depressing thought that I come to the end of my journey across the very top of Argentina. Heading ever further east towards the Atlantic Coast, a ten-hour drive will take us from Tartagal towards Asunción, the capital of land-locked, little-known Paraguay.

We leave Tartagal early in the morning, head south for an hour, then turn left onto a road that takes us a vast distance across this enormous country. A kilometre marker by the road reads 1,853km.

'Is that how far it is to the border?' I ask with a start. The distance is even greater than I feared.

'No,' says Gloria. 'That's the distance if you drive from here to Buenos Aires. Everything is measured from the capital.'

We are driving 1,300 kilometres to the town of Formosa, where we will rest for the night before crossing the border into Paraguay.

Ahead of us a straight road stretches into the endless distance. The landscape around is flat and dulled under grey clouds. Small patches of forest enliven the land. They are all that is left. For hundreds of kilometres along our route, the great forests and beautiful hardwood trees of this region have been chained and felled in recent decades.

To the south, the province of Santiago del Estero was devastated long ago. When the British built railways across Argentina, they chopped vast areas for use as railway sleepers. Losing the trees destroyed the province, now arid and desertified. But few trains currently run across Argentina; the network was cancelled almost overnight in the 90s after politicians bowed to pressure from the road-freight lobby. So railways rust, with tracks strangled by weeds, mud and sand. And all that wood has gone to waste.

Apart from stops to pee and a brief pause where the road crosses Capricorn, our only break on the drive is in the tiny town of Las Lomitas, which has just been flooded with rain, and where the only available food is served in a grubby café called the Pasty House. We spent roughly eight hours in the car yesterday, nine today. My bum is numb and I fear the muscles in my legs are atrophying. We are tired and sick of driving, and although the owner of the Pasty House insists on playing thrash heavy metal music at festival volume, and the meat we are served has the grey pallor of death and tastes like something caught in the sewers, we briefly consider breaking our journey and staying in the town overnight. But then I spot the waiter eyeing a plump rat running around outside, and we decide to head straight for Formosa, near the border with Paraguay.

11 · PARAGUAY

EVERY SOUTH American seems to have something bad to say about land-locked Paraguay. Crossing the continent, I lost count of the numbers who warned me about travelling to the hellhole of the hemisphere. Paraguay is dangerous, they said, riddled with disease, smugglers, corrupt officials and swarms of bandits.

'Even my own relatives, who live abroad, won't come to Paraguay,' says journalist Andrea Machain, my new guide, as we drive into the capital Asunción after crossing the border from Argentina. 'I've offered to buy them a ticket, but they're scared to come here.'

Her own relatives?

Crossing from Argentina was fairly uneventful, even though the border was packed with devout souls making an international pilgrimage for Paraguay's main religious festival. And as I stand in the main square in Asunción, the country doesn't look too bad. Rather welcoming, in fact.

Asunción sits on high ground next to the Río Paraguay, a peculiar body of water that drops just 30 centimetres over more than 1,500 kilometres. The city has dilapidated colonial buildings, bubbling fountains, shopping malls and polite street hawkers. For five years running it has secured the title of least expensive city in the world. It remains the pleasant, quiet, steamy, humid capital of a sleepy country long forgotten by the rest of the world.

Andrea and I walk through one of the main squares and I ask if she thinks the country is isolated.

'Oh yes,' she exclaims. 'Definitely. It's like our most famous writer, Augusto Roa Bastos, said: "Paraguay is an island surrounded on all sides by land."'

It was not always this way. After the Spanish arrived, Paraguay became the launch pad for the conquest of the south of the continent. Asunción is known as 'the mother of cities'. By the nineteenth century Paraguay was one of the most developed countries in South America, with factories, railways, universities and military academies. But then Paraguay had the misfortune to become embroiled in a conflict called the War of the Triple Alliance, one of the bloodiest wars of modern history. The causes of the war, which ended in 1870, are still passionately disputed. Some say Francisco Solano Lopez, the Paraguayan leader, was responsible, some Brazil or Argentina, some even blame the British, who were doing all sorts of dastardly things at the time. But the consequences are clear.

'The war was incredibly destructive,' Andrea tells me as we wander around Asunción, 'we lost about 90 per cent of our men.'

I stop walking so quickly I nearly trip over my feet. Then I stand stock-still. It is such an extraordinary figure.

'Ninety per cent?' I exclaim. 'Nine zero?!'

'Yes, incredible, isn't it? At the end of the war boys were sent to fight, because there were no more soldiers. Just the women, children and old men were left. When it was over Paraguay became known as the Land of Women.'

Andrea tells me the remaining men were encouraged to take several women as their wives, just to get the birth rate up.

'Decades later there were still four women to every man. The effects were still being felt by my generation when I was growing up.'

Almost 140 years on, Paraguay has never fully recovered. 'Much of our best land was taken by our neighbours. We went from being an industrialised economy to an agricultural country. That war destroyed Paraguay.'

I ask Andrea if she thinks the British, who some historians have claimed wanted a new source of cotton during the American Civil War, were to blame for the Triple Alliance War.

'No, you were to blame for the Chaco Wars,' she says. 'Argentina never recognised Paraguay's independence and wanted to have us as their province. Brazil signed a secret pact with Argentina. And then Uruguay was drawn into the war.'

'So the Argentineans and Brazilians tried to wipe you out?'

'Yes, that was their plan, and they wanted to divide the country between them.'

'So what do you think of the Argentineans now?

'Well, they are stuck up, especially the people from Buenos Aires. They are very stuck up.'

At that moment we pass the Ministry of Finance. Andrea greets a large, matronly woman who comes bustling out of the building.

'That's one of our top corruption investigators,' whispers Andrea as the woman wobbles past us trailing a cloud of perfume. She is followed out of the building by a bodyguard who wears a light jacket under which nestle conspicuous metal bulges. He shoots fierce glances at the two suspicious characters loitering around on the street, namely Andrea and me, and then helps to ease the investigator into her car, a tiny vehicle into which she is having trouble squeezing her ample frame. Although corruption is endemic in Paraguay, from the look of her car it seems this is one woman who is not taking backhanders.

Yet despite corruption and the destruction of war, or perhaps partly because of it, Paraguay has been a land to which many have been inexorably drawn, principally fraudsters, felons, religious freaks, Australian utopians, White Russians, Mennonites, pacifists, fortune hunters, socialists, Graham Greene (who described the capital as a nexus of 'the exotic, the dangerous and the Victorian'), Aryans and hundreds of Nazis. Josef Mengele, Hitler's own Angel of Death, who conducted obscene experiments in Auschwitz, hid out here after the Second World War, protected by the dictator Alfredo Stroessner, a child molester who employed torturers that conducted interrogations while victims were dumped in vats of excrement, and ordered opponents to be cut up with chainsaws to the lyrical accompaniment of the Paraguayan harp.

The combined ravages of war and Stroessner's regime have left Paraguay devastated. Here is a fertile land, enormous in scale and rich with minerals, that still needs to import basic foods and has a national poverty line hovering just above destitution.

In this peculiar land, larger than Germany but with a population of only six million, there is the curious, the strange, the unusual and the horrifying. All in one isolated, extraordinary, backwater country.

THE FOLLOWING day we head to Caacupé, a town just outside Asunción. It is the weekend of the biggest religious festival of the year, a time for Paraguayans to make their yearly pilgrimage to see the Virgin of Caacupé, a figure with miraculous properties and powers, during the Feast of the Immaculate Conception. More than a million pilgrims will descend on Caacupé to ask the Virgin to cure their illnesses, find them a girlfriend, help them with an exam, or simply make them happy.

We drive out of the capital along a wide street with a lane reserved for pilgrims. By the side there are endless stalls selling gaudy statues and figurines: statues of the Virgin Mary, nativity scenes, Christ on the cross, alongside Teletubbies and Snow White and the Seven Dwarves. Their relevance is unclear. Along the road hundreds of people are trekking to Caacupé. Young and not so young, wearing T-shirts, baseball caps, football strips and carnival outfits and carrying backpacks and food and small barrels, like mini beer kegs, containing *tereré*, a Paraguayan tea made with herbs, and *yerba mate* (pronounced mahtay), a healthy alternative to coffee.

'When it's hot like this it cools you down and keeps you calm,' says Andrea.

Arriving in the town, we find tens of thousands of people wandering the streets and hanging around cafés and food stalls. Thousands more are in the square outside the Basilica of Our Lady of the Miracles listening to the choir and celebrations. It is all spectacularly colourful, with the feel of a celebration rather than a pilgrimage.

'It doesn't seem to be an exclusively religious festival,' I say to Andrea as we walk past huge snow domes containing the Virgin Mary.

'It's a national celebration. In many ways it's more important to us than Christmas.'

Through the long years of the Stroessner dictatorship, which lasted from 1954 to 1989, the church remained one of the most respected institutions in the country, although Stroessner tried to control the church and many priests bowed to his regime.

We stay late into the evening, listening to the archbishop giving an outdoor sermon, an overtly political critique of the ongoing poverty of Paraguay and the suffering of the poor.

'Many people feel we are still not making progress,' whispers Andrea.

One of the extraordinary facts about Paraguay, one of the *many* extraordinary facts about Paraguay, is that the same party has been in power for more than 60 years. It ruled during the dictatorship, and then retained power after the country became a democracy – only in name – in 1989.

It seems that however sunny and friendly the capital might be, this is a country with a rotten political core. A country where one president is in prison for fraud. Another president, who was only appointed after his predecessor was implicated in the assassination of his vice-president, was driven around in a BMW limousine stolen in Brazil; later he was sentenced to six years in jail for embezzling millions.

For a brief moment, just before my visit, it looked as though new elections might result in a change of power. But then the current president released a jailed opposition leader, a man who had been involved in a failed coup, and the opposition immediately fractured. Only in Paraguay.

I want to know more about life during the dictatorship, so the next day Andrea takes me for lunch at Bar San Roque in Asunción, a smart, European-style café where opponents of the Stroessner regime used to meet and plot.

'This café was somewhere everyone knew each other and people could come without worrying about *pyragüe*, someone with hairy feet,' she tells me as we sip coffee.

'I'm sorry? Hairy feet?' I am completely confused.

'Si, hairy feet, it's the name we would give to eavesdropping informants because they would creep up silently to listen to secret political conversations.'

Sometimes Paraguay under Stroessner can sound like something of a joke, with the dictator himself playing the role of an absurd, tin-pot leader straight from the pages of a Gabriel García Márquez novel. But for those who opposed his rule, life could be terrifyingly brutal.

'The tactic of the Stroessner dictatorship was to go after the families of those who spoke out,' says Andrea. 'So even those brave enough to oppose the regime were terrified to speak out because their families would suffer.'

'What would happen?'

'First they would get a polite warning, perhaps from a friend or a colleague. Then they might lose their job, or their child or parent would be held in jail for a few nights. And then if they kept speaking out they would be arrested, tortured, and sometimes people would just disappear.'

Paraguay is still coming to terms with life under Stroessner. Many cars bear stickers that read: 'We were happy and we didn't know it', a claim that life was better under Stroessner. Opposing stickers read: 'I wasn't happy and I couldn't say it', a reference to the silencing of dissent.

On the site of one of Stroessner's torture centres in Asunción there is now a museum. Andrea arranges for me to meet Joel Filártiga at the museum, a doctor whose son was tortured and killed by Stroessner's men. The doctor is elderly now, of enormous proportions, and burdened by poor health and maladies resulting from being extensively tortured himself. He struggles to walk, so his grandson Alvara rolls him around in a wheelchair.

The museum is in a pleasant building off a quiet residential street near the centre of Asunción. The front doors open into rooms with high ceilings. Behind them there is a courtyard, along the side of which are photos of the disappeared, the tortured, the executed. Men and women, young and old, a cross-section not unlike the happy faces walking to Caacupé. Behind the photos, Dr Filártiga shows more rooms with basic display cases revealing the paraphernalia of torture.

There is a soldering iron. There are rusty scalpels and simple extraction tools for removing fingernails and toenails, all neatly laid out. I grimace at the sight. There is a spiked sphere, like the ball on a medieval flail, with a note underneath explaining how it was used against backs or heads, causing incalculable pain and death. At the back of the courtyard there are barred cells. These were the torture chambers.

We pick one of the cells at random. It is a small room, about two metres by four. The floor is concrete, the walls are white. There is a dirty bath at the end of the room. On the floor in front of me is displayed a human form, wrapped tightly in filthy sheets, with a screw-tight ring around the neck.

'This is how they would dispose of a body,' says Dr Filártiga. 'Sometimes people would be dropped from helicopters into the rivers, or they would disappear in other ways.

'This,' he adds, 'is where I was tortured. The bath was larger, and the room was a little different. But I was brought here.'

'I'm sorry,' I stutter. 'I didn't realise.'

He doesn't seem to hear me.

'It could have been yesterday,' he says. 'I was forced underwater and then they passed a low electrical current through the tub. I lost control of my bodily functions and urinated and defecated in the water. And then I swallowed the effluent.'

Because he ran a free health clinic, spoke out against Stroessner and treated the families of dissident politicians, the doctor was beaten and tortured repeatedly. But the most devastating torture was losing his beloved son, 17-year-old Joelito Filártiga, who was kidnapped, physically tormented and killed by the regime. The doctor produces graphic, large-scale photographs of Joelito's battered corpse. His body was found with electric wires inserted up his penis.

Dr Filártiga conducted the autopsy on his own son. I find this the most upsetting fact. To lose a child is a devastating event beyond words. To take them apart physically after their murder is almost an act of self-mutilation. But the doctor needed to prove Joelito had been tortured. Looking at the photos, I cannot see how there could have been any doubt.

The doctor does not tell me all this without passion, but nor does he cry or break down. He is a tough, angry man. He still blames himself for the death of his son. It was a loss that tore his family apart.

But there is a postscript to the story, a tale that affords the Filártigas a modicum of justice for the desperate crime. Many years after Joelito was killed, the Filártigas took legal action in the US against the principal torturer, who was then living in Brooklyn, using the almost obscure Alien Tort Claims Act of 1789. Lawyers, acting for free, argued that some crimes transcend national borders, and that US courts could hear cases where foreigners take action against other foreigners for crimes that happened on foreign soil. The Filártigas won their landmark case, setting a precedent that has since been applied in scores of cases involving war criminals and dictators. The doctor was nominated for a Nobel Peace Prize in 2001, and was portrayed by Anthony Hopkins in an unsuccessful movie.

Dr Filártiga has sacrificed much for democracy in his country. I ask whether he is happy with the new Paraguay. Now he can only just contain his anger. He tells me a new evil is on the move. It is a seemingly innocent crop enjoying an incredible boom in Paraguay. Its name is soy. Vast areas are being given over to farming the crop, but Dr Filártiga views it as a modern curse.

'The poor are being driven from their land to make way for soy plantations, and the pesticides being used on the soy farms are causing disease and misery to thousands,' he tells me, jabbing his finger into the air.

The doctor still sees patients at a small free clinic in his flat in a smart Asunción apartment block. Where they once came to see him with injuries sustained by their opposition to the Stroessner regime, now they come with illnesses resulting from exposure to pesticides used in soy farming. So the next day I pay a visit to his surgery.

His thirteenth floor flat is busy with pictures, files, paintings, a flashing Christmas tree and a giant Nativity scene. There is a photo of the doctor in a grand chair with Sir Anthony Hopkins at his shoulder. And a drawing of Joelito in pride of place.

Half a dozen patients and assorted friends and family are waiting for their appointments. They have a variety of symptoms and complaints, but the consistent thread is exposure to powerful pesticides used on soy farms.

Carolina Alvarez, a vet who has worked for more than two decades in remote, rural communities, has been travelling to see the doctor since she developed symptoms she describes as chemical AIDS. 'Nobody has been able to help me except Dr Filártiga,' she says. 'I feel so alone in my suffering. Nobody in Paraguay wants to talk about the illnesses we have. The media is controlled by people with huge areas of land.'

When it is my turn to see the doctor, he is adamant. Soy is as bad for Paraguay as Stroessner. Clearly we will have to look into this.

So NOON a couple of days later finds Andrea and I at an airfield outside Asunción. We have hired a small plane to fly us northeast, to an area of Paraguay close to Capricorn, where soy is being grown in vast quantities.

At first it appears the pilot is a young lad with long hair and the dishevelled, trendy appearance of an aspiring DJ. But he is just a trainee co-pilot for his father-in-law, who emerges from an office and walks towards his waiting passengers with the reassuring swagger of experience. The real pilot is a rotund former major in the Paraguay air force with thousands of flying hours under his belt, which I find immensely reassuring.

We take off and fly over a huge expanse of rural Paraguay. It is hot up in the sky and the major sweats with the proficiency of a waterfall. Rivulets cascade from his brow, affecting his vision. As I do not want to die because he has not spotted a flock of birds heading for our propeller, I hand him a handkerchief, which he folds carefully and props on to his eyebrows and over his ears like sunglasses. Thumbs up from the major.

As we jog along, I spend most of my time on the flight looking at the ground. Modern international high-altitude travel leaves a passenger completely disconnected from ground they can rarely see from 35,000 feet. But a small plane, hobbling along below clouds at low altitude, lets you see and sense the land. Below me are a few remaining patches of forest, with a kaleidoscopic range of greens. Mostly there is an unnatural bright green, like an explosion of unpleasant fluorescent paint, marking vast soy plantations that dwarf the farms of Devon or Dorset.

'When I was young – in fact, when I was not so young – this was all still forest,' muses Andrea. I had a similar conversation with Batsola as we flew across Madagascar. The two countries have both suffered colossal rates of deforestation. In the last couple of decades the forests in Paraguay have vanished. Those naysayers who say humans are too insignificant a species to affect our global climate should travel around the Tropic of Capricorn and they will see the endless damage wreaked by our 'insignificant species'.

After an hour or so in the air, we circle an airfield a soy ranch is kindly allowing us to use. As we come in to land there is a small shape on the short, grassy runway. The major makes a snorting noise as he spots a challenge. There is a sheep grazing happily in the middle of the airfield. At first I accept this calmly. Then the next second I realise the danger. There is a sheep on the runway!

The major pulls back on the controls and the nose of the plane rises a few degrees. We pass just over the sheep with a satisfying whoosh of air and hit the ground, racing along towards a fence at the end of the field. For a moment I have a nasty feeling we are about to meet with an unfortunate accident. But the major's bulk provides useful ballast. We rumble to a stop.

In this remote area of the country, hours from the nearest town, Andrea has arranged for me to meet Diego Segovia, a smart, young, earnest sociologist, educated in Rome, who works for Base-IS, a Paraguayan campaign group investigating the impact of soy on the land and the people.

Together we drive out to the edge of a huge, hilly soy field, an ocean of the stuff, and walk along a track between young soy plants with the threatening appearance of geraniums. Soy now comprises more than 50 per cent of Paraguay's exports. Diego tells me that Paraguay is going through a soy boom and has become the world's fourth largest exporter of soy after the US, Brazil and Argentina.

'What's the soy being grown for here?' I ask Diego.

'Two things,' he says. 'First is mainly for Europe, where it's used to feed pigs and cattle, and the other is for use as a biofuel. To grow the soy for biofuel, we're chopping down huge forests, which will contribute to global warming. It's crazy! And land that is being used for farming is being transformed into land for soy. You can't take food from poor people to make fuel for cars. That's not right. During the last few years, millions of hectares of woods, peasant and native territories, have been turned into a huge green desert where no other form of life subsists but soy.'

For an apparently harmless plant, extraordinary controversy surrounds soy. Forty per cent of a soybean is protein, a remarkably high rate. A farmer with an acre of land can produce around 18 times as much edible protein by farming soy compared to farming beef.

But while soy has a reputation as a food for vegetarians, who love the protein it gives them, most of it is actually bought by livestock farmers and consumed from troughs.

In Europe, where the Mad Cow crisis finally forced farmers to stop perverting nature by feeding ground-up animal carcasses to herbivores, demand for soy as a livestock feed has rocketed. In China, where meat consumption has more than trebled in the last 20 years, soy imports increased by a factor of ten between 1999 and 2003. For as people are lifted out of poverty, they want less rice and more pork. And pigs need to be fed.

Yet the resulting soy boom is benefiting just a few wealthy landowners in Paraguay. Across the country, activists claim that around 100,000 small farmers have been forced, bought or harassed off their land, as powerful soybean farmers, many of them Brazilian, snap up estates and create huge industrial farms. Protest has been silenced. More than 100 Paraguayan peasant leaders have been murdered and hundreds more have been jailed for dissent. Paraguay now has the most unequal rate of land distribution on the continent, with around 75 per cent of land owned by just two per cent of the population, and rampant corruption ensures few of that two per cent pay taxes that help the country. In fact, in a recent corruption study Paraguay came 144th out of 159 countries. Meanwhile, thousands of peasants are being forced from their land and many of those that remain are being poisoned by the excessive use of chemicals.

'The pesticides that are being used are killing everything – people's animals, their crops, and even their children,' says Diego angrily.

We reach the top of a low mound, the middle of the field. I can see for miles in every direction. All is soy. This soy boom is built on greed and gluttony: the desire of Europeans for cheap feed for their intensively farmed pigs and cattle, and the demand of the emerging Chinese middle-class for meat. There is a direct connection between the food we eat in Europe and the deforestation of land for soy in South America.

But, as Diego explains, there is a second, increasingly important reason for the soy boom in Paraguay and across South America. It is the result of one of the most important shifts in global agriculture for decades, perhaps ever.

The EU, US and China want ten per cent of car fuel to be substituted for biofuel, made from soy, wheat, sugar cane and similar crops. The British government has said five per cent of fuel sold in petrol stations must be biofuel by 2010. As a result farmers around the world are switching from growing food that can be eaten to growing crops that can be used as fuel. Vast tracts of forested land across South America and Asia are being cleared for biofuels. By 2020 demand for soy will have increased by at least 60 per cent. In Paraguay landowners are planning to almost double soy production in the next few years. Where will they find the land?

Some see soy and biofuels as a greener alternative to oil and petrol, and a means of mitigating climate change. But to reach the goals set for biofuels we will need to turn one-sixth of the agricultural surface of the planet over to their growth. As the population of the planet keeps increasing, what are people supposed to eat? Something will have to give.

I for one am hugely sceptical about biofuels for a host of social and environmental reasons. If we use biofuels made from soy or wheat to fuel our cars, we are immediately setting the one billion people in the world who go hungry every day against the one billion wealthy motorists. The purchasing power of the drivers means the hungry poor do not stand a chance. And this is the situation now, when there are 6.5 billion of us. What happens as that figure rises to more than 9 billion by the middle of the century? What will all those billions of extra mouths be eating if we are growing less edible food than we are now? Small wonder that Jean Ziegler, the UN's special rapporteur, has described the use of arable land to grow crops for fuel as 'a crime against humanity'. Ziegler sees a disaster looming, because when rich drivers in the West fill their cars with biofuel they will be depriving the starving poor of a meal.

So why has this happened? Partly because our politicians are terrified of asking us to reduce our energy consumption, and partly because they cravenly follow the demands of big business. When the European Union had a chance to force car manufacturers to make their cars more fuel efficient they baulked, and instead decided to increase the use of biofuels.

But biofuels are not even good for the planet. Major university studies show that biofuels produce less energy than is used to grow and process them. According to one report from scientists at Cornell

University and the University of California, Berkeley, making biodiesel from soy results in a net energy loss of 27 per cent. Which means touting soy as the answer to our energy problems is sheer madness. Palm oil, another biofuel, appears to be even more dangerous. One study by the respected Dutch consultancy Delft Hydraulics shows that a ton of palm oil results in 33 tons of carbon dioxide emissions. That's more than ten times worse than petrol. Ten times!

The consequences of the biofuel boom are already becoming apparent. The price of wheat has doubled in the last year, the price of maize has doubled over the last 18 months. There have been empty shelves and violent protests over food prices in Central and South America, India and Africa.

As ancient forests and land used for edible crops are cut to make way for biofuels in countries like Paraguay, the era of cheap food is coming to an end. It is a dangerous experiment. I fear the consequences will be messy. This competition over land for food or fuel seems likely to be one of the epic issues of the century.

DESPITE THE best efforts of soy farmers, there is still forest in this region of Paraguay. Not much, but it does still exist. The Mbaracayú Reserve, a 64,000-hectare chunk of land, still close to Capricorn on the Brazilian border, is privately owned by Moises Bertoni, a Paraguayan foundation.

A long drive on cratered roads through rich, undulating land farmed for soy and cattle, takes Andrea, myself and the rest of the team to the main reserve lodge, where we meet up with René Palacios, a warm Paraguayan biologist who runs the foundation's work out here.

The offices are a collection of wooden thatched buildings in a large woodland clearing. Around the clearing is the start of the forest, one of the few remaining chunks of the extraordinary Atlantic forest, an enormously important ecosystem with biodiversity comparable to the Amazon rainforest.

'Everyone has heard of the forest in the Amazon basin, but not enough have heard of the Atlantic forest,' says René.

René explains that it gets its name because it once stretched from the Atlantic coast inland across southern Brazil, Paraguay and Argentina. It used to cover 1,000,000 square kilometres, four times the size of the UK. Now it has been felled into near oblivion, suffering proportionately much greater destruction than the Amazon basin. Less than ten per cent survives.

'What's the difference between those two great forests, in simple terms I can understand?' I ask René.

'Well, the Amazon forest is up on the Equator and is entirely tropical. And the Atlantic forest is down here, further south, fed by the Río Paraná and Río Paraguay, and it's sub-tropical here, even temperate in some parts. There's also just one season on the Equator, whereas here we get summer and winter, and that helps to encourage an incredible variety of plants and animals.'

We stand on the steps of the main lodge building and René points out at the remaining Atlantic forest.

'Out there,' he says proudly, 'are more than 2,500 species of plant, and more than 400 species of bird.'

More than 90 per cent of the amphibians in the Atlantic forest are found nowhere else. In one recent survey, a single hectare of forest contained more than 450 different species of trees. Mbaracayú is home to some of the most fascinating creatures on the planet: jaguars, pumas, pig-like tapirs, harpy eagles, armadillos, collared anteaters, red-billed currasows, three-toed jacamars, seven-coloured tanagers, the web-footed capybara, the world's largest rodent, and the mysterious bush dog.

But we have lost so much in the last couple of decades.

René takes me into the kitchen of the lodge, where a poster is headlined 'Avance de la Deforestación'. Six maps of Paraguay, labelled from 1945 through to 2005, show, in graphic detail, the spreading deforestation across the eastern half of the country. In 1945 there were 8 million green hectares. Then colour seeps away like receding flood waters. By 2005 there are just isolated pockets, totalling 1.1 million hectares, none capable of supporting a rich variety of life. Except, that is, for the Mbaracayú Reserve. Thankfully, funding for this forest comes from a trust fund established by an electricity company in Hawaii that offsets its carbon emissions by protecting trees here in Paraguay. The rock group REM also made a healthy donation the reserve uses to fund its administration. The reserve is selling more carbon credits, if anyone is interested.

And they need the money. WWF describes the Atlantic forest as one of the world's most endangered tropical forests, under greater threat even than the Amazon rainforest. Paraguay had the second-highest rate of deforestation in the world until 2004, when new protection laws were introduced. Logging and clearing has since dropped by up to 85 per cent, but there isn't much left to lose. Most of the forest has already been felled.

René wants to take me into the forest, to see what his foundation is still protecting from the advance and ravages of the soy farmers. We decide to head towards an area where a community of indigenous people, the Aché, live on the edge of the reserve. They still hunt in the forest, using traditional methods such as bows and arrows.

After a night on a camp bed at the lodge, where I was attacked and bitten by insects the size of helicopters and hoglike tapirs snuffled around outside, we are back in the four-wheel drives, and back on the bumpy tracks. We circle the edge of the reserve through verdant land culled for farming.

'This was once all forest,' René tells me sadly. 'It was covered in trees.'

Four hours later we arrive on the outskirts of the Aché community. Gates are opened and we pass signs indicating we are entering a protected indigenous area. Then finally we are driving through the edge of the Mbaracayú forest and into Kuetuvy village.

The Aché have had an extraordinary history. Peaceful and gentle, they have also been capable of barbarism. In the past children born with dark skin, a bad omen, were often killed at birth. Adults haunted by the spirits of the dead would exorcise the demons by sacrificing a child. And until just a few decades ago this ancient forest tribe were practising cannibals. It is a term long used by colonial powers around the world as a smear to justify subjugation or extermination. The great anthropologist Pierre Clastres lived among the Aché in the 1960s, and concluded their cannibalism was based on a ritual, an almost spiritual desire to store and internalise relatives and friends after their death. But it was still cannibalism.

The drive into their community is familiar. The last time I entered a remote indigenous village was just ten days ago, when I spent a couple of days with the Wichí in northern Argentina. This community is similar, but with an air of permanence and modern development. There are huts, horses, small gardens, short electricity pylons, a couple of village lights, even a satellite dish, and as we roll along a narrow track between homes and come to a halt next to a community hall, I can hear a stereo booming traditional music to a large group of locals who regard us with warmth and curiosity.

As I enter the community for the first time, the historical cannibalism of the Aché encourages a certain frisson of danger. But this new, unfamiliar element of risk quickly dissipates as wide-eyed, smiling children run towards our car to welcome the visitors. They have light skin, vaguely oriental features, and a strange desire to use me as a climbing frame. Kids here appear cleaner and healthier than Wichí children, and in an infinitely better state than youngsters in the Australian indigenous communities I visited.

In the centre of the community a group of young adults are slaughtering a hog, cleansing and removing the skin. The local reserve ranger tells René and me that a father and son died recently in the community, and villagers believe they have assumed the form of wild pigs. I wonder if feasting on the pig is an updated, twenty-first-century version of their cannibalism, a more socially acceptable form of internalising their loved ones. But it is not the time to ask.

As we wait for the arrival of the *cacique*, the village chief, Andrea and I hand out a few footballs as presents for the children, who run off to play on a makeshift pitch on the edge of the community, and Andrea gives me a sense of the suffering experienced by indigenous people in Paraguay.

'It's terrible,' she says, 'but indigenous people weren't even viewed as citizens of the state until 1991, after we became a democracy and brought in a new constitution. Many people in Paraguay still think they are some sort of subhuman group. I remember talking to a very respectable family, and they said they had forced indigenous people off their land by killing their dogs so they could not hunt.'

In terms of its contemporary treatment of indigenous minorities, Paraguay strikes me as the most backward nation I have visited on Capricorn. The isolation of the country, the dictatorship, the greed of farmers all seem to have encouraged genocidal campaigns waged against the first people of the nation. Tens of thousands were slaughtered. Some early hunters kept the skin of their victims to use as hammocks. During the 1970s, foreign hunters were still being taken on shooting tours targeting indigenous tribes. Andrea pauses before delivering her bombshell.

'Even well into the 90s there were areas of Paraguay where indigenous people were still hunted like animals.'

'The 1990s?' I exclaim.

I find this appalling, staggering and, given Paraguay's remoteness, somehow entirely believable.

'Yes. So I ask you. Who are the savages?'

Then Margarita Mbywangi, the Aché *cacique*, appears. She has a fever, but has forced herself out of bed to greet the visitors. She is in her 40s, round, light-skinned, barefoot, a couple of feet shorter than me, as, I can now empirically conclude, are most indigenous people along Capricorn, and blessed with a face that radiates warmth and kindness. She is also, to my surprise, a woman, one of the first female indigenous leaders in the country, democratically elected by this community to act as their central point of contact with the outside world.

It is dusk, and Margarita, René and I take a stroll around the village, and we discuss the extraordinary changes this community has endured and embraced in just the last few decades. Some Aché communities did not meet white folk until 1978. Photos from around the period apparently show an Aché woman breastfeeding an orphaned monkey. After contact with the outside world came roads, violence as they were hunted and killed by Paraguayan farmers and soldiers, then segregation on small patches of land, followed by lives of occasional farm work, money, electricity, satellite television and democracy. As Margarita explains all this, I shake my head in appalled wonder. There can be few groups on the planet forced to adapt and change so quickly.

Margarita's personal story is as extraordinary as the tale of her people. When she was five years old her village was attacked by Paraguayans and razed to the ground. She was found hiding nearby and kidnapped, sold into servitude on a farm ranch. Aché children were highly prized as slaves by Paraguayan families, thanks to their pale skin. After years suffering alone Margarita found herself with a family who gave her an education, and eventually she returned to her community to give them leadership and wisdom learnt from contact with the outside world. Now she is working with the Paraguayan opposition and looks likely to be elected as a Paraguayan senator. By the time you read this, Margarita might just be sitting in the national government.

As I talk with Margarita, one of the rangers runs up and motions René aside. I was hoping to spend more time chatting with Margarita and then sleep in the Aché village, but there is another, smaller indigenous community nearby. Apparently they are drunk, jealous and unhappy about our presence in the Aché village. They demand we leave immediately, and so we drive to a nearby ranch and camp among fields of soy.

DAWN THE next morning and I am brushing my teeth under a bloody, crimson sky. It is a good omen for hunting. Before the jealous locals wake from their drunken stupor, we slip back into the Aché community and meet with Margarita.

Margarita is still barefoot and still poorly. But she has arranged for us to go hunting deep in the forest, and by 7 a.m. René, Brian, Dominic and I are joined by five experienced hunters carrying long-bows and six-foot arrows made of light bamboo and topped with metal knives. I lift one with my finger. It balances perfectly. The men are dressed in dirty Western cast-offs. Three are barefoot. But as we march out of the village and into the forest, they set a blistering pace.

It is my first time in the hot, humid Atlantic forest and my senses are overloaded by a cacophony of sounds and new smells. Floating through the trees comes the intense sound of bird song, followed by clacking as thick 15-metre-tall bamboo stems clatter together in the wind. We pause by a path and one of the hunters hits a thick tree with his bow. Tiny bright orange fruits plop to the ground and the Aché stoop and fire them down their throats, sharing them among them-selves and with their wheezing guests. The fruit is sweet and delicious, but the greatest thrill for me – a privilege of life-affirming dimensions – is simply to be following Aché hunters doing what they have done for thousands of years, feasting on fruits, berries and seeds as they go in search of bigger game.

And then we are off again, trotting together at speed along narrow, overgrown paths. Short and wiry, the Aché slip under fallen trunks and between thick bamboo like the wispy forest breeze. I, by contrast, stumble, duck under logs and fall over branches like an ogre with arthritis. Within an hour of trekking and fighting our way through the undergrowth, sliding across log bridges over forest streams and clam-bering up low hills, I am utterly drenched in sweat and the numbing, poisonous taste of Deet insect repellent is running down my face and into my mouth. But my suffering is nothing compared to that of Brian, who bravely insists on carrying his 13 kilogram camera on a hunt that turns into an exhausting full-body workout.

We walk through the forest for nearly five hours, but see nothing on the ground bigger than a small lizard. I sense desperation among the Aché, a tribe unable to display their skills and the bounty of their forest. But the truth is their world has changed.

Eventually we find ourselves on one far edge of the forest. It is an extraordinary sight, a boundary between two worlds. On our side of a new fence the forest world of the Aché hunter-gatherers is pressed up tightly against a field of grass. Beyond that are fields and fields of soya.

One of the hunters, the youngest, speaks Spanish. Through René I ask whether he feels the world of the Aché is getting smalller.

'Yes,' he replies, 'we feel like we are losing our home. We really need the forest, and it's our right. Without the forest there is no hope for us. The biggest change has been the soy plantations. Soy farmers take a huge area of land and use massive amounts of chemicals and pesticides, which is bad for the soil, and the water, and the people. The government is not seeing this, so we feel like we're alone, fighting against soy in this area.'

I grip the wire fence. 'This feels to me like the barrier between two worlds. Does that make sense?'

He nods. 'We used to find our food in the forest, and we were happy and healthy. Now it is completely different, and now we have a lot of problems. This used to be forest, and now it is like different worlds in the same area.'

The Aché are not hugely interested in the world beyond their boundaries, beyond this fence. But they are fully aware their own world has changed. After pushing them to extinction, Paraguayans and soy farmers across this region have taken their best hunting land.

We have caught nothing on our hunting trip, and we have seen nothing, just empty holes where armadillos once lurked. Then one hunter spots chubby green membe fruits high in a tree next to this border fence, and the Aché shin up the trunk and lob the fruits to the ground. There is a palpable sense of relief among the hunters. We will not return to the village empty-handed.

Back among the huts, I snatch a few more moments with Margarita. I ask if she has any advice for other indigenous groups. Her world is the forest, and she talks movingly of the need to protect and conserve the environment.

'Indigenous people have been treated so badly over the years. Such discrimination,' she says. She is talking of Paraguay, but it could be any country. Now the Aché have a patch of land they can call their own. But it was only secured after their near-annihilation by farmers who tracked and killed them. They have learnt to fear European Paraguayans. The Aché tell me one of their old legends says that at the beginning of time, when the Great Jaguar told all the people what they were supposed to do on Earth, he left the whites out. He was afraid of them himself.

It was only when Aché numbers fell to a tolerable level, and the prospect of their extinction was proving politically and internationally embarrassing, that they were finally given protection. So the price of their independence has been astronomical. Will the Wichí have to endure virtual obliteration before they are given protection and land? Will the San in the Kalahari? What if they just face the former and never benefit from the latter?

I would have gladly spent another few days in the community

chatting with Margarita. But the future senator is leaving, barefoot, to visit a distant Aché community, and we must get back on the road and head to Ciudad del Este, a Paraguayan town on the Brazilian border.

I am gathering both my thoughts and my bags when Margarita gives me a treasured necklace made from old monkey teeth and the molar of a snuffling tapir. A gift of the forest. I have only functional offerings to make in return. But we hug, and she wishes me a safe journey across to the Atlantic coast. Kilometre by kilometre, my journey is coming to an end.

THE ROAD to Ciudad del Este takes us hundreds of kilometres through eastern Paraguay. Every dozen kilometres or so there is yet another huge soy silo with trucks and lorries waiting to be filled with produce they will truck overland to the coast for export. Once this area of the country was home to villages, small farms, families and schools. But soy needs the tending care of fewer labourers than other crops, so families have left and the schools are empty.

The driver of our car is a former Paraguayan stand-up comedian with a routine distinguishable only by its complete lack of humour, in any language. Unfortunately, he thinks Andrea and I are a captive audience for his old material. Eschewing politeness, I attach earphones to my laptop and make notes about the green desert. A depressing sight, it spreads for millions of acres across plains and hills, and runs right up to the road for long stretches, a clear breach of Paraguayan laws that state farmers should leave a safety gap between the ground they spray with chemicals and areas where people drive and live.

Together we all roll through land reeking of decay and rot – the stench of herbicides and pesticides – and villages that are shrinking on to ever smaller patches of land. All around, the ground is covered with soy. Even patches of land between houses are growing soy. It is the same fever, the same hunger for money, that I saw infecting Malagasy in the gem-rush town of Ilakaka. An infectious desire.

By late evening we finally reach Ciudad and check into a quiet hotel on the outskirts. The next morning we are out early to wander through the town.

Ciudad del Este is a town unlike any other in Paraguay. Essentially a huge shopping hell, it was set up by the dictator Stroessner as a duty-free zone to milk Brazilians and other visitors of their cash. Shopping malls here sell everything from fine French champagne and perfumes to grand pianos. Ciudad is now the third largest tax-free zone in the world after Hong Kong and Miami. But while those temples to consumerism have clean shops and tarmac on the streets, Ciudad is a crazy, crowded, claustrophobic sort of town where a jumbled jungle of stalls and vendors sell trainers, football shirts, inflatable paddling pools, tents, porno DVDs, umbrellas, sunglasses, pirated CDs, medicines, electronic gadgets and gizmos, marijuana, car parts, power tools, all by the side of dingy streets and sometimes in the middle of the road. It is dirty, dusty, smelly and frenetic. It is also one of the great smuggling centres of the world.

Taxes in Paraguay are among the lowest in South America, at around four per cent. In Brazil, just across the border, they are the highest on the continent, often around 80 per cent. So bulk whole-salers in the backstreets of Ciudad, often Lebanese or Chinese, sell to small-time smugglers, known as 'little ants', who shuffle to and from Brazil carrying small loads of goods under the £150 limit allowed by Brazilian customs for sale in Brazilian cities often hundreds of kilo-metres away. Some ants make 20 trips a day.

Along with a shady reputation for smuggling, Ciudad has developed a darker status in recent years. American intelligence agents claim the infamous tri-border region between Paraguay, Argentina and Brazil is a major centre for funding terrorism. They allege that militants from the Hezbollah group, which has killed scores of Israelis in the Middle East yet also runs hospitals and schools in Lebanon, have been raising huge funds among the tens of thousands of Muslim Lebanese who have come to live here and make their fortunes. The claims emerged after the attacks of 9/11, and have been variously confirmed, denied, then confirmed and denied again.

What does seem to have happened is that Lebanese expats in Ciudad have been sending huge sums of money back to their families in the Middle East. Some of the money has doubtless ended up in the hands of militants the US and Israeli governments view as terrorists or terrorist supporters. Separately, Hezbollah has operated protection rackets in Ciudad, demanding a cut of the profits made by import–export businesses, on pain of identifying those who refuse as 'Israeli agents' – with difficult consequences for individuals in Ciudad and their families back in Lebanon. Certificates were even given confirming receipt of payment to those sensible enough to pay. But wilder allegations of terrorist training camps around the area, or that al-Qaeda has been trying to establish itself in the tri-border region, seem far-fetched.

On the day I wander around Ciudad, the local paper has a story claiming Hezbollah is still raising huge sums in the town. Andrea suggests I take the story with a pinch of salt. Paraguayan papers are notoriously inventive. The next day one of the national newspapers runs a story directly contradicting the local Ciudad paper. Who knows what to believe? Local investigators do not have a single

Arabic-speaker on their staff, and American intelligence has, to say the least, been somewhat discredited of late. Israeli agents have been trying for years to link Hezbollah with al-Qaeda, connecting as it would one of their great enemies with the group threatening to anni-hilate the West, but with little success.

So until someone produces concrete evidence of terrorism here Ciudad del Este will continue to be just a fantastically dodgy town; a home to all manner of nefarious activity. Wandering around the shops I see knock-off versions of Microsoft computer programmes and fake brand-name mobile phones. No wonder the Americans, so beholden to their huge corporations, would like to see this place shut down.

The Friendship Bridge links Ciudad, on one side of the Paraná River, the second-largest in South America, with Brazil on the other. It is time for us to leave Paraguay. Our passports are stamped, we say goodbye to Andrea, and we turn our cars towards the final country on our Capricorn journey.

12 · BRAZIL

CROSSING THE dirty Paraná River into Brazil is a culture shock. We drive from crazy, claustrophobic Ciudad del Este into the emerging superpower that is modern Brazil.

The rest of the world thinks Brazil is one endless party. A land of beaches, bottoms, sunshine and cold cocktails in primary colours. A country where the national essence can be distilled into a single word: *Carnival!*

But this is a vast country, the size of the continental United States, and wider at one point than the distance from London to Moscow. It is a country with serious aspirations, a country with a space programme, a resource-rich country that could light and feed half the world, and which sees itself, along with China, India and Russia, as a powerhouse of the future.

So the customs point on the Brazilian side of the river is a huge new bus depot sort of a place with a high roof and a carefully tended garden with bright magnolias in flowerbeds. Smart young Polícia Federal agents, dressed in black with Glock handguns strapped to their legs, are studying the hundreds of Paraguayans who cross on foot, on an endless stream of motorcycles and motorbike taxis, and in the cars and trucks that constantly flow past. Despite the frenetic activity, there is an immediate sense of order and control, a marked contrast with the eccentricity of Paraguay. I am going to miss that steamy land.

As my passport is being stamped, the last entry mark it will receive on this Capricorn journey, there is a flurry of movement at the side of the bus depot and Fernando Cavalcanti, my energetic, dreadlocked Brazilian fixer and guide, who was waiting for us here at the border post, tugs me towards an area through which motorcycles are being funnelled and checked.

'They've caught a smuggler,' he says breathlessly as we jog towards a black-clad agent still handcuffing a swarthy young man he has taken from the back of a motorbike. The smuggler was carrying a small, innocuous plastic bag, which is searched in a customs office. Inside the bag, among clothes and socks, are small packets wrapped in newspaper. An agent produces a sharp knife and cuts one open. There are rows of .38-calibre bullets. Around 28 in each pack. The smuggler just shrugs. He has the attitude of a man who considers arrest an occupational hazard.

'Why did you decide to stop this particular guy?' I ask the arresting agent.

'Well, he had tattoos and he looked like a criminal!' he responds. No doubt there then.

Two minutes later the agent stops another motorbike passenger, less visibly criminal this time. The agent pulls up a baggy trouser leg, exposing dozens of slender white boxes taped together with Sellotape. It is an extraordinary sight. Again, the man accepts his fate calmly. The agent opens one box with a penknife. Computer chips. Worth about £100 per box on the Paraguayan side, where taxes are low, they would sell for at least twice the price in Brazil, where taxes are high.

'If a motorcyclist is bringing these across, what on earth is coming across in the trucks and lorries?' I ask the agent.

He nods thoughtfully. The police know they only catch a fraction of the smuggled goods. Brazil misses hundreds of millions of pounds each year in lost tax revenue thanks to Ciudad.

'Most of the smuggling happens along the river,' he says. 'That's the hardest area for us to monitor.'

So Fernando checks us into a hotel in Foz do Iguaçu, the city on the Brazilian side of the tri-border junction, and we arrange to meet up with the federal police for a river patrol along the border.

Fernando and I have just enough time for a beer and a chat about our journey across the country. My new guide is an informed and friendly photographer, the same age as me, who spent years living and working in London. Together we will make a few stops in the tri-border area before heading to the vast metropolis of São Paulo, Fernando's home town, which straddles Capricorn like a colossus. Roads east will take us to the coast, the solstice, and the end of my journey. We clink bottles and wish each other luck. For the first time I can now make out the finishing post in the distance.

As we natter about places we have visited, Fernando tells me that when he was younger he went on an exchange programme to Argentina. 'I have tons of friends there,' he says.

I can't resist asking.

'So what do you think of Argentineans?' Surely he must be a fan.

'Oh, they're lovely people,' he replies, 'and Buenos Aires is an amazing city. I love life there.'

But then he continues. 'Of course, they're completely stuck up. You know, the best deal in the world is to buy an Argentinean for the price that he's worth, and then sell him for the price he thinks he's worth.'

I can't help laughing. Fernando keeps going.

'And do you know what "ego" is?' he asks cryptically. 'Ego is the little Argentinean that lives inside all of us. Ah, but you have to love them.'

AT NINE that night we drive out of Foz to an unmarked police base on a quiet road near the vast Itaipu lake. Up to 13 kilometres wide, the man-made lake runs along the border for more than 170 kilometres. It is the perfect crossing point for smugglers.

The head of the river patrol unit, nicknamed the Black Panthers, is not happy to see us. We have been imposed on him from above, and he is worried about our safety and security. He does not want us to use his name or his photograph. He gives us a long briefing explaining the dangers of patrolling the water and the threats his men face. Then the armoury in the corner of his office is unlocked and the unit weaponry is produced. Heavy machine guns emerge, the sort mounted on top of large tanks, sub-machine guns, boxes of ammunition, grenades and grenade launchers, side arms and flares. Four police agents, short, muscular men wearing black combat uniforms, boots and flak jackets, are taking us out on patrol, along with an array of fearsome weaponry.

Leaving the base in large, blacked-out four-wheel drives, we drive down quiet roads towards the lake with our headlights off.

'Smugglers are always watching our base,' says one of the agents. 'If they spot us heading out on patrol, they'll cancel deliveries.'

A sleek, lean, matt-black motorboat is waiting at the lakeside next to a rickety wooden jetty. It has the sinister air of a boat used by the bad guys in a Bond film, a 'stealth' boat, built for speed. The agents begin mounting a large machine gun on the front of the boat.

'Is that really necessary?' I ask, wondering aloud how much of the weaponry is just a show for the visitors.

The captain of the boat gives me a steely, serious look. 'The smugglers have M16s, Armalites. On the shore they have heavier machine guns, with a range of more than a mile. Often when one of their boats is crossing, the gang on the bank lay down covering fire.'

'What, they just fire across the lake?'

'Exactly.'

I start to take proceedings a little more seriously.

Four of us are travelling with the agents. Fernando, Brian, Dominic and me, your scribbler. The captain produces flak jackets. I look at mine suspiciously. It is wafer thin.

'That's not going to stop a high-velocity round, is it?' I ask the captain.

'It will stop bullets from smaller guns,' he says. 'We need to have a balance between a jacket that can stop a bullet and a jacket that will drag you straight to the bottom if you go overboard.'

Ah yes. The other threat out on water. Over the top of the flak jacket goes a flotation harness with a buoyancy aid that emerges when a toggle is pulled. The whole get-up is heavy and restrictive, and the boat is small and lacking armour. I start to wonder whether this patrol is a good idea. But Fernando seems to be loving the experience. With camouflage combat trousers, thick dreadlocks down his back and a wispy goatee on his chin, he makes quite a sight.

'Apparently, the smugglers use tracer bullets when they fire at the cops,' Fernando says excitedly. 'It must look beautiful when there's a battle between the two sides.'

I shoot him a quizzical look.

'Beautiful? Are you mad?' I say. 'We might be stuck in the middle of that.'

He laughs. And I start to worry whether my new guide is in possession of a full set of marbles.

We clamber aboard the boat and the captain, a studious, bespectacled agent transformed into Action Man by the weapons and holsters strapped to his waist and thigh, ignites the engine. There is a throaty rumble, and we move slowly away from the jetty and out on to the dark lake, passing petrified trees illuminated by a waning moon.

'No lights,' orders the captain. 'We don't want smugglers to know we're on the way.'

We pass the final tree and the captain opens the throttle. The rumble turns into a roar, and the vessel becomes a powerboat. I sit at the back as we race across the water, the only light coming from the vast solar show above our heads, a million sparkling jewels. There are also shooting stars. Again and again they streak across the night sky, almost every time I glance up.

At the wheel, the captain guides our progress through the night with the help of a radar display. A young agent mans the machine-gun position at the front, night-vision goggles attached to his head, and the other two agents stand on each side, also using goggles to scan the water for smugglers. And so we speed across the water. On one side is Paraguay, just visible through the black night. Makeshift chutes on the bank enable smugglers to shift quantities of goods into boats or bales of drugs into the water. On the other side of the boat is Brazil, with a strip of trees along the water hiding dozens of smugglers' tracks and secret slipways. We rocket down the middle, moving faster than I have ever travelled on water. Something pokes my arm. It is the business end of one agent's Heckler & Koch sub-machine gun. The box I am sitting on is packed with grenades, flares and spare ammunition clips. I feel distinctly uneasy.

Then a bright shooting star skips along our atmosphere, leaving a wide trail through the heavens.

I glance at Brian, my friend and fellow traveller along Capricorn, and we share a wry smile. We both know our involvement on this patrol is a privilege. But we also know something could go horribly wrong: an accident; a silent tree-trunk floating in the water; a stray bullet; an accurate bullet. All could turn our Capricorn journey into a complete disaster.

As we speed through the night, Fernando and I chat with the captain, asking what the smugglers are taking across the water.

'There are guns and drugs, of course – weed and cocaine,' he tells me. 'But the risks for smuggling those are much higher. If a smuggler is caught with drugs they will spend years in jail. So the main goods they smuggle are cigarettes, pesticides and electronics. They can make as much money from smuggling them into Brazil as from smuggling weed. Not as much as they get for cocaine, but with much lower risks.'

'Pesticides?' I query.

'Yes, illegal Chinese pesticides. We have strong environmental rules in Brazil, but some farmers try to use dangerous chemicals to control their fields.'

Ironically, because Paraguay is land-locked, almost all of the smuggled goods originally entered South America via Brazilian ports. Shipped overland in sealed containers, they are unpacked in Paraguay, and then smuggled back into Brazil for sale. It is now just 12 days before Christmas, and nine days before the solstice. According to the captain, over the past few nights smugglers have been moving electrical goods for sale in markets in Rio and São Paulo.

After 15 minutes flying across the water, the captain cuts the engines and we drift to a halt.

'Now we wait,' he says.

And so we sit there, hushed, in the darkness in the middle of the lake, bristling with weaponry, ears open and guns at the ready. An agent passes me his night-vision goggles. They transform the darkness into green light. I scan the water, but nothing stirs. The captain keeps his eyes on the radar, looking for other boats on the water. Yet the radar has limitations. Our ears might detect what it cannot. Ten minutes pass. Then twenty. Undercover cops have told me their work is 90 per cent boredom and 10 per cent terror. Never more true than here.

We shift around in the boat. Eyelids acquire weight. My brain wants to stay awake and alert. There could be a gun battle at any moment. Yet the rocking motion of the waves and the black night are soporific, and I doze as we drift.

Then, after about half an hour, one of the agents taps my arm. The faintest of sounds is floating across the water behind our boat. An engine? A distant car? A boat? The sound is barely audible, muffled. But suddenly we are all alert, ready. The agents swivel their night-vision goggles, scanning the water. I cup my hands behind my ears, trying to locate the noise. It rises just a trace.

'It sounds like a scout,' the captain whispers. 'When they smuggle a large load across the water, the smugglers will send a smaller boat to check the coast is clear. We must be quiet, and patient.'

We wait. If the captain is right, a major load will be heading across the water. If he is wrong, we might be missing a smaller shipment of guns, drugs, stereos or car parts. All come across the water.

It is a tense experience. The agents are edgy and excitable, checking their weapons and slipping spare magazines into their pockets.

But, slowly, over long minutes, the muffled engine noise disappears into the darkness. And then we are embraced by silence. Again, we wait, this time hoping for bigger fish. Above the boat, the radar spins around and around, scanning for a target. Another 30 minutes pass.

'Perhaps they spotted us,' muses the captain. We wait again for another 20 minutes. Then at 3.30 a.m. the captain makes the call. He guns the engines, shattering the silence, and we head back to base. No catch tonight.

THE NEXT morning Fernando and I are invited to the Polícia Federal headquarters for a chat. It is a modern building housing elite Brazilian crime-fighting units. In the lobby two agents are drinking coffee next to a cappuccino machine. Sub-machine guns are slung casually over their shoulders. At the back of the police car park, beyond their armoured cars, are more than 300 vehicles confiscated from smugglers. There are new coaches, worth tens of thousands of pounds, trucks, lorries, new cars, old bangers and motorcycles. To the side are huge grey and green metal boats, great empty floating sheds, like D-Day landing craft, with powerful outboard motors.

'They can easily fit $2 million worth of goods in these,' says the plain-clothes officer who shows us around. 'Just one trip pays the cost of the boat. Anything beyond that is a bonus for them.'

The boats have small petrol tanks. They just need to get across the lake. They're not built for cruising.

'It's a game of cat and mouse,' says the agent. 'We can never know exactly where they will appear. But they always know we will be out there waiting for them. And we must be ready for whatever they use against us.'

The officer has a gun wedged into his trouser waistband, stuck in a dirty blue sock.

'It has a slim profile, which is vital if you're working undercover, and keeps the gun free of moisture,' he says with a smile. 'And I can fire it through the sock if I need to draw it in a hurry.' Clearly the police do things differently in Brazil.

With him is another agent, also hiding a handgun around his waist, who wears a T-shirt bearing a bold picture of a SWAT team raiding a house. I don't like to say anything, but I can't help thinking that if they are supposed to be working undercover, this rather gives the game away.

THE RIVERS of this region are home to smugglers and also two spectacular sites just a short distance apart. One is among the most extraordinary natural sights on the planet. The other is a man-made wonder. It would be folly to travel through this region without visiting both.

The first is approached by a road from our hotel that takes us through a forest, along winding roads full of tourist coaches, to a small car park where we leave our van. As we walk between tall trees, a low, thunderous rumble and a mist among the trees gives a tantalising suggestion of what awaits. We walk out of the forest on a metal walkway and emerge at the edge of the Iguaçu waterfalls, an entire horseshoe arc of roaring water that cascades over the edges of a gigantic canyon, thunders to the river below and races away through a Eden-like valley lined by lush tropical trees. My jaw drops. There are 270 waterfalls, the product of 30 rivers. The falls are taller and four times the width of Niagara. People have been known to weep when confronted by this sight. Eleanor Roosevelt said simply: 'Poor Niagara.'

Fernando and I walk to the edge of the falls, just metres from the water and close enough to see swifts slipping between the flow to their nests in the rocks behind. We walk down along another walkway that takes us over the very edge of the water. The water of more than five Olympic-sized swimming pools is being dumped over the falls every second. It is all most impressive. This is where they filmed the extraordinary opening scenes of *The Mission*, where a Jesuit priest plunges to his death down the falls while tied to a cross. These, surely, are the most beautiful falls in the world.

And so to the second sight, which we approach by helicopter, a luxury justified because we are filming and only height affords a true sense of scale. Paulo the pilot flies us from the Iguaçu Falls to the T-junction between the Iguaçu and Paraná rivers. On the left bank is Argentina, on the right Brazil, and opposite is Paraguay. We turn right, following the Paraná upstream, above the Friendship Bridge, past Ciudad del Este on our left and Foz on our right, everything in miniature beneath us, and then, after just a few more minutes, a great wall of concrete appears on the horizon in front of a vast lake.

Stretching for eight kilometres across the horizon, spread equally between Paraguay and Brazil, this is my second great sight of the day. It is an impregnable citadel, one of the great engineering wonders of the modern world, the Itaipu hydroelectric dam.

Construction of the dam used 15 times more concrete than was used to build the Channel Tunnel and 380 times the steel and iron of the Eiffel Tower. Embedded in the ground below the wall are 20 great whirring turbines that generate around a quarter of all the electricity used in Brazil, and all of Paraguay's.

The chopper carrying Fernando, Brian and me circles the dam, revealing the vast reservoir behind the endless wall where we patrolled the other night.

Then Paulo lowers us gently on to a landing pad just a mile from the concrete fortifications, where Fernando and I meet Professor Ildo

Sauer, an energy specialist who has kindly agreed to show us around. Academic and friendly, with floppy hair and banks of knowledge, the professor has briefed Tony Blair on energy policy. He bustles us into waiting cars and we hustle to the dam. Up close, at the base, it is the height of a 65-storey building and breathtaking. This is the most powerful hydroelectric dam in the world. At least it is until the Three Gorges Dam in China starts to churn power in a year or so.

The professor leads us along the base of the dam, explaining that to build this, a combined team of Brazilians and Paraguayans diverted the course of the Paraná River along a two-kilometre bypass by removing 55 million tons of earth and rock so they could begin construction. I find this engineering self-confidence astonishing, almost arrogance. Then they began constructing a miracle of engineering, all on a scale only possible when the governments involved are functioning dictatorships, or at least tinged with a strong streak of authoritarianism. More than 8,000 homes were flooded in the valley behind the dam and a waterfall rivalling Niagara was covered by the reservoir.

'They wouldn't get away with that now,' says the professor.

Jutting out of the colossal wall that towers above us are 20 giant metal pipes, called penstocks, more than 10 metres in diameter. I press my hand against the skin of the closest. It hums and pulses with life. The professor explains these tubes are carrying an astonishing volume of water, up to 700,000 litres a second, moving at high speed under intense pressure. The water inside pours on to huge turbines buried in a vast power plant below our feet at the rate of 160 tons a second, spinning giant steel rods, that run generators, which produce 12,600 megawatts of sparky power to light much of Brazil. The basic principle, of course, has changed little since the age of the watermill. A natural resource is harnessed and channelled for power. But before Itaipu an endeavour on this magnitude had never been attempted.

The professor takes us closer to the base, along a promontory in a wedge-shaped space that slims and narrows between the flanking buttresses propping up the dam wall. Everything is concrete. We approach a ledge, and I gasp. The promontory is a viewing point overlooking a space known as 'The Cathedral'. The dam wall rises and curves outwards above my head. It inspires a giddy feeling of insignificance, like standing outside a Tolkienesque castle. Below me the ground opens and falls away. I catch a glimpse of the bottom and my stomach churns and my knees wobble. I am struck with the sickening sensation of vertigo and the sensation of falling, of plummeting to the foundations. I try to steel myself and peek over the edge, albeit from a distance. On the floor of the Cathedral I can just make out rocks that once formed the bed of the river. The whole experience is dazzling and deeply disconcerting. This dam is that big.

I am more comfortable on top of the dam. But up there I shrink beneath the blistering sun. The professor laughs.

'This is what this is all about,' he says gesturing to the heavens. 'This is the tropical sun that drives the dam.'

Solar energy heats the Pacific. Water evaporates into the atmosphere, travels as fluffy clouds, then drops on to the forests of South America and flows down rivers like the Paraná into scores of dams like Itaipu. Brazil is completely dependent on hydroelectric power. It provides 85 per cent of the generating capacity for the country. But in recent years our changing planet has delivered lower rainfall to the forests and lower levels of water flowing through Brazil's dams. In recent years parts of the Amazon have dried up, even rivers more than a mile wide have become streams, prompting the Brazilian government to declare a state of emergency and reassess ambiguous environmental policies. Lorries have been needed instead of boats on dried riverbeds to ferry supplies to riverside towns hit by drought. It is the same throughout the world. As we monkey about with our environment, weather systems are becoming more unpredictable. And as droughts become more frequent, hydroelectric power becomes less reliable.

Yet still we continue with our environmental vandalism. Even Itaipu is not blameless. Although the water that gushes through this dam is nature's bounty, and does not emit carbon like coal or oil-fired power stations, the vast tropical reservoir behind the dam emits huge quantities of methane, a greenhouse gas more potent than carbon dioxide, as plant matter rots rapidly in the water. So it might still be doing more harm than good.

Standing on top of the dam and trying to take all of this in, I am struck by the realisation that it is in the tropics where much of our future will be decided. It is the region humans first emerged from, and where we might see the first glimmers of our end.

The tropics are perhaps the defining, driving force of our climate system. Mercilessly exposed to the furnace at the heart of our solar system, the region receives a much higher dose of the sun's energy than the rest of the planet. It is simultaneously the attraction of the tropics to outsiders, and the cause of much of the human suffering in the region.

More people will soon enjoy and endure these conditions, for the tropics, or at least the tropical conditions of the region, are expanding towards the poles. Scientists had feared this would happen. They predicted climate change would encourage the region to spread. But it is happening faster than their most severe predictions.

I have loosely followed Capricorn, identified as the southern border of the tropics by map-makers because it is the most southerly point at which the sun appears to be directly overhead during the summer and winter solstices. But even while I have been on my journey, scientists have discovered the tropical area of the planet has expanded polewards by more than 270 kilometres over the past 25 years. So the dry, arid areas of the world that we have passed through on our journey are expanding. Scientists expected this to happen, but only under an 'extreme scenario', and only by 2100. For this to happen already is terrifying.

Even energy experts like the professor cannot predict the consequences.

'This incredible area between the tropics of Capricorn and Cancer is the true home to the blinding sun,' he tells me as we squint at each other. 'The very existence of this dam is thanks to solar energy. And now the world wants to use the tropical sun between Cancer and Capricorn for biofuels, for ethanol, and, of course, for soy.'

'It seems that soy is becoming a curse for many in South America,' I say.

'Yes, but if we can find a way of producing it sustainably, it might be a silver bullet that helps us to reduce our carbon emissions.'

Most cars in Brazil already run on ethanol, obtained from sugarcane and sugar beet. Even more than Paraguay, Brazil sees itself as a major producer of biofuels. Vast areas of the country, areas larger than Britain, are being transformed by soy.

Back inside the dam, the professor talks of megawatts and kilowatts and takes us deep inside the guts of an engineering marvel, but I am still thinking of the tropical power outside. We see a vast rectangular chamber more than a kilometre long, the insides of a blackened turbine under repair, and the control room, with emergency shut-off switches that can cut the power to most of the country. Everything is huge, on a frightening, uncontrollable scale.

But the most extraordinary fact about this dam, at least for me, is the devastation it could cause if it fails. When it was being built the Argentineans suspected it was a secret weapon targeted against their capital. They talked darkly of Brazil's H2O bomb and started developing their own H-bomb. For if the dam wall breaks, perhaps after an earthquake, 29 billion cubic metres of fresh water will thunder down-river, creating a tsunami of biblical proportions that will rampage across the continent, wiping out Buenos Aires and potentially killing millions.

O N THAT worrying note, we leave the dam and aim for higher ground. Our next destination in Brazil is to the north-east, bang on Capricorn. We are heading for São Paulo.

An internal flight drags us across the country towards the great city. The plane is late, check-in staff are hopeless and the baggage-handlers try to throw our extensive consignment of camera equipment and luggage into the hold without tags, a sure guarantee we would never see them again.

The flight is full and next to me across the aisle is an elderly woman who sucks boiled sweets noisily throughout the journey and stares at me with evident distaste. I am tired now, weary of travel and overwhelmed by enough experiences and encounters on this journey to last my lifetime. I will not miss being cooped up in four-wheel drives and planes when I return to my normal sedentary existence at the end of this adventure.

But then we drop out of the clouds over São Paulo, and weariness leaves me as I am stunned once again by another Capricorn revelation, this time by the sheer scale of this enormous city, the largest on the line. São Paulo is, in fact, the biggest city in the entire southern hemisphere, the biggest city in the whole developing world. Officially, Greater São Paulo is home to 20 million Brazilians, putting it at number seven (behind Tokyo, Seoul, Mexico City, New York, Mumbai and Jakarta, if you're wondering). But another definition puts it at number two in the world and suggests there are nearly 30 million souls inside the metropolitan area. Either way, it is vast. The financial and industrial hub of the country, a home to more skyscrapers than New York and more helicopters than any city on Earth.

I strain my neck past the scowling old woman to catch glimpses of a city that sprawls from horizon to horizon. And then, too soon, we are landing and passengers are leaping out of seats to retrieve their bags with a haste suggesting they have previously been victims of onboard baggage theft.

Fernando drives us into his city in a rented plum-coloured van. We take a short detour to pass a Tropic of Capricorn sign on the outskirts of the city, and then we plunge straight into the urban heart. We drive along a four-lane highway that becomes an eight-lane motorway and dumps us into the centre of a fast-paced city drawn and quartered by endless stretches of tarmac.

How to capture a vision of a city the size of São Paulo? That afternoon we go for a drink at a bar on top of a hotel in the leafy Jardins district designed to look like half an enormous watermelon. No, really.

The view over my cold, sugary caipirinha, Brazil's national cocktail, is a revelation of the future. The Skye Bar at the Unique Hotel, one of a mere 30,000 hotels in São Paulo, looks towards a skyline like few others on the planet. From the top of the hotel, the Jardins area around me appears to be a park, with mansions popping out between trees. But a few miles to the west, at the edge of Jardins, are hundreds of towering blocks running from the left of my vision to the right. Whenever an opening threatens to appear, it is filled by another block. It is a thicket of housing and offices, with not a gap visible. It is a vision from *Blade Runner*, a sight that almost makes the New York skyline look bland and provincial. And it is the future.

São Paulo, as much as anywhere in the world, is the sort of mega-city urban life that awaits mankind. I have been making my journey in the waning months of our time as a rural species. At some point soon, more of us will be urban than rural. Perhaps the tipping point has already happened. Certainly by the time this book is out we will have become a creature of towns, of cities, of São Paulos. There are now 22 cities in the Third World that have more than eight million inhabitants and qualify for UN status as a 'mega-city'. By the end of the century, if we survive that long, almost all of our species will be living like Paulistanos. It is a frightening future, for I challenge anyone to avoid feeling insignificant in São Paulo, a gargantuan, daunting city on a scale like few others.

I ask Fernando what distinguishes his home town from the delights of Rio, a few hundred kilometres away on the coast. He strokes his goatee thoughtfully.

'We work, they play. They live for the beach, for the day,' he says, 'we live for the night, for the bars, for the restaurants, for the clubs.'

That evening, approaching the end of the journey, we follow the advice of a welter of reviews and head for a Japanese restaurant lauded as one of the best in the world. It is an achingly dull little place and we are seated in a cubby hole in the back at the least desirable table on Earth, next to a man in a tiny office who appears to be running a mini-cab firm and a kitchen door that is slammed, with surprising frequency, into the back of my chair. I would like to tell you the food was good, but luckily we realised our mistake and fled to a small, cosy bistro, where we ate like kings for £4.50.

But this city, of course, is not just a town of fancy restaurants, Skye Bars and skylines. It is a city of legendary traffic jams and 400,000 motorcycle couriers, who beetle along, weaving suicidally between cars and trucks; a city with the largest Japanese community outside Japan; a city that is shabby, elegant, dangerous and thrilling all at once. Most of all, it is a city where a few are rich, but most are poor. It is a city of high walls where I see young children pulling carts through the streets, while guards dressed like Gucci shop-staff stand outside million-pound mansions.

Fernando wants me to understand the reality of life in the peripheral city slum areas Brazilians call the *favelas*. The next day he takes me to a community project in a district called Jardim Angela, one of dozens of huge, poor, town-sized communities on the outskirts of São Paulo.

Just a few years ago, the neighbourhood, a home to 350,000 desperate, struggling souls, was well on the way to becoming a war-zone. Jardim Angela, in fact, had the unenviable reputation of being the most violent place on the entire planet. Death was a constant visitor.

We take the main road next to the Pinheiros River through São Paulo, passing the new business district, where tall, elegant office blocks are rising towards the skies.

'Does it feel to you like Brazil is changing, developing?' I ask Fernando.

'Yes, things are improving, but slowly. Not as fast as people would like.'

As the office and expensive housing blocks recede in the rear-view mirror, we enter Jardim Angela, a grubby area of cheap and ramshackle housing. I am nervous about our destination. We are so close to the end of the journey. My superstitious side fears this is just when everything could go horribly wrong.

But we arrive safely at a Catholic church off a main street and meet Osni Santos Gomez, a local community leader. He is welcoming, mixed race – like almost every Brazilian - and just a couple of months younger than me.

Together we trot up to the roof of the modern church building for a view remarkably different to that seen from the Skye Bar. Here I am looking over thousands of rooftops, as Jardim Angela sprawls around a hillside. It is not, to my eyes at least, a complete slum. Not compared to the shanty towns of Africa or Madagascar. But it is down at heel. There are tin roofs, ramshackle houses, dogs barking and engines backfiring.

For too long, areas like Angela were abandoned by the rest of Brazil. Businessmen didn't want to set up shop, teachers didn't want to work here, litter was not collected. Even the police didn't want to come here. Osni moved into Angela when he was a young lad.

I ask him what happened to friends from his school.

'About half are dead,' he says starkly.

By the late nineties Jardim Angela was a disaster zone. Most people were unemployed. Crime was endemic. The murder rate reached a world record and there was a massacre every weekend, usually connected to the drug trade. Infant mortality reached an astonishing 40 per cent. There was no hospital and no doctors were prepared to work in the health centre. The young had no future, no opportunities, no chance.

Then, with the help of Father Jim Crowe, an inspirational Irish priest known to all as Padre Jaime, residents decided enough was enough. Under the leadership of the church, they came together and fought for their community, marching in their thousands to reclaim the streets from drug dealers and gangs. Social centres were opened at weekends, bars were forced to close at 11 p.m., toy guns were exchanged for balls and there were amnesties for real weapons. The police began retaking the streets, one by one, introducing officers to families and using community policing tactics learnt from Japan. A real sense of society and community began to develop. And as the police and families retook the streets, so the pimps and the dealers and the gunmen were squeezed out.

'Things used to be really bad here and they were always finding bodies. Every morning, people would walk around the corpses,' says Osni as we look across the rooftops. 'But now life is slowly starting to improve. A hospital and a school will open soon, and there are a few more jobs, banks, a post office. They all make a huge difference.'

Osni offers to take us to see teenagers from the area who are learning new skills at a community centre in the heart of Angela. He had asked Brian to leave his main, hugely expensive camera at our hotel because of the ongoing risk of hold-ups, and now Osni worries that the tinted windows on our rented van might make locals think we are a raiding SWAT team. So instead we pile into the church VW van, a battered old thing lacking seats and essential mechanical parts, and with a fart from the engine we head down narrow streets, trailing black smoke.

Hiding in the open is the best way of travelling around Angela. Osni takes us to 'Quiet Hill', an area still infested with gangs, where locals are forbidden to talk to the police. There are basic houses cluttered together. Women, families and a few mean-looking men sit out on the shaded streets. It is midday on a Wednesday and nobody even glances at the church van.

The reputation of Angela reminds Brian of tough years spent working as a cameraman in Soweto, the South African township just outside Johannesburg.

'Mondays and Tuesdays are probably the safest days to be round here,' he tells me over the noisy engine, 'because people are still recovering from heavy weekends.'

'Good point. And the worst time?'

'Well, in Soweto it was just before the weekend. People needed to get the money to pay for their hangovers.'

Listening to Osni and watching the streets, it seems the same is true here. There are bars everywhere, far more than are needed in a community of this size. They offer temptation and an expensive ride towards oblivion. For all the sadness I feel about the suffering of the poor, I know that far too many families in places like Angela are condemned by their own addictions and behaviour. Too many, or at least too many men, drink and fritter away their meagre earnings. Studies show the rural poor in Mexico spend 8.1 per cent of their money on booze and tobacco. In Indonesia it is 6 per cent; in Udaipur, India, 5 per cent. It is simply not good enough to say 'Oh well, they deserve a drink.' The behaviour, almost always of men, helps to trap families in poverty and denies children nutritious meals, education and attention. But with intelligent, gentle leadership and a firm, benevolent hand that removes weapons and discourages the availability of temptations such as alcohol, so much is possible.

Osni takes us through another area of Angela where it is still too dangerous for us to stop, let alone wander around. As we pass, I catch glimpses of noisy bars, with drunks sprawled across broken tables. And then we are through the area and passing a newly built school, soon to open, that Osni prays will offer new hope and options for youngsters in the area.

We drive a few more kilometres to the other community centre, a series of well-lit rooms on a hillside under another Catholic church. Osni leads us into an area where several dozen black and mixed-race teenagers of both sexes are hanging around, chatting and putting on white aprons. We have arrived just at the start of a pizza-making class, and so of course Fernando and I join in and knead dough while chatting with the kids from the area.

I am one of the world's worst cooks, so Luis Fernando, a fresh-faced 17-year-old black lad, is assigned as my teacher. He lives on one of the most dangerous streets in Angela, in an area still rife with drug dealing. He dabbled with weed and then cocaine a few years back, but with the help of the church he has turned his life around. Even making pizzas can be imbued with deeper meaning. It is a task and a skill that gives Luis purpose, respect, a sense of achievement. He guides me, watching closely.

As Luis talks of the dangers he faces in his community, the temptations that line his path in life, a roomful of youngsters listen carefully, respectfully. He is talking for all of them. Just being here, surviving into their late teens, is a great achievement.

Fernando and I roll the pizza bases and smear tomatoes, meat and cheese over the results. And then, as the pizzas cook, we pop upstairs, where more youngsters are being taught to be hairdressers. To one side, a couple of young, tough guys are learning the essential art of crimping. Fernando declines to have his thick dreads trimmed, but my own mop comes under their scissors. They all giggle and laugh, and I submit willingly. They give me a quick cut and insist on styling the results with a pound of lard that smells like engine grease.

Back downstairs, Father Jim Crowe arrives to judge our pizzas. He arrived here in 1969 as a 24-year-old and is over 60 now. But he is light on his feet with the face of a boxer.

'It was a military dictatorship back when I arrived, of course,' he says, his Irish accent still distinct. 'Very nasty.'

After Jardim Angela fell apart, the father helped put the pieces back together again. He is one of those wonderful Catholic emissaries from the Emerald Isle who have spent a lifetime spreading goodness and salvation. For that is what has happened here. Jardim Angela has been transformed. It is still far from a suburb of Copenhagen, but the contrast with the situation a few years back is astonishing.

'It has been a hard slog,' says Father Jim. 'But the job here has been helping to give people freedom. Delivering them from death to life.'

The father tells me he is still battling, this time for more money for the community. As Brazil gets wealthier, the developed, middle-class areas of São Paulo have received huge boosts in council funding, while Jardim Angela has only received a marginal increase.

Finally, we remember the pizzas. Fernando and I are both confident we have won, and I foolishly bet Fernando four caipirinhas I will be the champion. The father thinks differently. He votes for the offering of my dreadlocked friend. A teacher at the centre votes for me. It is all down to Luis, who has the casting vote. His fingers stray towards my pizza, then pass over to my rival's.

'Yeeees!' roars Fernando.

I protest. 'I thought we had a great future making pizzas together,' I tell Luis.

'But I have to be just,' he says with calm wisdom.

As dozens of youngsters from the project tuck into our pizzas and a batch prepared earlier, cups of fizzy Brazilian drinks are poured and passed around, music is turned up, and I look around at the bright, smiling faces in the room.

There is such potential in this *favela*, such promise. Remove the vices and create opportunity and options for the youngsters here, and they can become engineers, doctors, teachers. Or pizza-makers, bakers or hairdressers. Through education they can become a productive part of their communities, not drug dealers with a life expectancy that hardly reaches beyond their teens.

The reason for hope in Angela is because families have fought for the community, for the very streets of Angela, for their new school and new hospital. They have fought for the right to be part of Brazil.

And the lesson they offer me here, I think, is that in other *favelas* in democracies like Brazil, and by extension the shanty towns and slums of Capricorn countries like Namibia, Mozambique and Madagascar, or – further off the line – India, Indonesia and Nigeria, the poor and the downtrodden need to gather together and demand change and improvements for their communities. They need to be more belligerent. But often the problem for the global poor is that they do not fight as one. And they do not revolt enough.

A ND SO to the final furlong. It is 21 December, the day before the solstice. We rise early and take the backstreets that wind out of São Paulo towards the east and the coast. We are heading for the town of Ubatuba, where Capricorn leaves South America and heads across the pond towards Namibia. Barring an extraordinary mishap along the way, it looks like I have made it.

The drive to Ubatuba takes four hours, time for reflection. To reconsider. From the start of this journey I wanted to know more about our world, and I feel I've achieved my aim. From China in Africa to gem mining in Madagascar, from a forgotten genocide in Namibia to bleaching on the Great Barrier Reef, from the suffering of Australian Aboriginals to deforestation in South America, I have learnt so much.

I have certainly seen and experienced more than I could ever have hoped for. There was so much to discover on the journey I could have filled a series of books. I am coming to the end of my trip, but I am left with a strong bond with people and places that previously only existed for me on a map. I know I will forever have an interest in what happens in countries and lives along the Tropic of Capricorn.

Soon Dominic, Fiona and I will be on a flight heading back to warm homes, Christmas in the UK and a cold January. Brian will be heading towards the coast of South Africa and Christmas in the sunshine. No doubt Anya and I will soon find ourselves poring over a map of the planet and wondering wistfully what mysteries there are in other remote parts of the world. Perhaps there will be other adventures ahead. Who knows?

The road east is broad motorway. But drawing closer to the Brazilian coast, we peel off on to narrow, hilly roads that rise gradually through mist and hilly forests, then start a long, winding descent towards Capricorn through a verdant green land. Through a gap in the mist I spot water: the Atlantic, the finishing line. I started this journey in southern Africa during winter in the southern hemisphere, and now I am finishing it during a Brazilian summer in December. But there are grey clouds above. Will they ruin my chance of witnessing the solstice? I am hoping to illustrate the event by standing under the sun at solar midday. If it is directly overhead I will have no shadow.

'What are the chances of sunshine tomorrow?' I ask Fernando.

'Not great,' he says. 'I've been coming here since I was three. My cousin has a place here. We call Ubatuba *Uba-chuva*. *Chuva* means rain in Portuguese. It's always raining there.'

That night we stay in a little hotel on the edge of Ubatuba. It is just a few days before Christmas and all other rooms in the town are taken. A stereo plays 'Jingle Bells' on a loop.

'BBC?' says the young hotel manager with excitement. 'London! Woody Lane! I was a despatch rider in London, on a motorbike.' Then his face darkens as he remembers why he left. 'I had accident!' He lifts his trouser leg to show me a long, hideous scar. 'When police found me they said "Oh dear, oh dear." Foot pointing wrong way. Now I have British metal in my leg!'

Any mention of traffic accidents makes Brian and I quiver. Near the end of our journey, we are superstitious about our safety. I try to change the subject.

'Any chance of sunshine tomorrow?' I ask.

He purses his lips and twists his mouth, then leans forward conspiratorially.

'It is true that it does rain here. Quite a lot. Some terrible people call this town *Uba-chuva*, because...'

'Yes,' I interrupt, 'so I've heard. Oh well, fingers crossed.'

The next morning Fernando drives our car towards the edge of Ubatuba, to where the Tropic of Capricorn leaves South America. The weather is cloudy and grey.

'If I remember right, there's a Capricorn monument just up here,' says Fernando as we nose along the bumpy beach road, between shops selling cheap beach clothes. 'I remember seeing it before. But where is it?'

We pass a couple of cafés and bars, then the buildings stop and a small park appears on our right next to the sea. Young skateboarders are doing stunts in a half-pipe. Beyond them, teenagers are leaping around a basketball court. Between the pipe and the court is a metal globe sitting on top of a concrete star showing the points of the compass.

'There it is!' says Fernando triumphantly. 'That's the monument marking Capricorn!'

He stops the car and we leap out together, joined by Brian, who was in the back of the car filming our approach.

Just beyond the globe, a sandy beach leads down to the Atlantic. We are in the middle of a circular bay around which low beach houses and hotels gaze out over the ocean. At the edges of the bay, forest covers every inch of land, with humps of small islands covered by trees that fringe the salty sea. Into the distance, further around the coast, low, lazy clouds float around forested hilltops. An old fishing boat bobs in the water. It is spectacularly beautiful. A real destination.

'We've made it,' I say. I cannot quite believe we are here.

We walk towards the monument. The skateboarders keep skating, the lads playing basketball score a basket.

I want to celebrate the end of my travels, to shout. Or at least raise my voice. But as I finish the journey of a lifetime, daily life in Ubatuba just keeps going.

I circle the Capricorn globe, tracing my fingers along three thick metal lines marking the Equator, Cancer and Capricorn.

'We started there on the coast of Namibia,' I say to Fernando, my finger pointing at southern Africa, 'and we crossed the continent, then crossed Madagascar, went through the middle of Australia, then hit the coast of South America in Chile and travelled all the way across the desert and the Andes to Argentina, Paraguay and Brazil. All the way to here.' My finger jabs at the outlines of the continents.

'There we are!' exclaims Fernando. He points to the coast of Brazil, where a small hole is crossed by the Capricorn line. 'There's Ubatuba!'

'Yep. This is it. This is the end.'

Fernando and Brian walk the final metres with me. Beyond the globe are a few bushes. I walk between them towards the sandy beach. And as I do the sun glares brightly through the clouds, just for a few moments, and I bask in the solstice sunshine.

I have made it.

It is an intensely emotional moment. I have a lump in my throat. We all have a hug. Backs are slapped.

My Capricorn journey is over. I feel an enormous, fulfilling, life-enhancing sense of privilege.

We all step on to the beach, and I walk towards the sea.

ACKNOWLEDGEMENTS

A while ago I dropped by the office of Karen O'Connor, then the Creative Director in the Current Affairs department at the BBC, and found her at her keyboard pounding out a proposal for a TV series which would have seen me making five epic circles around the planet: the Arctic, Antarctic, Tropic of Cancer, the Equator, and the Tropic of Capricorn. I thought she was joking. I had just finished making a series for the BBC called *Places That Don't Exist*, an idea of mine which had seen me travelling to a group of countries unrecognised by the international community, the UN, FIFA or the organisers of the Eurovision song contest. I had already proposed a journey around the Equator to the BBC, and when it became clear that sending me around the planet five times for a single TV series might be a tad expensive, the original five journeys were boiled down to just that one: the Equator. The resulting series, shown on the BBC in 2006, encouraged the BBC to commission this journey around Capricorn. So thank you, BBC and all who pay for it, thank you, Karen, and thank you to Roly Keating, the controller of BBC2, and George Entwhistle, the former head of Current Affairs at the BBC, for choosing and backing the Tropic of Capricorn project.

Out on the road along Capricorn I would like to give special thanks to directors Sophie Todd, Chris Martin, Louise Turner and Dominic Ozanne, to cameraman Henry Smith, who helped out for a week when Brian had to dash home, and to assistant producers Simon Boazman and Fiona Cleary. Huge thanks to Brian Green, who filmed almost the entire journey and, as my mother reminds me, does almost everything I do, often going backwards while carrying a heavy camera. Many is the time Brian's good humour and charm saved me on this journey – often during tedious encounters with officialdom. He is a wonderful travelling companion and a fine cameraman. Thanks also, of course, to his wife Lulu and sons Rupert, Jack and Oscar, for putting up with his trips away from home.

Back in the office Sam Bagnall, the ever-positive series producer of Tropic of Capricorn, and Lucy Hetherington, the executive producer, put the show on the road and kept our eyes on the goal. Gary Beelders, Jules Cornell and Adam Richardson were the fantastic editors of the series, and patiently sat through hours of my televisual warblings, looking for the occasional intelligible sentence. May Abdalla, Georgina Davies and Marina Brito were key researchers who helped to spot extraordinary places and people we could visit along the way. Jane Willey, the Capricorn production manager, and Luciano Piazza, production coordinator, organised us, looked after us, and juggled the needs and demands of the team with aplomb from HQ at White City.

Hearty thanks to everyone we met and all those who helped us along the road. Most are mentioned in this book. A special mention for Jason at the Nomad Travel Clinic, Tony Effik, Gael Somerville, Cindy Vallis, Grant Wootton and Frauke Jensen in Namibia. Special thanks to Mick Ashworth and Kenny Gibson from *The Times Comprehensive Atlas of the World*, of which Mick is editor-in-chief. (Mick also happens to be a past president of the British Cartographic Society, just the sort of person you want on a pub quiz team.)

At PFD in London, and now United Agents, huge thanks to Rosemary Scoular and Robert Kirby, my wonderful agents, who are ably assisted by Chris Cope and Katie Bayer. I have long relied on their skill, suggestions and counsel.

Enormous thanks to everyone at BBC Books who worked miracles to get this book on to shelves in such a short space of time, particularly Martin Redfern, the unflappable editorial director, Eleanor Maxfield, the skilled and patient project editor, and Sarah Bennie and Claire Scott, who made sure people knew the book existed. I am indebted to Justine Taylor for incisive editing, to Jonathan Baker who designed the book at great speed, and to Neil Gower for the beautiful maps which grace these pages.

In my own clan, my brother James helped to keep me going, read early emailed chapters of this book, and made some fantastic suggestions, as did Dimitri Zenghelis. Lotte, Peter, Elsa, David, Ragi, Louis and Boris all gave huge support. My mother not only read my emailed reports from the road but enthusiastically requested more words, which kept my spirits up and kept me scribbling. Thanks Mum.

Finally, endless thanks to Anya, my wife and partner, who read and edited my words, took a number of the photographs, and was an angel on the road as the assistant producer on the second and third Capricorn trips. Without her this book, the Capricorn TV series and just about everything else in my life would be utterly impossible.

Thanks to one and all.